Complete Book Of Whitetail Hunting

By Toby Bridges

With: Larry Weishuhn, Dick Idol, Harold Knight, David Hale, Jim Shockey, Mark Drury, Will Primos, John Sloan, Tom Fegely, Richard P. Smith...and other whitetail hunting experts

Stoeger Publishing Company

Title: *Complete Book Of Whitetail Hunting*
Editor: *William S. Jarrett*
Cover Art Design: *Ray Wells*
Book Design And Layout: *Lesley A. Notorangelo/DSS*
Project Manager: *Dominick S. Sorrentino*
Electronic Imaging: *Lesley A. Notorangelo/DSS*

Published by Stoeger Publishing Company
5 Mansard Court
Wayne, New Jersey 07470

ISBN: 0-88317-222-4
Library of Congress Catalog Card No.: 99-072948
Manufactured in the United States of America

Distributed to the book trade and to the sporting goods trade by Stoeger Industries, 5 Mansard Court, Wayne, New Jersey 07470

In Canada, distributed to the book trade and to the sporting goods trade by Stoeger Canada, Ltd., 1801 Wentworth Street, Unit 16, Whitby, Ontario L1N 8R6.

Toby Bridges has been hunting white-tails since 1963 and is today recognized as the dean of black powder hunting writers. The author of seven books, this is his first on a topic other than muzzle-loading or hunting with muzzleloading guns. Since he first began writing in the early 1970s, Toby Bridges has also authored more than 1,000 magazine articles, many of which have been on hunting the white-tailed deer with modern gun, muzzleloader and bow. In addition, Bridges has been actively involved with the hunting industry for more than 25 years, working as a technical advisor and catalog editor for Dixie Gun Works, head of public relations for Bass Pro Shop, and director of market development for Knight Rifles. He has also worked as an advisor for several major bullet and firearms makers, tree-stand manufacturers, deer call and scent suppliers, and camouflage designers. His knowledge of deer hunting equipment and white-tail hunting tactics are readily evident in the following pages.

Toby Bridges tracks down another whitetail.

About The Author

From The Author

I can well remember the first time I walked into a deer camp. Forever imbedded in my memory is the smell of strong coffee, the sight of hunting guns hanging on the wall, piles of old outdoor magazines stacked in every corner, and the sounds of good friends enjoying each other's company. It was obvious that this place was one they all held dear in their hearts. I was just 13 years old then, and by far the youngest hunter in camp. Most of the others were in their 30s and 40s, with a few in their late 50s. Still, no one treated me like a kid. I was one of them. And while I did not fill my deer tag that first fall, I went home knowing that I was a deer hunter. I've been one ever since.

Since those days as a skinny teenager, I've been fortunate to have enjoyed days and nights at various deer camps all across North America, spending a lifetime in pursuit of whitetails with modern gun, muzzleloader and bow. I've had good days in the deer woods—and I've had bad days. But that's deer hunting, and I wouldn't have it any other way. During more than 35 years spent chasing whitetails, I've been fortunate to know many legendary hunters, including Larry Weishuhn, Jim Shockey, Harold Knight, David Hale, Dick Idol, Mark Drury, Will Primos and many, many others whom I consider good friends. And from each one of them I have learned a little more about hunting the magnificent white-tailed deer.

When I sat down to write this book, I didn't want it to come off as "Deer Hunting According To Toby Bridges." Instead, I've asked dozens of the most respected and recognized deer hunting and shooting experts in the U.S. to share their knowledge of hunting this great game animal. In the following pages, you will have access to more than 1,000 years of shared deer hunting experience. The how-to information these men have contributed, their deer hunting savvy and experiences together make this one of the most complete books ever written on hunting whitetails. I feel especially fortunate to have had the opportunity to compile this wealth of deer hunting knowledge, with special thanks to the following men who contributed so much to *"COMPLETE BOOK OF WHITETAIL HUNTING"*:

Tom & Rhonda Baker:
Owners, Buck Hollow Ranch

Kurt von Besser:
President, Atsko/Sno-Seal Inc.

Marvin Briegel:
Nebraska Farmer & Deer Drive Expert

John Burgeson:
President, Wildlife Research Center

Sam Collora:
President, Mrs. Doe Pee's Buck Lures

Jim Crumley:
Founder, Trebark Camouflage

Mark Drury:
President, M.A.D. Calls & Drury Outdoors Video Productions

Dave Ehrig:
Outdoor Writer & Pennsylvania's "Mr. Flintlock"

Tom Fegely:
Noted Outdoor Writer & Photographer

Toxey Haas:
C.E.O., Haas Outdoors/Mossy Oak Camouflage

David Hale:
Co-Founder, Knight & Hale Game Calls

Brad Harris:
Promotional Director, Outland Sports, Inc./Lohman Calls

David Hale:
Co-Founder, Knight & Hale Game Calls

Dave Henderson:
Firearms Expert & Outdoor Writer

Dick Idol:
World Renowned Whitetail Authority

Mike Jordan:
Public Relations Manager, Winchester-Western Company

Harold Knight:
Co-Founder, Knight & Hale Game Calls

Russ Markesbery:
President, Markesbery Muzzle Loaders, Inc.

Tom McIntyre:
Outdoor Writer

Brian Murphy:
Executive Director, Quality Deer Management Association

Stanley Potts:
Bowhunter & Private Wildlife Manager

Will Primos:
President, Primos Hunting Calls

Terry Rohm:
Marketing Director, Wellington Products

Eddie Salter:
Member, Hunter's Specialties Pro Staff

Ted Schumacher:
Owner, Lone Wolf Outfitters

Jim Shockey:
Canadian Outfitter & Outdoor Writer

John Sloan:
Expert Bowhunter & Outdoor Writer

Richard P. Smith:
Whitetail Expert & Outdoor Writer

Ottie Snyder:
Promotional Manager, Horton Manuf.

Ronnie Strickland:
Vice President-Promotions, Haas Outdoors/Mossy Oak Camouflage

Bill Vaznis:
Noted Bowhunter & Outdoor Writer

Larry Weishuhn:
Noted Outdoor Writer & Whitetail Biologist

Grant Woods:
Consulting Whitetail Biologist

Toby Bridges

The Remarkable Whitetail

Of all the big game species roaming around the world, it's doubtful that any have been studied and researched more than *Odocoileus virginianus*—the magnificent white-tailed deer. The number of magazine articles written about this great game animal in just the past decade easily runs into the tens of thousands. Likewise, the volumes of books, research papers and biological reports devoted to hunting and managing the whitetail would altogether weigh tons. Today, whitetail hunting titles outsell every other outdoor video, with those featuring hunts for this favorite of the deer family rated among the most-watched outdoor television programs.

Thanks to the proliferation of the whitetail wherever it's found, an entire segment of the hunting industry has been established. Camouflaged clothing, calls, treestands, travel monitors, game feeders, hunting scents, specialized knives, footwear, taxidermy supplies, optics, ammunition, rifles and shotguns, are all now available only because the whitetail has enjoyed such huge popularity. We can all thank this growing whitetail population for the outstanding selection of muzzleloading and archery equipment now widely available. The revenue generated annually through the sales of deer hunting equipment and licenses runs easily into the hundreds of millions of dollars.

Still, with all the ongoing research concerning our attempts to manage the species successfully, plus educating the sportsmen who pursue it so feverishly, the abilities of white-tailed deer continue to amaze us. No other big game animal has ever adapted so well to the encroachment of humans on its habitat, actually benefiting in many instances from man's takeover of the world's large forests. Despite centuries of such intrusions, the resilient whitetail is still with us in even greater numbers than were present when the Pilgrims landed at Plymouth Rock. Depending on which

source you're using, whitetails in the U.S. now number close to 20 million!

As hard as it may be for some to consider a world without whitetails, not too many years ago we nearly lost this great resource. In many states, whitetails had all but disappeared by the end of the Great Depression of the early 1930s. Many whitetail managers claim that as few as 200,000 remained before modern conservation practices could be put into play. But even after reintroducing whitetails into their historic home ranges—not to mention the strict enforcement of game laws and tightly controlled harvest during early hunting seasons—it took more than 50 years to reestablish the whitetail in the numbers it had reached before the first white man took aim with his 16th century matchlock or wheellock and dropped the first white-tailed deer with the aid of a firearm.

As a teenager growing up in the Mid-west, I developed an early fascination for the whitetail. There simply weren't many deer in Illinois during the early 1960s. Moreover, my dad had

Thanks to modern conservation practices and game management, more whitetails roam North America than when the Pilgrims landed at Plymouth Rock in 1620.

The author was 15 when he took his first whitetail with a bow. This was at a time when the deer population in his home state of Illinois was barely 20 percent of what it is today.

winter, spring and summer of 1963, the thought of some-day hunting whitetails was all I dreamed about. Little did I know that my parents and several friends of the family had applied for, and received, my first deer permit.

The trouble was, less than half of Illinois was open to deer hunting, and my home county wasn't one of them. My permit was good only for a county nearly 150 miles to the southeast in the Shawnee National Forest. It was there that I spent three glorious days chasing whitetails with some fellow hunters. On the second afternoon of my first season, I actually shot at a small whitetail buck at about 80 yards. My old full-choked 30-inch-barreled Winchester Model 121 was great for dumping ducks and geese, but it wouldn't throw two slugs in the same place no matter how hard I tried. At 50 yards, I could barely keep three shots inside 12 to 14 inches, but the inaccuracy of that old Model 12 didn't dampen my spirits one bit, so I kept on hunting with undaunted enthusiasm. Although I ended the hunt without taking a deer, I was more excited than ever about hunting whitetails. Even before we arrived home, I was already looking forward to the next season.

I took my first whitetail the following year. I was now hunting with a side-by-

never hunted deer in his life, so when I came home from fishing a small local creek one day and excitedly blurted out that I had actually seen a whitetail buck, my dad gave me an understandably skeptical look, for he himself had never seen a deer in the wild.

By the time I was twelve, I was hunting squirrels on my own and spent every possible moment sneaking along the wooded creek bottoms and hardwood covered ridges near my home, something I still enjoy. That same year, I managed to slip up on three groups of whitetails, and during the following

side Stevens 12 gauge when, on that first morning, a big doe and yearling button buck came running past my stand. My second shot clipped the young buck, and in my excitement I leaped down from my stand and literally tried to run down the deer. I actually caught up with the button buck about a quarter of a mile away, but I missed it twice more. I then realized I'd left the remaining slugs in my coat pocket back at the stand. Suddenly, as I was about to turn around, someone yelled at me. A hunter carrying a long barreled muzzleloader approached and let me

put in a finishing shot with his front-loader. I had downed my first whitetail!

In 1964, some 14,000 hunters throughout Illinois harvested around 4,000 whitetails out of an estimated total of 50,000 or so. How things have changed. Today, my Prairie State is home to some 700,000 whitetails, with every county open to hunting (those counties making up the Chicago metropolitan area are open to archery hunting only). The annual whitetail harvest in Illinois is now around 200,000. Not bad for a state which many wildlife professionals once

A banner proclaims "Whitetail Days" in the small rural community of Nebo, Illinois. It represents similar celebrations occurring wherever whitetail hunting represents a boost to local economies.

Deer hunters travel the country in search of new ways to hunt whitetails. Dave Ehrig traveled from Pennsylvania to Missouri to take this ten-pointer.

claimed would never amount to much because of its dense human population and urban development.

This success story has been repeated all across the country wherever the whitetail can be found and hunted. In some areas the deer population has exploded beyond the game managers' wildest expectations. White-tails are now hunted just about everywhere east of the Mississippi, throughout all of its traditional western plains and low mountain habitats. They have either expanded their range into, or have been introduced to, regions where historically they had been seen. Large number of whitetails have now become established in Finland and New Zealand,

with several other smaller herds scattered throughout central Europe. Someday the whitetail, thanks to its ability to adapt, could become the world's most dominant species.

The most amazing examples of the whitetail's adaptability are now witnessed inside the city limits of major metropolitan areas, including New York, Chicago, Atlanta, Minneapolis and Philadelphia. A few decades ago, you had to head for remote farm country or the wilds of the north woods to spot a monster whitetail buck; but today, specimens can be found inside large city parks, metropolitan forest preserves, greenbelt areas, even in the backyards of many urban neighborhoods. In fact, the largest whitetail buck on record, scoring 333 7/8 Boone and Crockett points, was found dead in a small agricultural area inside the metro city limits of St. Louis, Missouri! Limited hunting in these areas often allows bucks to reach a much riper old age, hence a much fuller antler development.

Several years ago, while living in a town of about 7,000 people in southern Iowa, I encountered one such "super buck." It was in late October when I

Exceptional bucks like this 16-point Kentucky non-typical taken by muzzleloading hunter Wes Stone are what a deer hunter's dreams are made of.

noticed one day that my 3-D deer targets on the wooded lot next to my home had been knocked down and scattered all over that piece of land. It was the week of Halloween and so my first reaction was to put the blame on several local boys with a reputation for making pranks. That night, as I gathered up the buck targets, a neighbor who lived down the road stopped by to inform me that he had spotted a huge ten-pointer sparring with my foam targets early that morning. The next day I was up before first light, sipping my coffee and watching out a bedroom window when, sure enough, a huge typical buck in the upper 170 or 180 class waltzed into the yard and immediately began to disassemble the targets. I bowhunted that deer for nearly two weeks, perched each morning in a stand I'd hung up to practice with my bow. Unfortunately, as the rut progressed, the buck visited the lot less frequently, and then only at night. Then one afternoon, as I was pulling into my driveway after work, there in the wooded lot stood the buck. It was the last time I ever saw him.

More than one whitetail management professional has likened the adaptability of the whitetail to that of the cockroach. The deer have learned to conform to man's development of their habitat, to the point where they live quite comfortably among the hustle and bustle of big city life. Perhaps a little too comfortably. Homeowners who were once thrilled at the novelty of seeing "Bambi" scamper across their backyards have now grown weary of expensive ornamental shrubbery and gardens turned into browse for the ravenous whitetails, or fruit trees destroyed by bucks simply as a place to rub their antlers, not to mention the crumpled fenders as commuters collide with deer intent on crossing the road.

Several states now boast whitetail populations of 700,000 to 1,000,000 animals, all living in areas where wildlife biologists would feel much more comfortable with herds half that size. Fortunately, in some regions the herds show signs of leveling out. Still, old habits are hard to break. Throughout the 1960s and 1970s, hunters in many states were not allowed to shoot does, or at least the doe harvest was closely monitored and well-regulated. Whitetail populations were just beginning to grow in those days, and managers were afraid to over-harvest this fragile but expanding resource. Today, game managers are faced with an entirely different problem: too many deer. In some states, the deer herd is a long way from slowing its growth. We need to harvest more does in those areas, because the hunters simply aren't shooting enough of them. So for most white-tailed deer hunters, these *are* the good ol' days. The hunting seasons are generally long and bag limits are liberal, especially for hunters who are willing to harvest a few does (shooting bucks only is not going to halt the growth of deer herds). Most whitetail states provide sportsmen with a long archery season, an early and late

COMPLETE BOOK OF WHITETAIL HUNTING

muzzleloader season, and a firearms season. In many regions, hunters who've learned to take advantage of all three seasons can pursue whitetails for three months or longer.

A major contributing factor to the rapid growth of the deer herd has been the continued breakup of huge tracts of timber. Deep, heavily wooded expanses—especially the huge hardwoods forests of the South and East—satisfy the needs of whitetails. During years with a heavy mast crop, food is plentiful, and in even old growth forests whitetails can find suitable protective and bedding cover. The trouble is,

whitetails love to live on the edge. They prefer areas where the woods and fields come together. Throughout much of the country, what were once endless tracts of trees is now a patchwork of large wood lots and farmland. The nutritional value of soybeans and corn often raised on these cleared fields adds greatly to the health of today's whitetail herd.

These cleared lands help create the critical "edge" whitetails prefer, providing still more cover for more deer.

As rosy as the current status of the whitetail may seem, especially for hunters, there's a downside as well. Game managers who were once faced with reestablishing deer herds are now faced with the problem of managing too many deer. In heavily farmed regions, especially in the Midwest, whitetails play havoc with crops. It's not uncommon for agricultural lands to sustain a 30- to 40-percent loss of early soybeans to deer. Where their density reaches 50 to 60 deer per square mile, entire fields are lost to hordes of whitetails converging on those tender young plants from morning to night. One farmer I know in western Illinois owns close to 1,000 acres in an area known for its unusually high number of trophy bucks on his land. Some evenings it's not unusual to see 40 to 50 deer feeding in his fields. Each fall, in years when the white oak mast crop fails, the deer feed instead on his soybean and corn crops. It's not unusual for a 50-acre field to be totally decimated by these hungry whitetails. Fortunately, the farmer has learned how to make up for the lost crops. He charges a fee for hunting on his properties! The fees he charges

MOSSY OAK BRAND CAMO
MEGA BUCKS TV
10 Exciting Hunts including a successful spot and stalk bowhunt for a Boone and Crockett Whitetail!
Racks & Reasons

to hunt his farm offset the lost crop revenues, and they keep the farmer's land from being a total loss. Moreover, the hunters who pay the fees enjoy some of the finest deer hunting in the U.S.

Man's attack on the land is now beginning to eliminate some of the natural whitetail habitats. Rich river bottom timbers throughout the Midwest and South annually produce some of the country's most impressive bucks. Unfortunately, that same rich black soil, which contains the mineral elixir that contributes so much to those bony crowns, also produces some of the highest yields of corn and soybeans. Each year, tens of thousands of acres of river bottom timber are lost to the bulldozers as farmers continue to clear more of their valuable crop land, eliminating the old habitats forever. Instead, there's an ever expanding grain desert offering plenty of feed for deer, but only for a short period of time. Missing are the much-needed winter protective and bedding covers. It's difficult for deer to

Whitetail enthusiast Jon Blumb of Kansas took this wide-racked seven-pointer in the last light of evening as the buck grazed in a hayfield. Both deer and deer hunters have benefited from the efforts of American farmers.

exist in habitats that lie barren for four or five months of the year.

Across the south, valuable hardwood forests are turning into deserts of another kind. Slow-growing, mast-producing hardwoods—especially oaks—are being cleared and replaced by softwood pines that mature much faster, meeting the needs of lumber and paper producers. For several years after a large stand of hardwoods has been cleared and replanted in young pines, the undergrowth of honeysuckle, greenbrier and other low-growing bushes provide a great food source. But as the pines begin to mature 20 or so years later, the canopy prevents sunlight from reaching the ground, eliminating the much-needed ground growth. As pretty as an endless expanse of southern yellow or loblolly pine may appear, huge tracts of these softwoods offer little in the way of nutrition for whitetails. Unfortunately, the commercial production of southern pines tends to leave little room either for proper wildlife management. Short rotation of timber growth more often than not fails to take into consideration the needs of wildlife, including whitetails. In fact, deer are generally considered a nuisance because of the damage done to the young trees.

Fortunately, some of the more responsible producers of southern softwood timber are beginning to leave healthy stands of hardwoods intermingled with those of planted pines. The size of the average clear-cut has begun to shrink, too. In some regions, restrictions on the number of acres within a cleared area are now being imposed. The result is a more uneven grid of growths of varying levels of maturity. Instead of a thousand-acre expanse of maturing pines, which slowly force out the deer, the same acreage now may include 200 acres of newly cleared forest, another 200 acres of two- to five-year-old trees, another 200 acres with trees that are 6 to 10 years old, another 200 acres with 11- to 15-year-old growth, and the remaining 200 acres of mature or nearly mature pines. This kind of management produces the same amount of lumber and pulp wood, while doing a much better job of providing habitat for wildlife. This is especially true where the timber companies leave 10 to 15 percent of the land in old growth hardwoods.

As we head into the next millennium, whitetail managers face still more challenges. Should they permit deer hunting inside city limits, or should they revert to hired sharpshooters? Can deer be fed pellets containing a contraceptive that prevents them from procreating? What can be done to improve deer densities amid stands of southern pines? Must we now start managing for quality instead of quantity? Will trophy whitetail bucks become a money-making crop for Midwestern farmers? What can be done to keep deer from destroying our crops? And with such an abundance of whitetails, how do we prevent the spread of diseases that could wipe out whole herds in some areas? These and other persistent questions will command the attention of wildlife professionals in years to come.

The more we research and study the whitetail, the more we come to realize that we don't know as much about this adaptable creature as we thought we did. Whitetails can be simple animals, like the old doe and her twin fawns who bed down in the strip of shoulder-high brush along the far end of my field, and who come to browse every evening in the orchard next to the barn. They can also be exasperatingly complex, like the mythical buck that only appears in the middle of a bright moon-lit night, like some apparition, only to disappear to its secret hideaway long before first light. These are the deer that big buck hunters dream about and who keep hunters headed for the deer woods each fall.

No one alive knows all there is to know about whitetails. Anyone who claim to is only fooling himself. This book includes the input of some of the most respected deer-hunting authorities alive. As up-to-date and complete as the information on these pages may be, the whitetail deer can be counted on to prove to us that it still has a few tricks up its sleeves. We humans are the ones who will have to adapt. ■

Table Of Contents

Understanding Whitetail Behavior And Movement

WITH ■ *Larry Weishuhn, Whitetail Biologist & Writer* ■ *Brian Murphy, Executive Director, Quality Deer Management Association* ■ *Dick Idol, Whitetail Expert* ■ *Tom Fegely, Outdoor Writer & Photographer*

An eerie fog clung to the lake's surface as I navigated the 24-foot pontoon boat—more from memory than from what I could see of the shoreline. It was early January, and in less than an hour, some 30 volunteers would gather at a boat ramp nearly 20 miles away to begin submerging Christmas trees in Table Rock Lake. It was part of an annual fisheries habitat project I'd inherited upon becoming public relations manager for Bass Pro Shops (Springfield, Missouri). The day before, I had piloted one pontoon boat to the ramp and left it here overnight, but the second boat was needed to sink more than 6,000 trees left over from that weekend. Despite the dense fog, I knew I could find my way; I had, after all, spent a lot of time on that lake while working with the habitat project.

Out on the open water of this huge reservoir (built by the U.S. Corps of Engineers), the fog occasionally lifted, enabling me to get my bearings on small islands and points. I was just breaking the heavy mist when suddenly I spotted something swimming nearly a quarter-mile away. As I slowly maneuvered the boat toward the object, which was now less than a hundred yards away, I was amazed to discover that the mysterious object was a dozen or so whitetailed deer, apparently swimming from one shore to the other. Even at that point, the lake was nearly a mile wide and the water close to 150 feet deep.

One of the deer, I noticed, carried a very handsome rack. Wanting to get a better look at the buck, I throttled the boat back and moved slowly toward the deer. Much to my astonishment, the big 160-class buck immediately peeled away from the does and fawns and began swimming in the opposite direction while the remaining deer kept on swimming toward shore. The buck had instinctively reacted to my approach, breaking away from the women and children by taking a completely different course. Every time I've led a deer drive since then, I've thought back on that

A lifetime of studying the behavior and movements of whitetails has enabled the author to be in the right place at the right time before bringing down this late season Nebraska buck.

morning, wondering where a buck might head once the pressure was on. One thing I've learned for certain: when a doe or fawn exits out the other end of a cover, there's probably a really good buck no longer sharing the thicket with them. He'll be leading me, and others like me, in the opposite direction!

Observing whitetails has become a lifelong passion for me. Whether it's from a stand while hunting, or when pulling off the side of the road in mid-summer to glass whitetails feeding out in a soybean or hay field, I've always enjoyed watching deer. They fascinate me. I'll almost always stop what I'm doing to observe their movements and behavior. To me, there's a lot more to being successful at hunting whitetails than simply climbing into a stand on opening day and dropping the first buck that happens along. Shooting a

deer with a modern rifle, a muzzleloader or a bow is a personal thing. Filling a tag every year usually means that a hunter has spent many hours watching deer. He has learned their movements and behavior patterns well. In other words, he knows the ways of the deer.

One of my favorite deer hunting partners has long been outdoor writer Tom Fegely. Over the years we've shared many deer hunting camps in Missouri, Iowa, Minnesota, Kentucky, Wyoming and other whitetail haunts. Tom is also a 30-year-plus veteran of the deer woods and has taken his fair share of good bucks because he knows how to be in the right place at the right time. Like me, Tom's not a professional deer biologists, but he has spent enough time studying this particular game animal to have earned a doctor's degree in whitetail ecology. "It's no secret that the most successful hunters are also students of the whitetail." he will tell you. "They spend the off-season patrolling the deer woods, usually with camera or binocular

development encroached on its habitat. By the end of the Great Depression of the 1930's, whitetail populations in many states were down to a mere 1,000 to 2,000 animals statewide. Thanks to modern conservation efforts and strict enforcement of tough game laws, we

Tom Fegely

in hand, trying to unravel the mastering of this complex animal."

Tom Fegely feels that a serious deer hunter must first understand the animal being pursued. The first step is in knowing how and why we can enjoy hunting this adaptable animal. Thanks to uncontrolled hunting, we nearly lost the whitetail. Subsistence hunting, market harvesting and poaching took its toll on whitetails, especially where human

quickly discovered how fast whitetail can reestablish population levels that rival— and even surpass—herd numbers that existed in many areas where the first white settlers arrived. "As evidenced by the phenomenal growth of deer populations in suburbia over the past couple decades," Tom Fegely points out, "deer are capable of rapidly expanding their ranges and maintaining a high reproduction rate in suitable habitat."

Even in areas where whitetails enjoy minimal hunter pressure, such as on this large ranch in Texas, older, mature bucks are still quite nocturnal and are rarely seen during daylight hours.

As far as whitetail populations are concerned, man is the only true predator—and predation is an essential element in the management of wild game populations. Gone, for the most part, are wolves and mountain lions east of the Mississippi River, and even the ever-growing range of the coyote has had little impact on whitetail populations, which are still on the rise in many parts of the U.S. In most states, controlled hunting and vehicular deaths are now the main factors controlling herd size. To a much smaller degree, harsh winters, diseases and fawn deaths will occasionally impact whitetail populations in certain geographical locations. The whitetail is a social animal, preferring the

company of other whitetails, but in small groups rather than large gatherings. It's not uncommon, though, for a hundred or more whitetails to converge on the same food source during winter. Tom Fegely points out that this is due primarily to the availability of certain foods containing proper nutrients and enough calories to generate body heat where winters are severe.

Tom also observes that the most common gathering is matriarchal in nature, usually consisting of the doe, her fawns of the year, and quite often a yearling female offspring. He says to forget the Disney image of a big-racked buck, submissive does and a couple of

Bambis napping in the summer woods. Unless he's sustained an injury to his genitals during the previous fall or winter while carrying that big rack, you simply won't find a "hard-horned" whitetail buck in the middle of summer. Most often go their own way at this time of year. Even young bucks from the previous year generally leave the matriarchal group, while young does stick with their mother until the next breeding season.

During the warm weather months as many as a dozen or more bucks may form what is referred to as a "bachelor group." There seems to be no real rhyme or reason why some of these groups consist largely of bucks belonging to an older age class, while others may include bucks of all age classes, or still another of all 1- or 2-year-old-bucks. In spring and summer, when antler growth is still soft and blood-filled, bucks from one of these groups establish a hierarchy by occasionally standing on their hind legs and actually boxing at each other with their front hooves. Most acts of dominance don't tend to show up until early fall, however, when bucks within a bachelor group begin testing each other, usually sparring with one another in a casual way. Other than a blow to one's pride, there are seldom any injuries incurred.

One of the biggest misconceptions about whitetails concerns their home range. It is amazing how many modern hunters remain convinced that a whitetail will always stay within a mile or two of where it was born. Nothing could be farther from the truth. Whitetails, espe-

cially bucks in certain parts of the country, tend to move around quite a bit. In that connection, I decided during the mid-1980s to take an inventory of the bucks who still remained after the close of hunting season. In late January, the bucks in my part of Illinois still carried antlers. After several weeks of frigid temperatures and almost a foot of snow had fallen, the whitetails were forced out into harvested crop fields to forage for corn and soybean remnants. The deer became quite visible, often hitting the feed areas as early as two or three in the afternoon. That gave me plenty of time to drive around on back roads and glass herds of 30 or more deer. One buck with an unusual rack really stood out. His brow tines curved inward and nearly touched, while the tips of his main beams actually crossed, passing each other by several inches. When I first spotted this buck, he was in a cornfield just outside town. A week later, I spotted the same buck more than 15 miles away; and before the deer began dropping their head gear, I saw him once again, another seven or eight miles from where I had first spotted him. That area is now heavily populated by coyote hunters with their large packs of hounds to track and run off the predators (some of these dogs make no bones about chasing deer). It's possible that this particular buck, or the group of deer he hung with, had been pushed by coyote hounds into new territory. As Tom Fegely notes, "The ranges of individual whitetails vary from season to season and within the diverse habitats that make up my home state of Pennsylvania. While most whitetails there don't migrate, studies show long-distance movements, as much as 50 miles, during the winter in the vast tracts of forest that comprise much of the northern tier."

As long as a whitetail's home range provides all its needs, there's a good chance a deer will never wander far from where its mother doe gave it birth. With plenty of food, water and protective cover, a deer can—and often does—live its entire life within a few square miles. But because of man's changing demands on the land, whether it's hunting or some other kind of pressure, whitetails make no bones about picking up and moving to a new "home range." Another factor that will cause deer to move great distances is, of course, the availability of food. Whitetails consume a tremendous variety of plants, and they readily change feeding habits as more desirable food sources mature. Tom Fegely is one of those hunters who pays special attention to what's "ripe" and what's not, and by knowing how to identify what the deer are feeding on. That's what makes this whitetail hunter so successful as he moves his stands around accordingly.

Various grasses generally make up the bulk of a whitetail's diet from the time they begin to sprout in early spring until being replaced by different herba-

The author took this "town buck" in his own back yard. Modern whitetails have found suburbia to their liking.

ceous plants, or forbs, through much of the summer. Later, in the fall, a whitetail's food preference generally turns to mast crops and fruits. Deer are very selective feeders, and when offered a variety of foods they noticeably display special preference for some over others. In the Midwest, where I do the bulk of my whitetail hunting, I've noticed that deer that have fed primarily on soybean and clover crops quickly abandon these foods in favor of ripening white oak acorns. As soon as this mast crop begins to drop, the deer make the switch almost immediately. Even when the forest floor is literally covered with acorns, the whitetail continue to feed selectively beneath their favorite trees.

I've been truly fortunate to live in the middle of some great whitetail hunting areas for most of my life, including northern Missouri, not far from the Iowa border. Despite what uninformed hunters may think, this area is not one big, flat cornfield; indeed, it offers some great expanses of hardwood forests, primarily white oaks. From early to mid-October, deer hunting here depends on whether or not the bowhunter knows how to scout for and hunt preferred white oak stands. One of my old favorite spots was a long abandoned house site. Ringing what was once a backyard stood ten or more huge white

Even the harvest of farm crops can alter the manner in which deer move through a given terrain.

oaks with a canopy covering more than an acre. During a good mast crop year, these trees produced tons of big, succulent acorns and were therefore among the first to be hit by the local whitetails. Throughout the summer, I rarely saw deer browsing near the old half-fallen down house and outbuildings. But once the acorns began to fall, the deer began showing up in numbers, as many as 20 or 30 feeding there each evening.

From my stand I have more than once watched whitetails come across distant open ridge tops on their way to those trees. Some, I knew, had walked a mile or more through seemingly identical white oaks to reach the old house site. I never could determine why until one day an older and more experienced hunter told me that it was because an old outhouse had once been located among those trees. He was, moreover, aware that once a privy hole was filled, the homeowners would dig another and relocate the old outhouse over it, a process that was probably repeated every years for 30 or 40 years. These old outdoor toilets sitting among the oaks all those years had fertilized the soil to the extent that the acorns produced by the trees were invariably bigger and meatier. I now spread garden fertilizer around several big oaks on my own property— and it works!

Actually, deer will feed on whatever is available. Studies reveal that a deer's diet generally contains some woody stemmed plants, but that

they prefer more succulent plants. Mostly, they feed on a wide range of plants, including milkweed, crown vetch, honeysuckle, persimmon, sassafras, mulberry, spruce, willow, dandelion, rhododendron, wild grape, dogwood, nettles and even poison ivy. Commercial crops like alfalfa, clover, corn, soybeans, winter wheat, rye, oats and other crops also make up a large part of the whitetail's diet. And it's their consumption of agricultural crops which often get the deer into trouble. In many areas, they have caused millions of dollars in damage to farm crops.

SENSE—AND NONSENSE

The whitetail's keen sense of smell is generally recognized as its first line of defense. Many knowledgeable whitetail hunters feel that a deer can smell a hunter a mile or more away. Not only does the deer's extremely sensitive olfactory system warn a whitetail of man's presence or some other kind of intrusion into its habitat, a deer's nose is also an important means of communication. Whitetails easily pick up the smells of other deer that may be nearby. Have you ever watched a buck raise his nose into the air and curl its upper lip? This is called "flehmening," and it's what a buck does when he's trying to pick up the odors of a doe. Once the smell he's

looking for is in his vicinity, the scent will be picked up by the epithelian lining of the nostrils and the Jacobsen's organ located atop the palate in the mouth. That urine smell he detects helps him determine whether a doe is in estrous and ready for breeding.

Tom Fegley shares some of what he knows about the scent glands of the whitetail:

The interdigital glands are located between the hooves of all four feet. Spread the toes on your next kill and look for the small, sparse-haired sac which, to my nose, emits a "sour citrus" smell, although others have described it as a "foul, rancid" odor. The "cheesy"

The more a buck travels, the more vulnerable he becomes. These Missouri hunters load a good buck taken as it worked a scrape line.

excretions from the sac aid deer in trailing one another and noting the presence of others in their territories. The scent evaporates and loses its strength over time, which explains how bucks trailing does—or even predators following a deer's trail—know how long ago that scent was made. It's believed that deer on the run emit more scent than when they're walking, because their hooves are splayed. It's also been said that deer who pound their front feet when disturbed—as in a face-off with a hunter—or are uncertain about what they're looking at,, create a detectable, interdigital scent in the air so as to alert others that something's amiss.

The metatarsal glands are set on the outside of a deer's hind legs, between its feet and knees. They are white, oval patches with hair tufts surrounding the small, hairless pores. Biologists disagree about the true function of these glands. Some believe their purpose is to leave scent on the ground when bedded. Others say their function has nothing to do with scent, rather it's a method deer use to detect slight vibrations in the earth caused by the movements of friends or enemies nearby. The tarsal gland is probably familiar to most hunters because it's the most important communication gland. Hunters—bowhunters in particular—should be aware of its location and function. It's found on the insides of a deer's hind legs, on both bucks and does. The tufts of elongated hairs are readily visible, especially on rutting bucks.

Glands beneath the skin are connected to hair follicles, which transfer fatty secretions, called **lactones**, to the hairs. It's believed this is a whitetail's fingerprint, indicating its sex, age and even physical condition. During the rut, frequent urinating over the glands, especially when a buck tends an injury, individualizes his trademark odor. The same holds true for does who allow urine to run down their legs at estrous time. Bucks sometime rub their tarsals together while urinating, performing a kind of mating dance. The odor from a tarsal gland is enhanced when a deer, buck or doe becomes excited. Specialized muscles make the hairs stand erect, releasing more scent into the air. This also serves as a signal to other deer with whom it may be traveling.

The odor of a buck's tarsal gland is most evident during the rut. Like many hunters, I've experienced a "reverse" of sorts when trying to smell a buck's presence. On one occasion, I was able to detect a downed buck from the breeze that carried the tarsal's scent to my nose. Secretions from the pre-orbital gland have been noted by many hunters who didn't identify them as anything more than a deposit at the lower corners of the eyes. These tear ducts, also called the **lacrymal** glands, are located in front of the eyes. Check out a whitetail mount someday and note the narrow slit below the eyes, where the glands are set. That yellowish or whitish waxy secretion is often visible on live deer. It is believed the pre-orbitals emit a scent which bucks rub on overhanging twigs and ground vegetation.

According to Tom Fegely, the only other gland of note is the forehead gland, which is actually a recent "new find" among biologists and hunters. Its purpose is not actually known, but many hunters have witnessed bucks rubbing their foreheads against scarred bark. Limbs, saplings and leaves are also rubbed this way. The skin in that region contains scent glands which often discolor the forehead, staining it dark. Deer who visit a rub will first smell the area, lick it, and then deposit their own forehead scent.

An entire segment of the deer hunting industry has been created for supplying hunters with a wide range of these scents. Many hunters will argue that, when properly used, the application of either natural glandular secretions taken from deer, or man-made synthetic scents that duplicate odors, provide the hunter with something of an edge. Others feel that hunters use too much scent—often it's the wrong scent at the wrong time. Surprisingly, there seems to be a growing number of hunters, particularly bowhunters, who seek to be as scent-free as possible, rather than trying to lure deer in or mask their own odors with bottled scents.

Most experts agree that whitetails communicate by means of soft, almost inaudible vocalization and through scents on a year-round basis, but it seems that the levels of communication heighten as the breeding season approaches, and that they peak right along with the rut. Perhaps it's because whitetails tend to be more active at these times as they search out suitable breeding partners and seek out their favorite food sources, all the while trying to elude an army of hunters who invade their habitats from August or September until late January or early February.

Knowledgeable whitetail hunter and outdoor writer Tom Fegely combines sound hunting tactics with careful scouting when looking for late season deer.

RUT PREPARATION

Dick Idol (Bigfork, Montana) ranks high among today's most recognized whitetail hunting experts. Since the 1970s he has been one of the strongest supporters of hunting big, mature whitetail bucks (known as "trophy hunting"). It's doubtful that there is another hunter in the U.S. who has spent as much time studying the ways of older bucks as Dick has. Through the years he has written enough magazine articles to compile ten books on the subject of hunting whitetails. In short, he knows what he's talking about. Dick feels that instead of breaking down the fall months into the commonly accepted "pre-rut," "rut" and "post-rut" periods, they should be divided more accurately into "rut preparation," "pre-breeding," "breeding," and "post-breeding" periods. He refers to this as the "four periods of the rut" and has written an excellent book on the subject. Some of his views on these very distinct periods follow:

Throughout most of North America's whitetail range, this initial period begins around the first week of September, when whitetail bucks typically shed the velvet covering on their newly hardened antlers. This period lasts roughly six weeks, ending sometime in mid-October. In extreme southern states—including Alabama, south Texas and on into northern Mexico—this period can extend into November. As the days lengthen, the velvet sheddingprocess is triggered by the flow of hormones. When this process begins, most bucks in a given herd will complete the shedding of velvet over a 7- to 10-day period. As the rut preparation period draws to an end, there is little if any change in the bucks; but mentally there can be dramatic changes in the bucks' attitudes as their primary interest shifts from food to does.

As the rut preparation period progresses, whitetail bucks become more anxious, preparing themselves for the new breeding season. At this time of the year, they often rub their antlers on shrubs

Mike Seay, a veteran muzzle-loading hunter from Iowa, went with his "best guess" when he caught up with this splendid buck. Educated guesswork often pays off when combined with obvious sign.

and small trees aggressively. The bucks tend to make rubs along most of the routes they travel, forming distinct "rub lines," which hunters use in patterning bucks during the entire period. Bucks that were visible in July while feeding in open soybean and hay fields suddenly seem to disappear. Actually, they have simply moved into a "woods pattern." In areas where early gun or bow seasons permit hunting, this is a great time to pattern and kill bucks who are now on regular, very predictable patterns—from bedding to feeding area and back again. Scrapes are usually established during this period, but most are boundary types made at random, not primary signs used for patterning.

PRE-BREEDING

In most places, the pre-breeding period begins around mid-October and runs three to four weeks in length. The period ends when the majority of the does begin to come into estrous, or are ready for breeding. In most northern and central states, and most of Canada, this usually occurs around November 10. In the deep South, this period may not end until breeding begins in mid- to late-December or even January.

The pre-breeding period is commonly marked by heightened buck activity. Whereas the does may still be a month or so away from breeding time, the bucks are ready now, and with their interest in does comes an escalation in scrape activity. Dick Idol says this is the time to use scrapes and scrape lines to pattern and predict the travel routes of

bucks. At this time their patterns usually denote regular circuits of scrape checking rather than the more rigid bedding and feeding patterns that are more prevalent during the rut preparation period. Dick also notes that during the preceding period a whitetail buck may travel only one to three miles in a 24-hour period. But during the pre-breeding stage, he may travel as much as 10 to 15 miles each day depending on such factors as the deer density, buck to doe ratio, habitat and terrain. Most of this activity is still centered around a buck's core center, i.e., wherever a buck tends to return at various times throughout the year.

Dick Idol

Many successful bowhunters feel that this pre-breeding period is, by far, the best time to take a really good buck. Dominant bucks have become extremely territorial, often challenging any intruders who invade their domain. At this time, bucks tend to respond quite well to calling and rattling, which can make even the wariest old buck extremely vulnerable.

BREEDING PERIOD

In nearly all states and provinces, this period is the shortest: approximately 12 to 18 days. In northern regions, the first does become receptive around November 8, and the final breeding takes place near Thanksgiving. In central Canada, breeding might begin around November 11 and end about November 24, while in south Texas, the dates are December 14-31. Assuming

there's an adequate number of breeding males, the vast majority of the does
will be bred during this short time span.
If not, unbred does will come back into
estrous in four-week intervals. When the
buck to doe ratios have gotten seriously
out of whack, with one buck per every six
to ten or more breeding does, late breeding begins to create some problems.

Dick Idol points out that the travel
patterns of most bucks change radically
during the breeding period—and so
should a hunter's tactics. As he says,
rubs and scrapes are not worth much
when trying to predict the travel patterns of bigger bucks; instead, they
move in tandem with their receptive
does. Predicting the travel pattern of an
individual buck becomes
especially difficult; hence,
this is not the best period
in which to kill a buck. It
is, however, a great time
to kill a random trophy.
The first two periods,
when patterns are more
predictable, are much
better times in which
to take a buck. Overall,
the breeding period is
the time when big bucks
are most vulnerable, and
no hunter should miss
the opportunity. In fact,
many states and Canadian
provinces schedule
their general firearms
seasons during the
breeding period.

THE POST-RUT

The breeding period
ends abruptly once the
primary doe estrous
periods have come to
an end. In most northern
zones, the post-rut usually begins around the first
of December. Dick Idol

figures the end of the post-rut period has arrived when the bucks have shed their antlers. Once the bucks are no longer concerned with pursuing hot estrous does, their attention reverts to feeding and surviving the winter. Some bucks will actually lose upwards of 25 to 30 percent of their total body weight to the rigors of the pre-breeding and breeding periods. Three to four weeks after the last doe has completed the primary estrous or breeding period, the secondary rut begins, in which unbred does enter estrous once again. This flurry of activity is considerably less than what goes on during the primary rut or breeding period. Just before the onset of the secondary rut, some bucks may freshen a few scrapes, providing hunters with one more shot at patterning a breeding buck.

With modern conservation practices and game laws resulting in an abundance of whitetails, the mindset of most hunters today has resulted in a lopsided ratio of does to bucks. Biologists profess different opinions about what the natural ratio would be if all mortalities caused by hunters and vehicular traffic were eliminated. Many knowledgeable whitetail experts feel, however, that bucks tend to suffer a slightly higher mortality rate whether they are hunted or not. Most feel that the birth rate of fawns is set at 50/50 for bucks and does. By the time they reach maturity (3 years), though, the natural ratio is actually closer to one mature buck to every 2 to 3 does. Private and professional deer managers in many parts of the country would be delighted to achieve such a balance. Unfortunately, aside from huge tracts of land or entire regions that are closely managed, such buck to doe ratios simply don't exist.

Western whitetails are often easier to pattern because of their limited range. Will Primos took this fine buck from a narrow strip of brush during the muzzleloading season in Idaho.

Through most of the 1950s and 1960s, the deer herds in many parts of the country were just beginning to grow. To ensure that this resource got the start it needed, early hunting seasons in many states prohibited the harvesting of does. After all, every hunter knows that these are the future mothers of a whole generation of whitetails. Even as population levels grew to the point of permitting an antlerless harvest, many hunters felt that shooting a doe was a "sissy thing" to do. The mindset stated that shooting a buck—any buck—was far better than harvesting a doe. Unfortunately, this led to an extremely large harvest of younger 1 1/2-year-old bucks who never lived to see their second rack or future trophy potential. In Missouri, for example, nearly 500,000 whitetail hunters annually harvest more than 60% of all antlered bucks. This pressure on the bucks has resulted in some extremely low buck to doe ratios. In many parts of this state (and others, including Wisconsin, Michigan, and Pennsylvania), large numbers of hunters take to the deer woods each fall with hopes of "bringing home a buck." As a result, the whitetail population now consists of as many as 20 to 30 does per breeding-aged buck.

Brian Murphy

Brian Murphy, Executive Director of the Quality Deer Management Association (P.O. Box 227, Watkinsville, GA 30677) comments:

When the sex ratio of a deer herd is out of balance, a number of potentially negative implications arise. When there are too many does for the relative number of bucks, does may miss their breeding cycles (primary rut) in the fall. For each cycle they miss, they must wait one month (28 days) before they can breed again. This is a special problem in southern latitudes where deer may experience three or four breeding cycles before a doe actually conceives. As a result, fawns are born late in the year, or at least later than they should be. These offspring tend to have low weaning weights and produce below-average adult deer.

The Quality Deer Management Association (QDMA) is a non-profit organization consisting of both professional and private land managers who have one goal in mind: to produce better quality whitetails for the future. Every hunter, they feel, holds the key to better hunting down the road: **the trigger finger**. It is QDMA's belief that hunters must now let younger bucks walk instead of harvesting them. And where the harvest of does is allowed, more emphasis must be placed on bringing the buck to doe ratio closer to what biologists feel is the natural balance of that particular whitetail herd. QDMA's origin springs from the determination among private land owners to do a better job of managing deer and other wildlife. Among its membership are more than 500 professional wildlife biologists, foresters and habitat managers who readily share their information with land owners.

COMPLETE BOOK OF WHITETAIL HUNTING

QDMA collects its scientific data and assimilates it into a format that landowners can easily understand and put into practice.

QDMA director Brian Murphy is among those who agree that deer hunters and land owners need reliable, unbiased information with which to make sound deer management decisions based chiefly on scientific research. In its endeavor to bridge the gap between land owners, hunters and researchers, QDMA publishes a distinguished quarterly magazine and offers excellent educational materials on whitetail management.

Sometime during the 1970s, a tall, red-headed and mustachioed young deer biologist and outdoor writer named Larry Weishuhn began fueling fires over the debate about stricter whitetail management. Since then, this deer-hunting buddy of mine has won the title of "Mr. Whitetail" among his professional peers in the fields of biology and journalism. As one of the most prolific writers on deer hunting, he bases his numerous articles and books on scientific research and practical hands-on hunting experiences, including the following realization:

The times have certainly changed. During the 1970s, no respectable deer hunter would even think about shooting a doe, even if his tag designated either sex. The manly thing to do was to shoot a buck, no matter if it was a spike, a small fork-horn, or a basket-racked 1 1/2-year-old eight-pointer. It was still a buck. Genetic research was just getting off the ground then, and many professional biologists openly backed the shooting of all spike bucks, claiming that they would never reach true trophy proportions. Today, these same experts realize the importance of harvesting adult does in order to bring a herd into balance—and to continue harvesting an equal number of does and bucks to maintain that balance. More than one researcher has proven that it's impossible to determine what future potential a buck many have from its first rack. Many spike bucks have matured into quite impressive record-book class bucks by the time they were 5 1/2 years old.

According to Larry Weishuhn, intense private management of whitetails has had both positive and negative

Larry Weishuhn

"Twenty years ago we were about to leave the age of deer hunting innocence and embark upon a broad new age of quality management. Deer hunting was different back then, Today, the average hunter is in his mid-40s, then the average hunter was only in his middle 30s. Kids hunted with their parents, grandparents and friends. If opening day of deer season fell during the middle of the week, most rural schools were closed during the first day of the season. Hunting with your parents was, in nearly all instances, considered an' excused' absence from school."

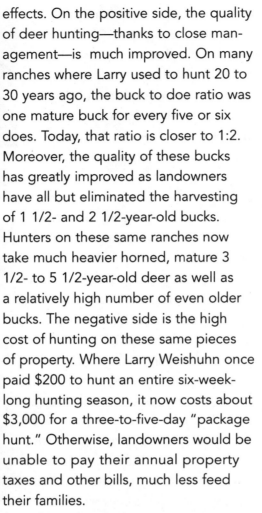

effects. On the positive side, the quality of deer hunting—thanks to close management—is much improved. On many ranches where Larry used to hunt 20 to 30 years ago, the buck to doe ratio was one mature buck for every five or six does. Today, that ratio is closer to 1:2. Moreover, the quality of these bucks has greatly improved as landowners have all but eliminated the harvesting of 1 1/2- and 2 1/2-year-old bucks. Hunters on these same ranches now take much heavier horned, mature 3 1/2- to 5 1/2-year-old deer as well as a relatively high number of even older bucks. The negative side is the high cost of hunting on these same pieces of property. Where Larry Weishuhn once paid $200 to hunt an entire six-week-long hunting season, it now costs about $3,000 for a three-to-five-day "package hunt." Otherwise, landowners would be unable to pay their annual property taxes and other bills, much less feed their families.

Unless a hunter happens to pursue whitetails on public hunting lands, the days of a "free ride" are quickly coming to an end. For the right to hunt on prime private properties, hunters must be ready to fork over hard-earned cash. As a result, they are beginning to form hunting clubs, or at least organizing themselves into close private groups when leasing private lands. In many cases, these hunters share a real desire to maintain and improve the quality of

hunting. Those who have leased sizable tracts of broken farm country often pay the landowner to plant specific food plots, or pay him for leaving a small portion of crops. Their well-intentioned goal is to attract more whitetails to more suitable tracts of habitat, and thus improve their hunting.

Whether the property is owned or leased, private deer management is changing the dynamics of today's whitetail populations. Where hunting restrictions require clients, club members or lease holders and guests to reduce the harvest of young bucks, where the antler-less harvest has been increased to balance the sex ratio of resident deer, and where honest efforts have been made to improve the quality of nutrition, the result is often not only more deer, but bucks of superior quality. State game department management has in some regions even begun to swing more toward producing quality over quantity. Whitetail deer management in the 21st century has gone hi-tech, including radio telemetry for studying whitetail movement, infra-red scanners for determining deer densities, and even DNA-testing to determine the blood lines of bucks that have sired offspring. Deer-hunting changed considerably during the last half of the 20th century. It will be interesting to see what the new millennium holds in store for the whitetail and those who live for the deer season each fall. ∎

Four Season Scouting

WITH ■ *Dick Idol, Whitetail Expert* ■ *John Sloan, Renown Bowhunter & Writer*
■ *Tom Fegely, Outdoor Writer & Photographer*

I first saw the big Illinois ten-pointer munching lazily on some clover late one evening in early September. The deer still sported full velvet on its massive rack. Even from a half-mile away, I knew right away that I was looking at a buck, with a massive rack that easily topped 190 Boone & Crockett points. Better still, the deer was eating his dinner on property on which I could hunt legally. A few weeks later, I made my first foray toward this record-book white-tail, quickly finding tracks that could have been made only by a big, mature buck like the one I had watched earlier in the clover field. After hanging several stands, I held off hunting the area until I found a more conclusive sign that I was indeed tracking down the same buck. By the third week of October, the deer was making rubs—and I do mean rubs. A cedar tree about one foot in diameter had been whittled down to less than half its original size. As the end of the month grew near,

the bucks began to make scrapes in earnest. After finally locating several scrapes near some huge rubs, I decided it was time to place an arrow into this monster.

Once you've set your sights on holding out for a buck-of-a-lifetime, it's really difficult to take a shot at an average-sized specimen. That's when other good bucks tend to show up, offering easy 20-yard shots to test your will power. A solid week of hunting from several different stands offered several good opportunities, all of which I reluctantly passed. Then, late one evening just as the sun was setting, there was my buck, hot on the trail of a big doe. Immediately, I grunted several times. The buck stopped, threw up his head and stared in my direction for several minutes. Then he dropped his nose to the ground and disappeared over a wooded rise several hundred yards away. While taking that buck with a bow (or with a rifle during gun season in mid-November, or during the December muzzleloader season) never materialized, just having the opportunity to hunt such a deer that close was almost reward enough for all the time spent scouting and placing stands.

The last time I saw anything of that buck was well after the close of the muzzleloader season. I had just ended my bow season by taking a good eight-pointer on Christmas Eve. Then, as my son and I gathered up a dozen or more stands, we were shocked to find one of the buck's huge antlers lying on the ground less than 50 yards from the same stand where I had arrowed the eight-pointer on Christmas Eve. That single antler scored 96 3/8. Given the estimated 22- to 24" spread of the rack, with the other side being about the same, the buck I was after would have grossed somewhere around 214 to 216 Boone & Crockett points.

While finding that shed antler told me the buck had survived the season, I never saw it again—and I certainly never heard of anyone who claimed he had spotted a potential world-record whitetail in the same area, let alone harvest one. Big bucks do live a charmed life, or so it seems; but they do leave sign so that even the most secretive whitetails can be spotted on occasion. Knowing when and where to observe off-season whitetails or to look for sign—whether it's shed antlers in late winter or early spring, or trails, scrapes, rubs and bedding areas before or during the hunting season—is knowledge acquired from years of studying white-tails. Neither this chapter, nor one entire book on scouting, will supply everything you need to know about sign—but it's a good start. The following section offers some sound advice from several extremely knowledgeable and successful whitetail hunters, not to mention some observations made by yours truly during more than 35 years spent chasing the white-tailed deer.

POST-SEASON SCOUTING

Many hunters will swear that post-season scouting is a waste of time; that determining where the deer were and what they did a whole season ago is of no value and doesn't say anything about what the deer will do next fall. On the other hand, some well-respected experts on whitetail hunting feel just the opposite—that determining travel and feed patterns from the season past tells them everything they need to know to start patterning the deer they will hunt come next October or November. Serious big buck hunters like Dick Idol claim there's no better time to take inventory of trophy class whitetails. He feels that finding sheds from a big mature buck—or locating someone who has—is the best evidence in determining rack characteristics that can help trophy-minded hunters to identify the same buck come fall. One reason why most hunters fail to find many sheds is that they start looking for them too late in the year. "The best times to find sheds," Dick says, "is immediately after they drop, or in the case of snow country, just after the snow melts." By early spring ground grasses are generally

so high that it's impossible to find a shed—unless, of course, you actually step right on it. By then, the squirrels and other rodents will likely have chewed away much of the antler.

Deer in different regions of the country tend to shed their antlers at different times of the winter. Dick Idol points out that in northern wilderness areas, bucks tend to shed their racks a lot earlier than do those in farmland areas, due probably to the quality of feed available combined with the rigors of winter in the big woods. In most areas of the Northwest, Canada and even parts of the Northeast, antlers begin dropping in late December, with the majority falling off in January. In the richer farmbelts, many bucks will carry their antlers well into February, with some

even dropping them into late March. Personally, I've learned to associate extreme cold spells that last for weeks as the reason why many bucks shed their antlers early. During a few late December bowhunts in northern Missouri (and muzzleloading hunts in Iowa during the first part of January), I've observed many bucks who had already shed their antlers. In those years when the bucks dropped their antlers early, temperatures had dropped to -10 to -20°, with wind chill factors as low as -40 or -50°.

When temperatures drop that low, the deer must feed. In western Illinois where I live, the whitetails are quite visible toward the end of January, nearly a month after all the hunters have left the field. Even the big bucks hit the corn

When combining scouting for deer sign with other outdoor activities, such as squirrel hunting, you'll discover more hot spots where whitetails gather.

and hay fields then, putting away some extra groceries to generate the body heat needed to survive an extended cold spell. Most of the bucks at this time of year still carry antlers, making this a good time to take inventory. During the first hour or two in the morning and the last couple of hours almost every evening, I like to ride around looking for deer through my binoculars. It's not uncommon to glass several hundred deer in a single day, many of them bucks. At this time of year, bucks also tend to hang together. Once the battling for the rut is over, they tend to be ol' buddies again. I've seen five or six 140 to 160 class bucks feeding together. Sometimes I can even spot cast antlers from my pickup through a pair of 10 power binoculars. The one thing I've come to realize from observing post-season bucks is that where I see them, and where they drop their antlers, is usually far from the places where I hunt. Winter deer band together, often moving miles from their summer and fall ranges. So just because you spot a monster buck or find its shed antlers in an area where you like to hunt doesn't mean he'll be there come fall.

Glassing is a great way to locate bucks. Watching feed areas from afar through a good pair of binocular can help eliminate spooking whitetails.

"Shed antlers tell me nothing," exclaims outdoor writer John Sloan, "They are no value to me in killing a trophy buck."

Despite his comment above, there's not a stronger supporter of post-season scouting than veteran bowhunter John Sloan, who maintains a sizable deer hunting lease near his home in central Tennessee. If a buck doesn't frequent the acres he manages, it's of little value to him. John also knows that a buck in his area may spend late winter far from where that same deer will appear next September and October. Like all ardent deer hunters, he relishes finding a good shed while scouting his hunting area in February, but he doesn't place much value on what this means to him during the next hunting season. John has come to the conclusion that most trails "lead to" something rather than "from" something. He contends that deer may come from several directions, but at one point these travel routes will merge into one at whatever destination they had in mind originally. Furthermore, when most deer leave whatever it is that drew them, they do so using different exits. Where there are exit trails, John has found them less noticeable than entrance trails. Most trails, he contends, lead ultimately to either a feeding or bedding area. And crossover trails tend to link with heavily-used travel corridors. Knowledge of these crossovers may be more valuable to a buck hunter, especially during the pre-rut and rut periods when a buck is on the move in search of receptive does. In February, the woods in John Sloan's country are mostly barren, allowing him to observe where these trails are headed, plus those land forms that can cause a trail to go around, over or through an area. As John points out:

In short, post-season scouting allows a hunter to see what he cannot see when the foliage is on and crops are in. Whitetails are creatures of habit and, all things being equal, they will normally return to the same feeding routine year after year. This is especially true where mast crops tend to do well each season. You can bet that when John Sloan finds a distinct trail leading to a stand of big white oaks, where the trail suddenly fans out or all but disappears, this season-wise bowhunter will know instinctively that here is a favored feeding area, one that he will duly note in the small notebook he carries during his post-season scouting. Somewhere, he knows, there will probably be a tree-stand come next fall.

John Sloan

SPRING AND SUMMER SCOUTING

According to Dick Idol, the warm weather months of late spring and summer are easily the most overlooked scouting periods of the year. Beginning in late April or early May, bucks begin to grow new racks, a process that requires large amounts of high protein

"When the trees are barren and the ground is open, I can see the terrain features. I see the low spots, the dips, the grown-up logging roads. I can glass the ridge tops and see the saddles, bowls and cuts. I can glass down from the ridge tops and see the thicket's creek bottom crossings. I can glass from the edge of crop fields and see the undulations in the land contour and tree line. In the winter, while the land is still naked, I can see the underwear. . . the foundation garment that is going to make a deer adhere to instinctive travel patterns."

foods. As they munch on newly sprouted soybeans, clover or specially planted food plots, the deer often become extremely visible. Unfortunately, most hunters at that time of year are too busy fishing, playing softball or going on family vacations to do any scouting. In most areas of the country, Dick points out, by the end of the first week of July a deer's main beams have developed to the point where they begin to turn forward. That's when trophy-minded hunters begin to get a feel for the potential and characteristics of the rack. Dick also believes that a whitetail's rack has fully developed by the first week of August, with most bucks beginning to shed the velvet covering during the first ten days of September. According to Dick Idol:

"Bucks tend to be very visible in the heaviest growth stages of June and July, and they begin showing themselves less and less as August progresses. I normally concentrate my scouting—or "looking" as it's better described—from the last week in June through the second week of August. The summer months offer the added bonus of possibly seeing several bucks at a time, because those in similar age classes tend to reside in bachelor groups. This behavior is part of nature's design to establish dominance ranking by non-lethal means. I have on special occasions seen as many as 8 or 10 big bucks feeding in the same field, though it's more common to spot only two or three together."

I'm one of those people who loves to watch whitetails, no matter what time of the year. I cannot think of a more pleasant way to spend a late afternoon or early evening in mid-summer than riding the back roads glassing for bucks out in the soybean or hay fields. Not only does it allow me to see some of the biggest bucks I'll encounter all year long—such as that big Illinois ten-pointer discussed earlier—it also allows me to see what crops the farmers have planted. The annual rotation of crops, especially soybeans and corn, can play a big role as to where, when and how the deer will feed in certain areas. To

me, late spring and summer scouting is just another part of understanding completely the world of the whitetail.

PRE-SEASON SCOUTING

This is the time of year when the vast majority of hunters—whether they hunt with a bow or gun—do all of their scouting for the upcoming whitetail seasons. This is also a time when many deer hunters actually rob themselves of a chance at a buck they've patterned successfully. Once we step into the deer woods and hang around too long or make too much noise, or disturb the area unduly, every deer inhabiting that stand of woods will know that a hunter

is—or was—close by. The more we hunters tromp around through good deer cover, the less likely we'll ever actually see the buck we're after.

Several season back, I spent much of late October helping Ruby Custer, a western Iowa outfitter, scout and hang stands on several thousand acres she manages. On one afternoon, I located a heavily used travel corridor in a big bowl near the end of a large corn field. The deer were passing through the area, morning and evening, going to and returning from Ruby's heavily cropped farm fields. Into the middle of all the deer sign, Ruby and I carried a strap-on climbing pole and chain-on

During mid to late summer, bucks who gather in bachelor groups are usually quite visible. It's a great time to glass fields and timber edges to check on the quality of bucks to be hunted.

type stand. While we kept our chit-chat to a bare minimum, we did make more noise while hanging the stand than we should have. While Ruby worked on getting the stand in place 20 feet up the tree, I used a pruning pole to clip away a few branches that might deflect an arrow. Suddenly, I heard a noise and looked up to see a good 140 class buck standing just 20 yards away, watching our every move. With that, the deer spun and left. Not ten minutes later, another 130 class buck came to investigate the chain rattling on the stand and the rustling of the underbrush as I continued to chop a shooting lane. It came to within 25 yards of the stand before bolting. I was sure the spot would produce a good buck for one of Ruby's clients, but during the remainder

of the archery season, and all during the shotgun seasons, not another buck was ever spotted from that stand.

It's extremely important, John Sloan warns, to realize that deer will begin to pattern hunters during pre-season scouting. He feels that a hunter's goal is to key in on a stand location in anticipation of deer movements. In other words, he should place a stand when no deer are in the area, but with the knowledge that deer will later be using the trail, the feeding area, travel corridor, cross-over, or what have you; in other words, preparing to hunt a pattern before the pattern itself actually develops. He often bases his decision on where to put stands from information garnered during post-season scouting. He seldom wastes time in a sector where his hunting area is totally void of deer sign. The average whitetail hunter simply cannot devote months every year gathering information about a deer he may hunt only one or two weeks in the fall. *For those with a limited amount of time, outdoor writer Tom Fegely suggests the following plan of action:*

1 The first order of business is to zero in on the area in which you plan to hunt. Establish travel patterns to and

from feed areas and bedding areas. Study the tracks to see where the larger, more mature bucks enter feed areas, cross creeks, and move from one travel corridor to another, or even bed. Often in late September and early October, a big buck's movements are commonly different from that of does and fawns. At this time of the year, it's not uncommon for bucks to be traveling in bachelor

John Sloan took this buck as it traveled a rub and scrape line. He spent several days scouting this area before locating the travel corridor.

groups. If you do come across a large track of five or six deer, don't dismiss it as a bunch of old does. It's probably a bachelor group of bucks running together. When this many deer scramble up a creek bank one after the other, the crossing can appear well-used, even though they may never cross there again. In short, use some discretion in hanging stands whenever you see such sign.

2 In some parts of the country, bucks often begin making rubs and scrapes in late September or early October. Throughout most of its range, from mid to late October, the deer commonly begin to leave this sign in earnest, just before the start of the rut. In some regions, though, scouting hunters may not encounter scrapes until early November. During pre-season scouting, especially for an early archery hunt, the hunter may not encounter large numbers of rubs and scrapes. But if the deer fail to pick up on man's intrusion into the area, or if it is not spooked by close encounters with hunters, it's a good idea to recheck these areas at the end of October. Active bucks can really tear up an area in a short span of time. That's when a bowhunter should be in the stand. Early rubs made in September can be caused by anxiety among individuals within a group of bachelor bucks. The hunter who finds such sign early should always plan follow-up scouting jaunts to see if additional, newer rubs and scrapes have been made in the same areas. Often a buck may "shadow box" or spar with

saplings in preparation for the time when it will be battling others. Rubs found early can be the result of such mock battles. While small rubs are sometimes made by young bucks, you can rest assured that when a rub has totally debarked a 6- to 10" cedar tree, it wasn't a buck sporting his first or second rack who did it.

3 The existence of rubs lets a hunter know that at least one buck exists in the hunt area, but scattered and isolated rubs hardly establish a reliable pattern. The hunter should spend time to cover the area thoroughly and try to locate a "rub line." When you can locate a dozen or so rubs in what seems a distinct route, that's what hunters refer to as a rub line. A series of rubs may indicate a definite travel pattern. As the rut grows closer, it's a good bet you'll find a few scrapes along the same route. Field edges, along stream banks, skid trails, old logging roads and readily recognized deer trails must all be given special attention. Scouting hunters should carefully note the locations of rubs and scrapes on either a topographical map, a sketch of the hunting area, or simply in a notebook. As all the pieces of the puzzle slowly come together, the wise hunter can often detect well-traveled areas simply by noting where most of this sign was found. Bucks often take the most direct route, from one area to another. It's along these routes that one often finds the best spot to ambush one.

4 For those who must hunt on public land, it's likely you'll be sharing the area with other hunters, so locating deer sign may not be enough. You can bet that once you've located some well-used trails, rubs and scrapes—especially those close to easy access areas—other hunters scouting the same area have probably discovered the same sign. When faced with hunting in national forest or state hunting lands, or any other area open to the public, seek out the most inaccessible spots in the area and concentrate your scouting there. "Once, while hunting some property in northeastern Pennsylvania," Tom Fegely recalls, "I bought a topographic map and aerial photo of the area and discovered an alternate route into the backcountry. Using a canoe with a three-horsepower motor, a friend and I were able to cut an hour's walk into a 15-minute boat ride, placing us in a region where other hunters might push deer to us each morning."

5 Walking the edges of a field will often reveal where most of the deer enter to feed. If undisturbed, they will usually keep using the same routes, at least until they make the transition to another food source. Deer will often feed heavily on clover or alfalfa early in the season, then abandon these fields once the white oak acorns (the favorite food source of most whitetails) begin to fall.

When hanging a stand—especially if bowhunters with a 30- to 40-yard range limitation are involved—it's best to position it a few yards back from the edge of a field, rather than along its rim. Large bucks tend to linger in the fringe cover until darkness allows them to move with safety into the open in

Tony Knight caught up with this Iowa buck by scouting during the course of the season and shifting the location of his treed stand.

search of feed. A hunter who hangs a stand away from the edge of the field may not see where the deer have gone to feed, but he's more likely to see more bucks in the fringe.

6 Anxious hunters who have waited nearly a year for deer season to roll around again should take extra care to avoid polluting the area. Always wear rubber boots while scouting, and utilize cover scents or sprays that mask human odor. Avoid contaminating the hunting area with foreign odors carried on clothing and footwear. Use the same awareness of wind changes while scouting as you do when actually hunting. Get into the area, learn what you can, and exit without leaving a calling card. Scouting —and the degree to which it's performed —is a personal matter. Give it as much

time as you can afford, even if only for a day or two. The more knowledge gained about your hunting area in pre-season, the better your chances of being in the right spot on opening day.

INTERPRETING PRE-SEASON SIGN

For John Sloan, simply finding lots of sign isn't enough. Before he can take full advantage of what he sees in the hunting area, he must first know how to interpret what's actually there. Reading deer sign correctly is developed only by spending years in the deer woods, studying the movement and habits of whitetails. Following are a few of John's personal observations having to do with the subject of *rubs*, of which there are three different classifications.

1 *Incidental rubs.* Some hunters associate these with a buck's attempts to shed the velvet from its antlers each September. They are the same type of rubs Tom Fegely feels are made by bachelor group bucks trying to vent a little frustration. Whatever the reason, John Sloan considers these rubs incidental. They tell him only that a buck has been there and are of no real value in patterning a desirable whitetail.

2 *Cluster rubs.* These are important to note wherever rubs are all in close proximity, such as in a willow patch. Often there may be more than a dozen or so such rubs, all within sight of one another (I once found a heavy stand of willows along a slough near the Mississippi River where bucks had rubbed more than 200 willow saplings

in an area measuring only 30 feet by 30 feet). John feels these rubs offer slightly more information than incidental ones. They are usually the result of more than a single buck, an indication that the area is frequented on a regular basis. When enough other sign is located within the same vicinity, some cluster rub sites deserve consideration as good stand locations. Cluster rubs are often found near feeding or bedding areas, and therein lies the true value of locating this sign.

3 *Sign-post rubs.* According to John, these are the big, impressive rubs found by hunters. As such, they represent something of a guidepost allowing dominant bucks to travel along routes visited less frequently by other whitetails in the region, especially does, fawns and lesser bucks. Rubs that appear on trees of 10- to 12" diameters also serve as a kind of stop sign for competing bucks who seek to infringe on another's territory. Such large rubs are often used by more than one buck and are freshened on a regular basis through much of the fall. Since the travel route is usually frequented by only one, two, or three bucks, there is seldom any trace of a trail. But when scouting reveals a line of such rubs, a hunter has probably located an ideal place in which to hunt a good buck. When an experienced hunter comes across a major rub line located close to a probable feed area, he knows the stand is likely to be near an afternoon and evening location. But where a rub line is close to a known bedding area,

the hunter will usually do better by hunting in the morning. One way to tell in which direction a buck is headed is to note on which side of the tree the rubbing has appeared. Bright, barren rubbed areas nearly always face oncoming deer traffic.

Among whitetail hunters, there's a feeling that rubs tell you only that a buck was in that vicinity at one time. If you really want to shoot a good buck, you need to be hunting scrapes, not rubs. John Sloan disagrees. "In my years of hunting experience," he recalls, "the exact reverse is true. When finding rubs during your scouting and hunting, take time to analyze why the rub is there and what it means. It could be the key to the buck of a lifetime."

John doesn't discount scrapes altogether, he just doesn't base his entire approach to hunting an area on the existence of scrapes. Instead of letting the size and abundance of scrapes dictate where to hunt, put more faith into exactly where the scrape was located. To him, the best scrapes appear in or along a tree-line on the edge of a grown-up field. This usually puts a scrape close to bedding areas or along heavily traveled routes. His second choice is a scrape that appears in extremely heavy cover. In his experience, such scrapes are usually made by larger bucks. Such bucks, however, don't run right up and plant their noses in these scrapes. Instead, they will first pass slightly downwind, using their sensitive noses to detect activity in the scrape —whether it's an estrous doe letting a

dominant buck know she's ready for breeding, or another buck who is challenging that dominance. Thus, while scrapes are an important part of the overall picture, John still prefers to hunt rub lines and travel corridors that lead to the location of good scrapes, rather than hunt directly over the scrape itself.

SCOUTING DURING SEASON

Whitetail movement is influenced by several different factors, among them human disturbance of bedding and feeding areas, hunting pressure, thinning foliage, crop harvests, changing weather patterns, and other factors. Those hunters who think they can simply hang a stand in October and hunt the same spot all the way to the season's end in December or January are foolish indeed. Whitetails can quickly pattern a hunter who returns to the same location day after day and alter their movements accordingly. Through the pre-rut and rut periods, hunters should constantly scout these areas similar to those frequented by the deer at the start of the season. Once the gun seasons have put too much pressure on the whitetails, you may have to concentrate more heavily on remote locations or the thickest cover available within a given area.

As the primary rut winds down, usually in November or perhaps as late as December or January in the deep south, bucks have all but abandoned scrapes. There is commonly a second flurry of rut activity about two to three weeks after the end of the primary rut

(already referred to as the secondary rut). While the second rut may offer one more chance to pursue rutting bucks, the smart hunter at this time of year will usually turn to searching for food sources. Where December temperatures can plummet to below zero and stay there for extended periods of time, whitetails need to feed heavily in order to maintain body heat. Corn fields still laden with corn are a great place to concentrate; and where the ground is still free of snow cover, fields of hay and green grass will attract deer in large numbers. It's a good bet, too, that whitetails won't bed down all that far from heavily used feed areas late in the season.

Personally, I look forward to each scouting trip. There's no other way to learn what the deer in your area are doing. If you have no clue where they are feeding or bedding, you're entrusting the success of your hunting season to sheer luck. While I'm always joking that "I'd rather be lucky than good," the fact is, I don't ever have to explain why I succeeded in a whitetail hunt. I want to know enough about the deer I'm hunting so my chances of being lucky will put me in the right place at the right time. ∎

The Well-Equipped Deer Hunter

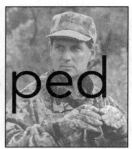

All About Hunting Rifles, Shotguns, Handguns, Muzzleloaders and Bows

WITH ■ *Tom Fegely, Outdoor Writer & Photographer* ■ *Jim Shockey, Canadian Outfitter & Writer* ■ *Bill Vaznis, Bowhunter and Outdoor Writer*

Chapter Three

Each year, hunters throughout the U.S. spend hundreds of millions of dollars on new equipment, most of which has been designed for their use while pursuing the white-tailed deer. In many states, the number of hunters who head out with dreams of hanging a trophy buck on the wall is far greater than those who seek other species of game. Even where deer hunters and small game hunters are nearly equal in number, the whitetail hunter spends far more on equipment than his counterparts. As outdoor writer Tom Fegely of Pennsylvania points out, "Visit your favorite sporting goods store, or flip the pages in all those catalogs that show up in the mailbox each fall and you'll find the widest selection of deer-hunting gear imaginable."

Not only is the selection of calls, tree stands, camouflaged clothing, binoculars, packs, knives, scents, cold weather clothing, boots, archery accessories, muzzleloading gear and a wide range of other deer hunting essentials available in abundance, but new products are being added every year. And as deer hunting experts and researchers keep discovering new facets of whitetail behavior and their habits, it's a good bet that more innovative offerings are not far behind. In recent years, for example, we've witnessed the growing popularity of deer calls, especially grunt tubes, along with such innovations as infra-red game finders (indicating the body heat of downed game), laundry detergents developed specifically for the removal and elimination of ultraviolet brighteners from hunting clothes, and even laser sights for bows (to make shot placement easier during low light conditions). Who knows what the future will bring? As long as there are hunters searching for an edge and who are willing to pay for products that hold the promise of success, there will probably

always be a demand for new gimmicks. Fortunately, bogus products are generally short-lived once hunters realize they've been taken. Trouble is, million of dollars are spent on fly-by-night products before they can be weeded from the market. Before any new idea is condemned, however, consideration must be given to the many widely used and trusted products that were met with great opposition and skepticism when they first hit the market.

All deer hunters have their own style, creating different demands on certain gear for hunters to rely on each fall and winter. Stand hunters will concentrate on tree stands that offer plenty of comfort for those long waits until the deer appear. Since hunters must often sit 20 to 30 feet off the ground, safety becomes a primary issue. The still hunter, on the other hand, is on the go, quietly slipping from tree to tree searching for the slightest movement that

Outdoor writer Tom Fegely feels that each time a white-tail hunter heads for the deer woods, a good quality pair of binoculars should be hanging around his neck. (Betty Lou Fegely photo)

Jim Shockey

The Thompson/Center Arms "Encore" carbine and pistol in the same caliber would be a handy combo for most whitetail hunters.

might give away the presence of deer nearby. The still hunter is concerned more likely with the quietness of his footwear and clothing, and with the clarity of his binoculars. These allow him to search the brush rather than rely on his eyes alone. Late season hunters during a muzzleloader hunt could also be faced with temperatures plummeting well below zero during late December or early January. Warm clothing and boots are a must.

One piece of gear every serious whitetail hunter should invest in, according to outfitter Jim Shockey, is a good pair of binoculars. Whether a hunter does most of his hunting from a tree stand, on foot, from natural or manmade landforms, or by using "spot-and-stalk" techniques, a clear, crisp binocular will allow the hunter to identify whitetails, whether at a distance or standing back in the brush. Too often, a hunter who packs a scoped rifle uses the optics on the firearm to check out unidentified movements, which could easily turn out to be another hunter moving through thick cover. At that point, he is aiming a loaded rifle at another human being! A good set of binoculars would—or should—eliminate the need to sight through a rifle scope. Jim Shockey hunts the big country of Saskatchewan, where covering lots of ground—either on foot or through the binoculars—is often a must. His favorite pair of binoculars is a big 10x50mm

Leupold glass, which can stand up to the daily demands of an outfitter who may spend each day from mid-September to the end of November looking for deer. The precision glass elements of his binoculars allow Shockey to spend hours each day peering through them without creating eye strain.

Not everyone spends as much time looking through binoculars the way Jim Shockey does, and few hunters care to pack around the extra weight of those 10x50mm glasses. One who does is bowhunter Bill Vaznis, a bowhunting writer who hunts several states each fall, spending practically all of his time on the ground still-hunting, stalking or tracking. According to Vaznis:

"Binoculars are a still hunter's best friend. When slipping quietly through good deer cover, a hunter must see the buck before it sees him if he ever hopes to be successful. A quality pair of field glasses can increase the odds in the hunter's favor, and then some."

Like many weight-conscious hunters, Vaznis favors compact binoculars, such as a handy 10x50mm pair from Nikon that weighs less than a 20-round box of .30/06 ammo. It's small enough to stay out of the hunter's way as he brings a bow to full draw, or while taking air at a distant whitetail with a long rifle. Nikon, Leupold, Pentax, Simmons and a few others market a wide range of compact binoculars ranging from 4x to 12x.

"When shopping for a pair of binoculars," says Tom Fegely, "try sighting on a distant object. Make sure the glass can be focused easily, remembering you may have to do so while wearing gloves. Is the eye relief comfortable? Does it cover the full scene? For those who wear regular glasses, be sure to fold down the rubber eyecups before testing. And be certain those 'second eyes' are around your neck whenever you head into whitetail country."

Just as different hunters will prefer different binoculars for different reasons, the same is true with clothing, whether it's footwear, a field dressing knife, a camouflage pattern, or any other piece of deer-hunting equipment. Never base the products you utilize solely on the needs of other deer hunters. Listen to what experienced whitetail hunters have to say about certain products or concepts that interest you. In many cases, what works for them will likely work for you, especially if you're hunting in the same basic terrain and whitetail habitat. Each hunter will eventually develop his own needs based on previous experiences in the deer woods, his observations of whitetail movement and behavior, his favored hunting techniques, and so on. We all will eventually turn to the products that best meet our needs. It's simply a matter of taste. Though we all may be linked by a common bond—hunting the white-

Bill Vaznis

tailed deer—we each have our personal preferences. Otherwise, no one would ever find his vehicle in the parking lot—it would be filled with pickup trucks!

In the following chapters, some of the world's best known whitetail deer hunters share the tactics and products they use in harvesting bucks. In the chapter on stand hunting, for example, we discuss some of the features hunters look for. There's another chapter on still-hunting, and others on the use of deer hunting scents, deer calls, knives, clothing, footwear, portable ground blinds and so forth. And finally, there's a chapter on managing property for better deer hunting, and others by recognized biologists and deer-hunting pros on products that can ensure more deer on the property you hunt.

Whether you're using a centerfire rifle, shotgun, handgun or muzzleloader, making a choice of one over another is generally a personal matter as well.

When it comes to firearms, though, certain calibers and bullet weights have become best-sellers for a reason: they work, and they take deer effectively. We will also turn to recognized shooting industry experts, such as Steve Hornady, (Hornady Manufacturing), Mike Jorden (former head of technical services at Olin-Winchester) and Russ Markesbery (president of Markesbery Muzzle Loaders), plus respected deer-hunting authorities Larry Weishuhn and Dave Henderson. They will all take a look at what products deliver the performance now demanded by today's deer hunters.

There's also a section on bowhunting in which we take a look at current trends in archery-hunting gear, and why today's bowhunter looks for ever faster, flatter arrow

flight. Hunting experts John Sloan, Will Primos and Richard P. Smith share their thoughts as well; and Ottie Snyder, a spokesman for Horton Manufacturing Company, takes a close look at the crossbow myth, with a compelling argument on why bows that are held horizontally should be made legal during all archery seasons.

Whitetail deer hunting is a sport in which opinions are like, well, favorite deer hunting spots. Everyone has one!

When voicing an opinion about products, be careful not to under- or over-sell anything. Don't jump on the bandwagon for or against specific products, ideas, concepts or tactics without first trying them out yourself. Half the fun of hunting deer lies in new experiences. If you hunt the same old stand and use the same old tactics with grandpa's same old .30/30 year after year, you are only cheating yourself. ■

Whitetail expert Larry Weishuhn knows the importance of heading for the deer woods with the right equipment. His modern in-line percussion rifle was apparently an ideal choice for this muzzleloader hunt.

PART ONE

Centerfire Whitetail Rifles

WITH ■ *Mike Jordan, Winchester-Western*
■ *Steve Hornady, Hornady Mfg.*

Everyone, it seems, has an opinion about which is the best, most ideal rifle for hunting deer. Tastes run from bolt-action rifles for long-range accuracy to fast-firing semi-autos for quick second and third shots at running deer, or short lever-actions for close, heavy-cover hunting situations. What is ideal for one hunter's favorite whitetail cover may be totally wrong for the overall hunting conditions preferred by another. When it comes to calibers best suited to your needs, some are much superior under certain hunting situations—no matter what style of rifle is chambered for a given cartridge.

One of the five best-selling centerfire rifle cartridges today is, believe it or not, the old .30/30 Winchester. It's not that this cartridge is a whitetail-stopping powerhouse, but one time or another many rifles were chambered for the cartridge, and still are. All told, more than 10 million Winchester Model 94 and Marlin Model 336 lever-action

rifles have been sold, most of them chambered for the .30/30 Winchester. What makes the cartridge truly significant is that originally it was, back in 1895, the first American small bore smokeless powder sporting cartridge, available in what was then the "new" Winchester Model 94 rifle. Through the years other rifles—including the Savage Model 99 lever-action, the Winchester Models 55 and 64 lever guns, the Savage 340 bolt-action, the Stevens 325 bolt-action, H&R's "Topper" single-shot rifle, the Thompson/Center "Contender" single-shot carbine—have all been offered in .30/30.

Some of the early Winchesters are now considered collector guns, and it's a good bet that most of them still see regular use. It should come as no surprise, therefore, to learn that this 100-year-old cartridge remains one of the top five sellers for Winchester-Western, Remington, Federal and other ammunition producers. A 170 grain roundnose

bullet is one of the more popular weights for whitetails. Winchester's popular Super-X "Power Point" and "Silvertip" bullets of this same weight leave the muzzle of a 20-inch barrel at around 2,200 f.p.s., with just over 1,800 ft. lbs. of energy. Such ballistics are comparable to the velocities and energies currently being produced by today's in-line percussion muzzleloaders. In the hands of an experienced marksman, a .30/30 rifle can take whitetails out to around 150 yards; but the .30/30 is not a long-range hunting projectile. By the time its blunt-nosed 170 grain bullets reach 200 yards, its energy levels drop to less than 1,000 f.p.s., while from 100 to 200 yards the bullet drops nine inches.

Due to the poor ballistics and excessive drop of the .30/30 cartridge, only a few centerfire rifles now being manufactured are offered in this chambering, including the Winchester Model 94 and Marlin 336, plus a few single-shot models. Centerfire rifle shooters want something with a much faster velocity, more knockdown energy, and a super-flat trajectory. They want a cartridge that enables them to hold dead on from 50 to 200 yards and drop a whitetail where it stands. Rounding out the five top-selling cartridges made by U.S. ammunition makers are the .30/06, .270 Winchester, 7mm Remington Magnum, and the .243 Winchester (not necessarily in that order). Mike Jordan, Public

Tom Fegely took this Saskatchewan ten-pointer with a Remington Model 700 in .270 Winchester.

Relations Manager for Winchester, says that the best-selling bullet weights for the .30/06 are a toss-up between 150 and 180 grains, while the .270 Winchester weighs in at 130-150 grains and the 7mm Remington Magnums at 140-160 grains. Winchester's best-selling bullet weight for the .243 Winchester is its own 100 grain bullet. Since the .243 was primarily developed as a longer range varmint cartridge, the popularity of heavier 100 grain bullets over 55 and 80 grain "varmint" bullets indicates that this sweet-shooting .24 caliber cartridge sees more use today on deer and other deer-sized game than the pesky critters for which it was developed.

For those who work within the shooting industry, where everything is available to shoot, it becomes increasingly difficult to know which rifle style and caliber are absolute favorites. Mike Jordan prefers a good bolt-action rifle, such as the Winchester Model 70 in .270 Winchester (topped with a high-quality 3x9 or 4x14 scope). His bullet choice depends largely on where he is hunting, whether in the close cover of Missouri, where he prefers the slightly heavier 150 grain bullet, to the open country of eastern Colorado or Wyoming, where he opts for the flat-shooting characteristics of the 130 grain bullet. Most modern centerfire lines include the .30/06, .270 Winchester, 7m Remington Magnum and .243 Winchester in the lineup of available calibers. Ballistics can be boring to those whose lives

Mike Jordan

don't revolve around numbers; nevertheless, the velocities, energies and trajectories of different cartridges and bullet weights can help shooters to select the caliber(s) that are best-suited for a particular type of whitetail hunting.

For years, rifle experts named the .30/06 as the perfect choice for the big game hunter who desires a one-rifle battery for all North American big game. Even though it has been around for nearly 100 years, no other single cartridge has matched its versatility. Factory-loaded cartridges are available with bullets as light as 125 grains for greater velocity and a flatter trajectory, and as heavy as 220 grains for maximum knockdown power and brush-busting shot placement. The handloader has an even wider range of bullets for special purpose loads. With lighter 125 or 130 grain spire-point bullets, most .30/06 rifle barrels produce a muzzle velocity of around 3,100 to 3,200 f.p.s., with approximately 2,750 ft. lbs. of energy. At 100 yards, the bullet smacks home with a little more than 2,100 ft. lbs. of energy and more than 1,600 ft. lbs. at 200 yards. In fact, this light bullet delivers more than 1,200 ft. lbs. plus of energy all the way out at 300 yards. The popular 150 grain bullet for this caliber usually leaves the muzzle at slightly more than 2,900 f.p.s. (with most factory loads) and about 2,800 ft. lbs. of energy. Out at 100 yards, the bullet is good for more than 2,200 ft. lbs. of energy, close to 1,800 ft. lbs. at 200 yards, and about 1,450 ft. lbs. at 300. In fact, this bullet is still good for

1,000 ft. lbs. of knockdown power at 400 yards. The big 180 grain factory loads are usually good for around 2,700 f.p.s., with 2,900 ft. lbs. of energy at the muzzle. Remaining energy at 100 yards is over 2,400 ft. lbs., around 2,000 ft. 150 yards will hit only about an inch high at 100 and 2 inches low at 200. The same bullet will impact around 5.5 inches low at 250 yards and just over 10.5 inches at 300 yards. Sighted in the same manner, a heavier 150 grain bullet

lbs. at 200 yards, more than 1,600 ft. lbs. at 300, over 1,300 ft. lbs. at 400 yards, and close to 1,100 ft. lbs. out at 500 yards.

No one doubts that heavier bullets deliver greater knockdown energy levels, especially at longer ranges. But whitetail hunters should know that the bigger the bullet, the more it tends to drop once the range extends out past 200 yards. Light 125 grain factory .30/06 loads sighted to hit dead on at

will still be right at 1 inch high at 100 yards, close to 2.5 inches low at 200 yards, some 6.5 inches low at 250, and slightly over 12 inches low at 300 yards. The even heavier 180 grain bullets sighted on at 150 yards will impact around 4 inches low at 200, close to 11 inches below point of aim at 250, and more than 15 inches low at 300 yards. That's enough to miss a whitetail completely without compensating for the drop.

Open country, like this wide-open Wyoming prairie, offers a different challenge than one encounters when hunting the thick brush country of the Northeast. It also requires a totally different kind of centerfire rifle.

Steve Hornady

Hornady's "Light Magnum" load produces hotter factory loads closer to the performance level of carefully crafted hand-loads. The Hornady line includes 150, 165 and 180 grain InterLock boat-tailed soft-point bullets for the .30/06. The 150 grain bullet leaves the muzzle at a remarkable 3,100 f.p.s., while the 180 grain powerhouse still manages to leave the muzzle at 2,900 f.p.s. Corresponding muzzle energies are 3,200, 3,330 and 3,361 ft. lbs. Downrange at 200 yards, the remaining energy of the 150 grain bullet is 2,161 ft. lbs., with 2,428 ft. lbs. for the 165 grain bullet, and 2,500 ft. lbs. for the heavier 180 grain soft-point bullet.

Steve Hornady (president of Hornady Manufacturing Company), while claiming he doesn't really have a "favorite" rifle or caliber, often turns to the .30/06, using this caliber to take a number of good-sized whitetail bucks. On one hunt, he recalls firing a Browning A-Bolt in .30/06 to take a record-book Coues whitetail in Arizona. His rifle was equipped with Browning's BOSS (Ballistic Optimizing Shooting System), featuring a compensator at the muzzle to adjust barrel vibrations according to the bullet. Using Hornady's 165 grain "Light Magnum" loads,

Steve's rifle proved to be a real tack driver. On this whitetail hunt with outfitter Duwanne Adams he recalls vividly the following incident:

"We left Tucson, Arizona, in the middle of the night. It poured rain during the hour-long drive to where we planned to hunt, parking on a ridge top where we could huddle under ponchos in the back of the pickup while glassing a draw and along the side of a mountain. About half an hour into the hunt, the rain stopped. Duwanne quickly spotted a good buck making its way through the cactus and brush down below. I never did see the deer before it went out of sight. We grabbed our stuff and followed the buck as it headed up a draw. Eventually, we spotted the deer and, after a careful stalk, got to within 200 yards of the buck. It was lying behind a log, where only his head and neck were visible. As a result, I missed, whereupon the buck leaped to his feet and moved about 15 feet into the open to see what was up. I dropped him immediately with the .30/06 Browning A-Bolt."

I've hunted with a variety of rifles in every top-selling caliber—*except* the "thirty-thirty." At one time or another, I've owned a few collector guns in .30/30 but never considered it seriously as a choice for deer—not when there are much better calibers to use. One of my favorite rifles in the past was a tack-driving Sako Finnbear in .270 Winchester topped with a super-clear Leupold 3x9x40mm variable scope. When firing a Nosler 130 grain boat-tailed spitzer, that rifle consistently punched 1- to 1.5-inch five-shot groups at 100 yards. On extended range shooting, I could easily keep five shots inside 3.5 inches at 200 yards (or 6 inches at 300 yards). I know some shooters can make tighter groups, especially at longer ranges, but that was good enough for me. Every standing whitetail I shot—out to almost 300 yards—went down. The hottest handloads that still produced the kind of accuracy I wanted could push a 130 grain spitzer from the muzzle at just over 3,100 f.p.s., with about 2,775 ft. lbs. of muzzle energy. Those same loads were still hitting the target at 300 yards with more than 1,500 pounds of wallop. I learned my own range limitation long ago when hunting whitetails in Wyoming. For example, on one of my first trips to the wide open spaces out West, I attempted several shots way past 300 yards. I managed to hit one good buck at nearly 400 yards (using a 130 grain spitzer), but I lost the buck to a less-

then-perfect hit. I have no business shooting at whitetails past 300 yards—and neither should a vast majority of today's deer hunters.

More recently, the 7mm Remington Magnum has become quite popular, and for good reason: it's a great cartridge. When one of those big belted cartridges is placed next to a .270 Winchester cartridge, the 7mm Remington Magnum looks like an artillery round. Ballistically, though, it's not that superior proportionately to the old .270. For example, Winchester Super-X 7mm Magnum ammunition loaded with a 150 grain Power-Point bullet is good for 3,100 f.p.s., or only 250 f.p.s. more than the same bullet weight in the .270 Winchester. Remember, too, that some handloads can easily push 150 grain bullets from a .270 at 3,000 f.p.s.—and with considerably less recoil and muzzle blast—than the magnum belted 7mm Remington cartridge. Hot handloads with 150 grain bullets out of a .270 can raise energy

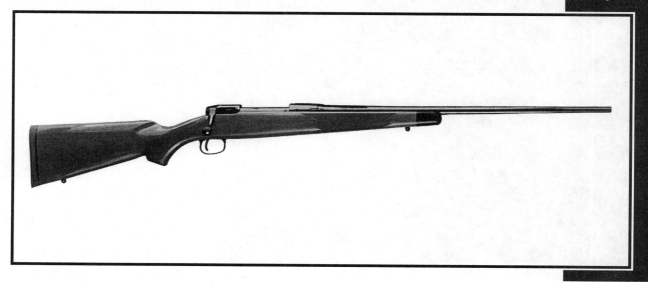

levels up to 3,000 ft. lbs., whereas most factory loads for the same weight bullet fired from the 7mm Remington Magnum usually fall in the 3,100 ft. lbs. range. A big whitetail buck standing at 200 yards will have no idea what hit him when struck by a 150 grain .277" diameter .270 bullet or a 150 grain .284" diameter 7mm bullet. At that distance, the .270 projectile delivers around 2,100 ft. lbs. of energy, while the slightly faster 7mm Remington Magnum cartridge comes closer to 2,400 ft. lbs. Either bullet when properly placed will definitely do the job. Don't get me wrong, I'm not putting down the 7mm Remington Magnum. I've taken several good bucks with an older Ruger Model 77 that I've owned since the first year that rifle was available. But just about any .270 is easier on the shoulder and ears than any of the "Seven Mags!"

Recoil is, in fact, one of the major reasons why the little .243 has been such a favorite with centerfire rifle shooters. Countless numbers of young shooters have cut their deer-hunting teeth with rifles in this caliber, as have many women deer hunters. Even with the heavier bullet weights available, the recoil of a .243 is still quite mild. Winchester Super-X ammo with a 100 grain Power-Point bullet leaves the muzzle at 2,960 f.p.s., with 1,945 ft. lbs. of energy at the muzzle. Out at 100 yards, the bullet still hits with more than 1,600 ft. lbs., with the bullet maintaining around 1,300 ft. lbs. at 200 yards and a little over 1,000 ft. lbs. at 300 yards. Beyond that, the small projectile can't maintain enough high energy levels to be successful on whitetails, especially big deer, with any consistency.

These cartridges have all been successful for a

David Hale (Knight & Hale Game Calls) show off a good Kentucky buck he downed cleanly with one shot from his favorite 7mm Remington Magnum.

variety of reasons, the foremost being that they are proven performers on whitetails. But they are far from being the only effective calibers for deer. There's still a strong following for such calibers as the 6mm Remington, 250 Savage, .25/06 Remington, .257 Roberts, .264 Winchester, .280 Remington, .284 Winchester, 7mm Mauser, .300 Winchester Magnum, .300 Savage, .308 Winchester, .35 Remington, .35 Whelen, .444 Marlin and even the old .45/70 Government. A few—such as the 6mm Remington and .280 Remington—nearly duplicate the ballistics of several calibers already reviewed, while others, like the .300 Savage, aren't really anymore potent than the old .30/30. A few top-rated brush-busting cartridges, including the .35 Remington and .444 Marlin, are much better choices than any of the top five best-selling calibers for use in heavy cover.

To my mind, the .308 Winchester has always been underrated as a whitetail cartridge. I've never shot a rifle of this

This Texas "Hill Country" nine-pointer was no match for Tom Fegely's Ruger Model 77 in .270 Winchester, a favorite caliber among whitetail hunters for several decades.

caliber that didn't punch tight down-range groups with readily available factory loads. Even with bullets of 180 grains, this stubby .30 caliber cartridge is gentle on the shoulder. Most factory loads with a 150 grain spire-point are good for around 2800 f.p.s. and 2,650 ft. lbs. of energy. The Hornady "Light Magnum" loads push a 150 grain bullet from the muzzle at 3,000 f.p.s. with nearly 3,000 ft. lbs. of energy. Out at 200 yards, the load hits with 2,000 ft. lbs. and more than 1,600 ft. lbs. at 300 yards. A bolt action Remington Model Seven in .308 caliber with a handy 18.5-inch barrel may be the epitome of a classic, close-cover whitetail rifle, one that can deliver a 150 or 180 grain bullet with lots of authority and accuracy out at 200 or more yards.

No matter what caliber is selected for whitetail hunting, be sure that it can deliver the knockdown power necessary to do the job at whatever maximum range pertains, either dictated by the type of cover, the cartridge itself, or the shooter's innate ability. Most deer-hunting experts feel that approximately 1,000 ft. lbs. represent the minimum amount of energy needed to harvest a good buck topping 200 to 300 pounds on the hoof. All cartridges discussed here are capable of maintaining this level of energy out to 150 yards. Most of them will do so all the way out to 300 yards, or even to 500 yards.

New bullets, such as the all-copper Barnes X-Bullet and Winchester's Fail Safe bullets have been engineered to ensure 100 percent weight retention—even when one of the bullets has been pushed into a big game animal at maximum velocity. The Barnes bullet is all-copper and longer than other lead-core bullets of the same weight. So are Winchester's Fail Safe bullets, which are mostly copper but with a steel insert that protects a lead core. Both designs are formed with deep hollow-point noses, causing the all-copper Barnes X-Bullet and semi-copper Winchester Fail Safe projectiles to expand fully even after they've slowed down at longer ranges. These bullets will not fragment when driven into a big game animal at close range and with maximum velocity.

Another exceptionally well-built bullet is Nosler's "Partition Bullet." Just as the name implies, it's constructed with two lead-filled cavities separated by a tough copper partition. The design allows the nose of the bullet to expand back to this partition, while the encapsulated lead-core base stays intact. This bullet, which is now loaded into some of Winchester's Supreme cartridges, is famous for its expansion and penetration. Swift Bullet Company (Quinter, Kansas) produces a similar design, known as the Swift-A-Frame, used by Remington in its Safari Grade ammunition.

As for the rifle itself, the market is filled with an outstanding selection of accurate centerfire rifles. Even some of the less expensive ones, such as the single-shot break-open models from Harrington & Richardson or New England Firearms, are capable of performing reliably and with acceptable accuracy. The market also includes some rather costly bolt action guns capable of knocking out one-hole groups at 100 yards. Some now even feature a steel barrel liner encased in tough but ultra-light carbon materials that help lower the weight of a hunting rifle. A number of old favorites, including the Remington autoloaders and the time-proven Model 70 Winchester bolt-action rifles, still survive. Other choices are the state-of-the-art lever action rigs like the Browning BLT and the Ruger No. 1 single-shots, not to mention Browning's new BPR pump.

There's nothing cheap about most new guns these days, especially when hunters are buying top-quality scopes for mounting on their rifles. You can

shooter can place the bullet exactly where it should go.

Just as various stands of whitetail cover, changes in terrain and different hunting situations dictate which rifles and calibers are called for in a given situation, so can these variations require different optics to be mounted on the rifle in question. A hunter headed for extremely thick cover—where close shots at running deer are more the norm than the exception—may want to concentrate on low-powered magnifications—something like 1.5 to 5 or a 2 to 7 power variable, or perhaps a fixed 2.5 or 4 power scope. The lower the power, the greater the field of view, which can mean the difference in finding a fast-moving target. Longer range shooting

spend as much on a top-of-the-line scope, bases and rings as you can on the rifle itself. Serious deer hunters should think of this as an investment, especially when shooting out past 100 yards. A hard-hitting, deadly accurate big game rifle is worthless unless the

calls for higher magnifications for more precise shot placements out at 100, 200 or 300 yards. The problem with sticking a straight 10x (or greater) magnification scope on a deer rifle is that when a buck suddenly shown up at 40 or 50 yards, the hunter will have a tough time

finding the deer in his scope. Not many scope makers today include high magnification fixed power models. Most have concentrated on variable models because they're more versatile. Easily the most widely used modern scope is the 3x9. About 90 percent of all whitetail hunting situations call for a scope that can be turned up or down quickly and easily within that range. At 3x, most any moving deer can be quickly spotted, while the higher 9x magnification is good for most shot placements out to 300 yards. Hunters who want slightly more magnification can choose between a variety of other variables, from 3.5x to 10x and up to 6.5x to 20x. Telescopic sights more powerful than that are simply too powerful to be of any real benefit to the whitetail hunter.

When selecting a scope for a favorite (or brand new) deer rifle, pay particular attention to the front lens diameter. Most fixed power scopes have a 24, 32, 44 or 50mm diameter. The larger the number, the bigger the front lens; and the bigger the front lens, the more light will be collected. When looking for a scope that collects more light in the early morning and at twilight, concentrate on models whose front lens are at least 40mm in diameter. But first, before rushing out to buy a scope with a large front lens, make sure it can be mounted without making contact with the rifle barrel. Rings of varying heights—low, medium or high—are available, of course, to permit most large front objective scopes to be mounted on most rifles. In general, many shooting authorities feel that the closer a scope is kept to the axis of the bore, the better it will maintain zero out in the field. ■

Slug Shooting Shotguns Come Of Age

PART TWO

WITH ◼ *Dave Henderson, Firearms Expert & Outdoor Writer*
◼ *Mike Jordan, Public Relations Manager, Winchester-Olin*

Chapter Three

For three mornings in a row, I had watched a huge Boone & Crockett class buck ease down a hedgerow and into a 20-acre stand of multiflora rose, locust, blackberry briars and a mass of thick brush. I could have kicked myself for not throwing a stand in one of the trees and bowhunting that bruiser before Iowa's shotgun season opened the next day. The slugs, I knew, would start flying as soon as the sun rose in the morning. Fortunately, I knew the landowner well, so I pulled into his farm and shared the information with him. He immediately got on the phone and a drive was organized in short order for 8 am the following morning. In Iowa, drives like this are often the preferred way to hunt whitetails—none of that sitting around for long hours on a cold, early December treestand for these Iowans. They create their own luck by covering lots of ground—and I do mean lots! I didn't have a shotgun permit, so I decided to hang around and witness the harvest of that magnificent buck.

When I pulled into the farmer's barn lot the next morning, I was amazed to see a small army of hunters assembled and ready to begin the day. First, several pickups drove a dozen or so standers to the opposite end of that tangle of brush, positioning them along several small creeks, fence rows, washes and points that might serve as exits for any deer being pushed from the thick cover. The rest of the hunters lined up at fairly even intervals and began to push through the heavy brush, with one hunter walking on the outside edge along each side. It was all very well organized.

The drivers, or pushers, were barely into the cover when the first dozen shots sounded. Then, a minute or two later, ten or more blasts were heard. I watched as a big doe and two fawns ran up to a point that intersected a fence row—straight at one of the standers. He dropped the larger deer with one well-placed rifled slug. Things

quieted down for a few minutes. Now and then I could spot through my binoculars the bright orange jackets of the drivers as they fought their way through the heavy cover. The drive was nearly 75 percent finished when all hell broke loose. One of the standers had ripped off three shots as fast as he could fire his shotgun, and I suddenly caught a brief glimpse of the huge buck I'd watched for three mornings.

The big whitetail was running toward the drivers, who immediately emptied their shotguns as the deer kept running parallel with the line of pushers. Now

the buck headed for a small creek that flowed down into the 20-acre refuge where two more standers waited. Another five or six shots roared, and I could see the buck racing back up over a point toward the hunter who had shot the doe earlier. He fired twice at the deer before it turned and once again ran back into the brush below. Five or six more shots rang out, then the deer broke out on the opposite side of the cover, not 40 yards from the driver who was working the outside edge. The hunter fired three times at the deer, missing ever time, but his shots forced the buck to turn and run along the edge of the cover, straight at another stander. As the buck roared past him in high gear, the hunter fired another three-shot volley. Still, the deer remained untouched.

Now it was crossing a harvested cornfield into another small creek drainage. Only one more hunter stood between the deer and freedom. Having spotted it only seconds before, I estimate the deer was about 50 yards from the stander. Three shots sounded in quick succession, followed by two more less than a minute later. At first, I thought the buck had been shot, but then I saw its magnificent rack appear on the horizon as it crossed another open field beyond the stander. I watched as the deer turned about in mid-field and ran for more than a mile into another small patch of timber. As the deer was crossing open ground, four more shots sounded from the upper end of the brush thicket, and I could hear the voices of the hunters as they congratulated themselves and made fun of those who had earlier missed easy opportunities. As it happened, the big boy had actually escaped unmarked, but at least the drive had given up three does and a respectable eight-pointer, all taken with single shots. Back at the farmhouse, as the hunters recouped with hot cups of coffee and relived the drive just finished, we determined that close to 60 rounds had been fired during the 30-minute drive, most of them thrown at the big buck at distances of 30 to75 yards. Before the day ended, the group made three more drives, and by day's end they were hanging tags on 14 whitetails, including two 160 class bucks.

As we broke for lunch, I took a look at the arsenal of guns at the scene, Remember, these were mostly farmers or residents of small towns in south central Iowa, home to some great pheasant hunting. So I wasn't too surprised at what I found. Of the two dozen or so hunters, only four were actually carrying "slug guns." The rest were relying on the same old pumps, autos and side-by-sides they used for upland bird shooting and waterfowling. Moreover, of the 24 shotguns I observed, less than half sported a full-choked barrel, while four or five others were of modified choke. It's no wonder that it took so many rounds to harvest 14 deer that day and that they actually missed far more deer than they hit.

Having grown up in Illinois—a real "shotgun state"—I have to question those who claim that hunting deer with a shotgun and slugs is safer than with a deadly accurate centerfire rifle. Sure, a stray bullet from a .30/06 or 7mm Remington Magnum may travel farther when a shot is taken at a deer topping a distant rise. But where centerfire rifles are allowed, the number of shots required for each deer taken is far less, as a rule, than shotgun hunting produces. That means less lead is flying around to worry about. Opening morning of the November season in Illinois, or in Iowa during a drive, sounds more like a combat zone than an enjoyable day in the deer woods.

Still, across the Midwest and along the East Coast, large numbers of white-tailed deer are hunted with "quail" guns. According to Mike Jordan (Public Relations Manager, Winchester-Olin) an estimated 3 to 4 million deer hunters in 26 states hunt deer with slug-loaded shotguns. Less than a dozen of these states (including Iowa and Illinois) are "shotgun only," while significant portions of other states, including Minnesota, Wisconsin and Michigan, are zoned as shotgun areas.

could hit an oil can with consistency at about 75 yards. He took his first southern Illinois whitetail—a big doe—with that gun at 50 to 60 yards.

Fortunately, shotgun slugs have improved tremendously since those days. According to Jordan, the two most significant improvements have been the introduction of modern plastic-saboted slugs, and shotguns with rifled barrels or rifled choke rubes. During the 1970s, several companies experimented with the sabot concept,

"These areas will continue to grow as urban areas keep expanding." Jordan explains. "Safety is the primary reason. Whitetails have adapted to the development of their habitat by humans, so that many live in peoples' backyards. With more folks building homes on a few acres out in the country, some of the best deer hunting often occurs within easy range of population centers. The maximum range of a shotgun armed with slugs is considerably less than that of a hot centerfire rifle."

Mike Jordan began hunting whitetails in Illinois back in 1958. Like most deer hunters, then and now, he packed a standard field gun. His old Winchester Model 12 was fitted with a field barrel with only a tiny round bead at the muzzle for sighting. Accuracy was problematic with those old rifled shotgun slugs, and when a hunter did make a hit the slugs often failed to produce good penetration. Shotgun slug fodder during the late 1950s and early 1960s generally had a maximum effective range of 60 to 70 yards, due mostly to a lack of accuracy and poor sectional density. The following year, Mike switched to a scoped Model 12 with an open choked barrel, and found that he

primarily for law enforcement application. Winchester was among the first major ammunition manufacturers to apply the idea to whitetail hunting. The saboted slugs now available are definitely an improvement over earlier designs, which often shot accurately enough out of the barrels but simply didn't expand sufficiently to merit use on deer. The new Winchester Super-X BRI sabot slugs still retain the basic "hour-glass" shape of the earlier examples, but they now feature hollow points and are formed from a softer lead for enhanced expansion.

Fired from a 3-inch, 12-bore shotgun, a 1-ounce saboted Winchester BRI slug (about 437 grains) leaves the

muzzle of a 12 gauge barrel at around 1,400 f.p.s. That translates into about 1,900 ft. lbs. of energy at the muzzle. The same slug out of a 2.75-inch loading is good for about 1,350 f.p.s. and about 1,765 ft. lbs. of energy. Out at 100 yards, the .50 caliber projectile can still generate 1,300 ft. lbs. of energy, or a little over 1,100 ft. lbs. for the 2.75-inch saboted slug load. Winchester also offers a 5/8-ounce 20 gauge sabot slug load along with a hotter 3-inch 12 gauge Supreme HI-IMPACT saboted slug load. It pushes a 1-ounce projectile

from the muzzle at 1,550 f.p.s. With 2 .75-inch ammunition the rate of f.p.s. is 1,450. This produces 2,330 ft. lbs. of energy for the longer case load, and close to 2,100 ft. lbs. for the shorter one. At 100 yards, the 3-inch HI-IMPACT saboted slug can still drive home with around 1,700 ft. lbs. of knock-down power.

The actual inside measurement of a cylinder-bore 12-gauge barrel is .729 inches. The actual diameter of a Winchester Super-X "Foster" rifled 12 gauge slug is basically the same when measured across the narrow lead band

States requiring the use of shotguns and slugs during the general gun season continue to produce some of the more impressive bucks. This monster was taken in Illinois with a Remington Model 11-87 slug gun with rifled barrel.

that encircles the base. When measured across the rifled "fins," though, the slug measures closer to .665 inches. As for design, the "Foster" style slugs are similar to the old "Minie" bullets used during the Civil War. The rear end of this big projectile is hollow-based, allowing pressure from the burning powder charge to expand and press

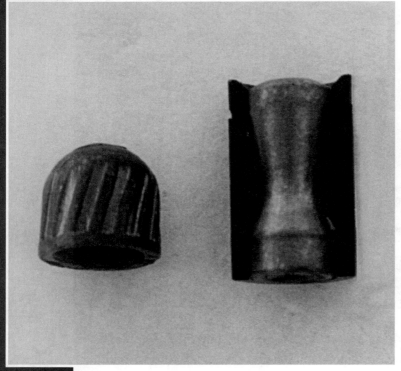

An older Foster-style slug, left, shown in comparison to a modern saboted "hour glass" slug.

the rifled fins tightly against the inside of the shotgun barrel. Slugs of this design perform best when fired through a smooth bore, especially a barrel that's cylinder bored from chamber to muzzle. Contrary to popular belief, shooting a soft lead slug through a choked bore will not cause the barrel to burst, nor will it ruin the choke.

At the muzzle, Winchester's Super-X Rifled Slug load turns in a more impres-

sive performance than do the saboted slugs. A 3-inch 12 gauge load pushes a 1-ounce Foster-style rifled slug from the muzzle at around 1,760 f.p.s., which translates into just over 3,000 ft. lbs. of energy at the muzzle. This slug is so big and so poorly designed aerodynamically that it sheds velocity and energy extremely fast. Out at 100 yards, the slug actually hits with 30 percent less killing energy than the slower 3-inch saboted slug of the same weight. Mike Jordan advises that a smooth bored 12-gauge with rifle type sights—or better yet, a good scope—should print today's improved Foster-style slugs inside of 3 inches at 50 yards. Mike's current choice for hunting in his home state is with one of the newer 12 gauge guns with a rifled barrel fitted with a good scope and loaded with saboted slugs. A quality shotgun with a good trigger should print 1.5-to-5-inch groups at 100 yards (75 yards is considered the maximum effective range for the older slugs).

Noted shotgun deer hunter and writer Dave Henderson adds this advice: "To my way of thinking, the first step in any accurizing procedure for a slug gun is to lighten and stiffen the trigger." Even if your gun is a 'buck special' with rifle sights and maybe a rifled barrel, it's going to have the same receiver, internal and trigger mechanism as its counterpart, which was designed for scatter shot. A shotgun trigger is meant to be slapped, not squeezed like a rifle trigger. And gun company insurance carriers like to see substantial creep in triggers that are also set up for a hearty slap. Dave points out that most shotguns come with a trigger pull that's somewhere in the neighborhood of 6 to 10 pounds. Moreover, the vast majority have an abominable amount of creep to prevent accidental fire during recoil. Shooters will also find differences in trigger weight and creep from one gun to the next as the same model comes off the production line. Until recently, shotguns were designed and built primarily for shooting at upland game, waterfowl and claybird targets. With a shot pattern that spreads 2.5 feet or more at 30 or 40 yards, minute-of-angle accuracy simply isn't all that important —unless you're trying to hunt whitetails with a solid projectile instead of with hundred of tiny pellets. "I don't care if you're the type who can crush cue balls with your fist," Dave adds.

"Nobody can wring full potential out of a firearm with an 8 to 10 pound trigger pull."

Dave feels that the ideal slug gun trigger should break at around 3 to 3.5 pounds, but he would settle for a 5 pound pull weight without any creep. Unfortunately, factory triggers found on most pumps and autos cannot be adjusted—not by the shooter or even the novice gunsmith. Hastings (Clay Center, KS) markets a replacement trigger that drops easily into the receiver of Remington pump and semi-auto shotguns. This product makes the adjustment needed to turn a standard field gun, or even one of the special purpose slug guns, into a much better performer. Replacing the smooth-bored barrel of most field grade pumps or autos with a rifled barrel is Dave Henderson's next recommendation for better accuracy with saboted slugs. If a hunter's sole purpose is to produce a more effective shotgun for hunting whitetails, Dave recommends

Dave Henderson

Modern slug guns, such as this rifled 12 gauge bolt-action Model 210F from Savage, have taken shotgun slug accuracy to a new level.

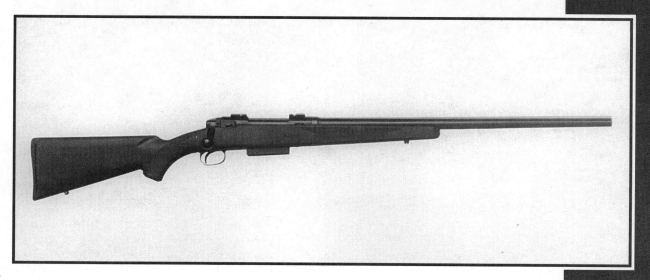

that a gunsmith pin or fix the barrel to the receiver. On many shotguns, this can be done with a set screw, or the barrel can be fixed with Loktite. Either way, a solidly mounted barrel won't move one way or the other once a slug hits the rifling. A barrel that's held in place only by a screw cap at the end of the magazine tube has enough play to make it virtually impossible to shoot tight groups down at 100 yards. "The new bolt-action guns are, right out of the box, more accurate than any other action," Dave says, "simply because the barrels are fixed to the receivers and the lockup is more solid . . . that's why the vast majority of custom slug guns are invariably built on a bolt-action receiver."

One of the most promising "minute-of-angle" slug guns currently available is the Savage MasterShot bolt-action 12 gauge. This rifled slug gun is built on the same action as Savage's long-standing 110 series of bolt-action rifles. Its trigger offers modest adjustments, but if a crisper, cleaner pull is called for the factory trigger can be replaced with a custom job from any of several trigger makers, including Timney Manufacturing (Phoenix, AZ). The Savage MasterShot is built with a 24-inch barrel rifled with a one-turn-in-

Dave Henderson wrings out a slug gun from the bench, shooting a variety of slugs.

COMPLETE BOOK OF WHITETAIL HUNTING

35 inches rate of rifling twist, which performs best with full bore-sized slugs. The popular saboted slugs, however, produce the most consistent accuracy when fired from a barrel with a noticeably faster one-turn-in-25 to 28 inches (Marlin's Model 512 Slugmaster and Browning Models BP-12 and Gold are bolt-action rifled with a one-turn-in-28 inches).

Another advantage of the bolt-action slug guns is the ease in which a scope can be mounted. Savage Master-Shot, Marlin 512 Slugmaster and Mossberg Model 695 all are factory-equipped with the receivers drilled and tapped for quick and easy installation of scope bases. Because the receivers on most

pump and auto shotguns are too thin to allow drilling and tapping, the current trend is threefold: use a mount that fastens to the receiver, use the same pin arrangement that holds the trigger assembly in place, or use a cantilever arrangement that mounts onto the barrel and extends back over the receiver. The trouble with those simple mounts attached to the receiver with push-type pins is that they allow the scope to move around, especially under the heavy recoil of slug loads. B-Square (Fort Worth, TX) markets a receiver mount that saddles the receiver rather than fitting it along one side. Instead of using those tight pins to hold the

Most shots at whitetails are typically 30 to 75 yards, which makes an accurate slug shooting shotgun deadly.

mount in place, this one is bolted on to eliminate scope movement.

Henderson jokes that nothing spurs technology into motion faster than the profit motive and competition. With the increased amount of whitetail habitats designated "shotgun only," a growing number of deer hunters must now use a shotgun and slugs to hunt their favorite deer woods. Accordingly, some significant changes have been made in the design and effectiveness of the slugs

now being used. According to Dave, slug shooting has come farther in the last decade than it did during the previous century. As he points out, the "rifling" grooves or fins swaged into the soft lead of Foster-type slugs are meant more for sales appeal than function. While it's true that rifled slugs don't spin, the fins found on the German-made Brenneke slugs do impart a slow rotation on the solid slug design. However, it's the nose-heavy design that stabilizes slugs of either the hollow-based Foster or solid-based Brenneke designs. "Even when the first sabot slugs hit the market in the late 1980s," Dave Henderson points out, "the primary factor in their stability lay in being nose-heavy." Certainly the spin that occurred when the barrel rifling gripped the plastic sabot had a stabilizing effect—but it was in addition to, not in place of, the nose-heavy design. The spin served more to prolong the stability of those projectiles."

Winchester, Federal and a few smaller custom slug manufacturers established the accuracy superiority and improved energy retention of the saboted slug. However,

COMPLETE BOOK OF WHITETAIL HUNTING

the development of the sabot concept didn't stop with the original projectile and its hour-glass shape that had evolved from the 1970s. Remington dared to introduce a slug that actually looked like a bullet, and when their Copper Solid slugs weren't banned by game departments (for not looking like a shotgun slug), other companies took notice, resulting in several other similar designs now on the market. Remington's all-copper slug, or bullet, is swaged from soft copper and formed with a deep hollow-point nose cut so that it peels back into four distinct petals upon impact. Federal now offers a similar slug, but instead of manufacturing its own all-copper bullet the company is loading with Barnes'

Expander-MZ bullet design. Instead of relying on a .50 caliber projectile, such as the original Remington Copper Solid, Federal asked Barnes to produce a special .58 caliber version of the Expander-MZ. Serious muzzleloading shooters have proven that the sabot concept produces the best accuracy when the slug is closer to actual bore size. The .58 caliber Barnes bullet that Federal loads into its sabot slugs must have been doing the same thing. Remington also now loads its "Improved Remington Copper Solid" with a projectile of similar size. Both slugs weight 1 ounce, or 437 grains.

Currently, several new slug designs and concepts have come onto the market, with most centered on improving

Today's modern shotguns with rifled bores can be amazingly accurate when matched with the right slug. Mike Jordan, of Winchester, checks out a bolt action shotgun with a variety of slugs.

the sabot idea. Hornady has entered the slug race with its HZK Heavy Mag slug—a soft copper, Foster-shaped projectile loaded in a uniquely shaped sabot wad. Another contender to watch, according to Dave Henderson, is the French-made Sauvestre Ball Fleche, a 397 grain .45 caliber saboted projectile with a muzzle velocity of over 1,750 f.p.s. out of a 3-inch 12-gauge loading, which calculates into nearly 2,700 ft. lbs. of muzzle energy. This aerodynamically-shaped projectile promises to retain energy well down range. At 100 yards, the .45 caliber bullet hits with approximately 2,000 ft. lbs. of authority. Winchester also now has a new 2 3/4" saboted slug which utilizes a 385 grain .50 caliber projectile that's good for 1,900 f.p.s. at the muzzle. Dave Henderson says it's the finest slug round he'd ever fired.

In conclusion, I've never been a fan of hunting deer with a shotgun. In places that are designated "shotgun only," I've opted for a muzzleloading rifle, specifically a scoped, in-line percussion rifle loaded with a saboted handgun (or all-copper) bullet. The result is better accuracy than I've achieved with any of the finest slug guns. It seems to me that manufacturers are now taking a back-door approach to the development of slug loadings,

most of which now utilize true bullets with higher velocities and longer effective ranges. With fully rifled bores and saboted slugs, today's state-of-the-art slug guns are in reality no longer shotguns—they are big-bore rifles. And as long as game departments permit these guns in areas designated "shotguns only" for safety reasons, why not allow hunters to use lower velocity centerfire rifle cartridges.

Many Midwestern and Eastern states that are "shotgun only," or which offer significant areas for shotgun enthusiasts, are now scheduling handgun seasons in which hunters use certain specified calibers for safety reasons. If the game departments in these states can designate legal calibers for handgun hunters, why can't they designate certain centerfire rifle calibers for use during the hunting seasons. Old-time favorites like the .30/30 Winchester, .35 Remington, .44 Magnum, .444 Marlin, and even the ancient .45/70 Government cartridges could provide hunters with a more accurate short range deer gun. In most cases, it'll be a lot more enjoyable to shoot than a slug-loaded shotgun that kicks like a Missouri mule. In the end, we'll have a lot less lead flying around, and much fewer wounded and maimed whitetails to escape and die later. ∎

PART THREE

Handgunning For Whitetails

WITH ■ *Larry Weishuhn, Outdoor Writer and Whitetail Biologist*

For too many years, hunting whitetails in Alabama had become an obsession for noted deer biologist and writer Larry Weishuhn. It's not that the deer hunting was so great there; it was because Alabama was one of the handful of states in which he had failed to bag a whitetail—and this in a state with an estimated deer population of two million! Through the years, Larry had spent some 75 days on deer stands in Alabama without ever getting off a shot. Now, as a good-looking ten-pointer slowly fed its way into a large food plot, it looked as if Larry's Alabama deer drought was about to end. He was working as an assistant for a video program on deer management and was accompanied by a cameraman who was perched on a tree stand adjacent to Larry's. Unfortunately, just as Larry eased around to grab the big handgun he was packing, the cameraman, in his rush to get the action on tape, moved his big video camera around to get a bead on

the deer. In doing so, the camera swung against the metal tree stand. Even though the buck was only 20 yards away, neither Larry nor the cameraman could recover in time as the deer spun around and crashed off into the thick Alabama underbrush.

The next afternoon found Larry sitting alone overlooking another food plot. It was the last day of his Alabama hunt, so when several does fed into the green field in early afternoon, he decided it was time to end his deer drought. Earlier, Larry had put together a special handgun rig for hunting whitetails. This unique conversion kit from Springfield Armory allowed him to take a Model 1911 .45 semi-auto handgun frame and transform the pistol into a hard-hitting, single-shot whitetail rig. The company offers its 1911-A2 S.A.S.S. (Springfield Armory Single Shot) conversion kit in a good selection of suitable whitetail hunting calibers, ranging from .223 to .358 Winchester. Larry had selected the

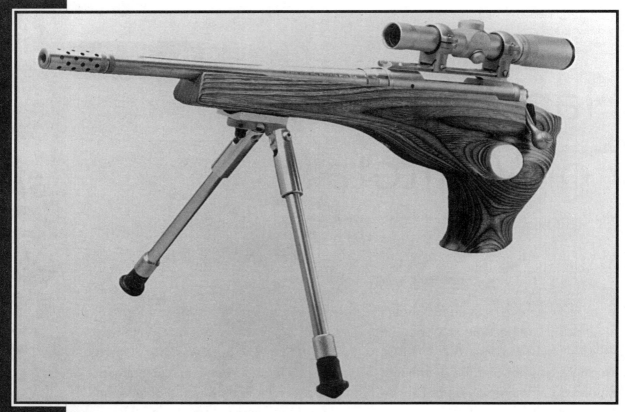

Whitetail
hunting
handguns
don't get
any more
serious than
the Savage
"Super
Striker."

7mm-08 Remington chambering for the 10 3/4-inch barreled conversion kit he had installed on the .45 auto frame. He had mounted on top a 2.5 to 7x long eye relief handgun scope, sighting the pistol (armed with Remington's 154 grain "Extended Range" ammo) to print about an inch high at 100 yards. The does were about 125 yards out when Larry decided to do his part for deer management. Taking a good rest, he centered the crosshairs on the shoulder of the largest doe and eased back on the trigger. At the roar of the big hand-gun, the deer collapsed in its tracks. Larry had just ended 76 days of deer-less hunting in Alabama.

The popularity of hunting big game—especially whitetails—with a handgun continues to grow, and hand-gun manufacturers have responded with an excellent variety of guns and calibers from which to choose. The conversion kit used by Larry Weishuhn allows Gov-ernment .45 auto owners to get "dou-ble duty" from one handgun. Today's deer hunter who is in the market for a handgun designed specifically for hunting deer and other big game can find one at his local gun shop--or his dealer can order whichever handgun will do the job.

Thompson/Center's single-shot "Contender" has long been a favorite of serious handgun hunters. It has been around since the 1960s and has been available through the years in a tremen-dous range of calibers. While some older chamberings are no longer around, Thompson/Center Arms has replaced them with new choices, including more than a dozen different calibers—from .22 Long Rifle to .45/70 Government—in 10-inch, 14-inch and 16-inch barreled models. The company also offers a similar break-open, single-shot design, known as the "Encore," with another long list of caliber choices, including the .243 Winchester, .270 Winchester, .308 Winchester and even the .30/06 Springfield. Any one of these designs enable a shooter to own several different barrels that are easily changeable from one to the other in just a few minutes. Since the sights or scopes attach directly to each barrel, the guns tend to hold zero no matter how many times a barrel is installed, removed and re-installed.

Among the most popular deer hunting calibers for Contender shooters has been the old .30/30 Winchester. Known primarily as a "short range" caliber when chambered in a rifle, it becomes an honest 100-yard performer out of a single-shot design like the T/C Contender. Shooting factory ammo, the company has found most 150 grain bullets will leave the muzzle of a 10" barrel at around 1,780 f.p.s. With a 14-inch Contender barrel the f.p.s. jumps to 2,128. Energy (with the shorter barrel) is 1,056 ft. lbs. For the sake of comparison, T/C has run the same loads through the longer 21-inch barrel of a "Contender Carbine" and found the 150 grain .30/30 factory cartridge produces 2,311 f.p.s. at the muzzle, with 1,779 ft. lbs. of energy. Obviously, the shorter the barrel, the greater the loss in velocity and energy levels. This is more noticeable when shooting "rifle" cartridges from a handgun than when shooting ammo designed specifically for handgun use. Take the .44 Remington Magnum for example: A 240

This 15-inch barreled single-shot Thompson/ Center "Encore" handgun is deadly accurate past 100 yards with a good rest.

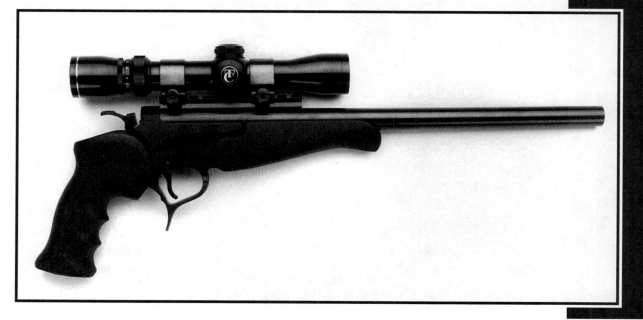

grain factory load leaves the muzzle of a 10-inch Encore barrel at about 1,540 f.p.s., with 1,260 ft. lbs. of energy. The same load from a longer 15" Encore barrel increases velocity only to 1,620 f.p.s. with 1,398 ft. lbs. of energy.

What about other hot rifle cartridges—the .270 Winchester, .308 Winchester and the .30/06 Springfield? What kind of velocities and energy levels should a modern handgun hunter expect? When shot from a 22" barreled Remington Model 700 bolt-action rifle, the .270 Winchester with a 130 grain spire-point bullet is good for 3,060 f.p.s., with 2,700 ft. lbs. of energy. When fired from a 15-inch T/C Encore barrel, the same load leaves the muzzle at 2,602 f.p.s. with 1,954 ft. lbs. of energy. By comparison, most factory 150 grain .308 Winchester loads can produce muzzle velocities of around 2,800 f.p.s., with close to 2,650 ft. lbs. of energy when fired from a 22-inch rifle barrel.

Out of a 15-inch T/C single-shot handgun bore, the same load produces a muzzle velocity of just over 2,600 f.p.s., with more than 2,300 ft. lbs. of energy. The popular .30/06 with a 150 grain bullet produces rifle velocities of around 2,900 f.p.s., with slightly more than 2,800 ft. lbs. of energy. When fired from a 15-inch Encore barrel, the bullet is good for 2,760 f.p.s. and 2,537 ft. lbs. of whitetail knockdown power.

Handguns chambered for hotter cartridges developed especially for shoulder-mounted rifles can get a little wild and uncomfortable to shoot. This is especially true when the handgun features a short 10 inch barrel length and the

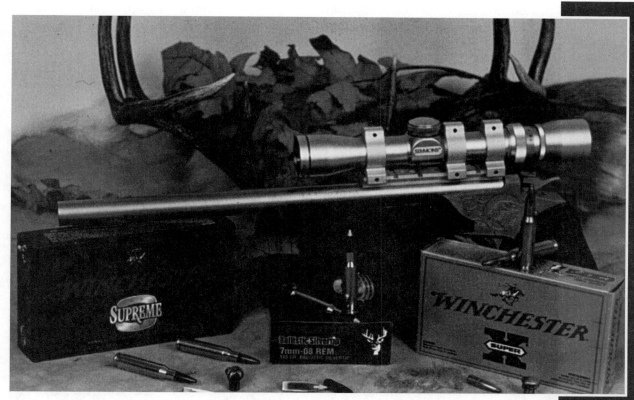

shooter elects to shoot one of the heavier bullets developed for a particular cartridge. Big 180 grain bullets for the .30/06 will certainly produce more muzzle jump and recoil than 150 or 130 grain bullets out of a handgun. For that reason, new interest has risen for shooting smaller caliber "bottle-neck" cartridges, such as .22-250 Remington and .243 Winchester. Some experienced whitetail handgunners question the wisdom of hunting deer with the light bullets often associated with these cartridges. Hornady offers one of the heaviest bullets available for factory-loaded .22-250 ammo with a 60 grain spire-point. The bullet leaves the muzzle of a 22-inch rifle barrel at around 3,600 f.p.s., with 1,720 ft. lbs. of energy. The ammunition fired from a 15-inch Encore

barrel hits less than 3,000 f.p.s. at the muzzle, with about 1,200 ft. lbs. of energy. While the ballistics seem impressive enough for use on deer inside 100 yards, the bullet simply isn't big enough to produce proper penetration with consistency. "When it comes to handguns and rifle cartridges," claims Larry Weishuhn, "my personal minimums are the 7mm cartridges—the 7-30 Waters and the 7mm-08 Remington."

The 10 3/4-inch barrel of Springfield Armory's conversion for the Government M1911-A1 handgun chambered for the 7mm-08 is good for just over 2,250 f.p.s. with the same 154 grain bullet Larry used to take his Alabama doe. At the muzzle, the bullet generates a little over 1,700 ft. lbs. of energy. The deer standing at 125 yards was hit with

The 7mm-08 has become a popular whitetail hunting cartridge in big single-shot handguns like the Thompson/ Center Arms "Contender."

around 1,300 ft. lbs. of knockdown power. "As I had expected," recalls Weishuhn, "the 7mm-08 Remington fired out of the short barrel of the S.A.S.S. was a real handful. It wasn't unbearable, though, and after a short time at the bench I had my scoped

Today's hunter in search of a hard-hitting, accurate whitetail pistol has access to the best selection ever offered.

Larry has always favored the Thompson/Center break-open, single-shot handguns primarily for their versatility. He could leave home on a month-long

Larry Weishuhn used a 15-inch barreled T/C Encore pistol in .30-06 to down this Kansas buck.

handgun producing close to two-inch groups at a hundred yards."

While that big Alabama buck still eludes Larry, he has taken some impressive bucks all across the country, shooting a variety of different calibers from various revolvers, break-open single-shot and bolt-action handguns. He has developed his own favorites, some of which are no longer available, or which have been custom-chambered for a noncommercial wildcat cartridge.

big game hunting tour with one or two frames, plus two or three different barrels, and still be ready for nearly any hunting situation. During one fall season, he became the first to take a big game specimen with the new single-shot handgun (a prototype of the T/C Encore) chambered for the .308 Winchester. Starting with Hornady's 150 grain Light Magnum loads, he took a huge 1,000 pound Maine moose at 100 yards. A week later, in Colorado, he shot

COMPLETE BOOK OF WHITETAIL HUNTING

a good Shiras bull moose at 75 yards with the same load. Then, with the new handgun re-sighted with 180 grain Winchester Fail-Safe ammunition, a weeklong elk hunt rewarded him with a 6x6 bull dropped cleanly at 125 yards. If the caliber and loads he used were enough to take such big game, it should be more than sufficient to harvest the largest whitetail buck.

Actually, Larry Weishuhn has developed something of a love affair with the .44 Remington Magnum. One of his favorite hunting rigs is a Ruger .44 Magnum Super Blackhawk with a 10 1/2-inch barrel topped with a Simmons 1.5 to 5X scope. Shooting loads with the 270 grain Speer "Gold Dot" soft-point bullets, his big handgun can easily hit inside 2 inches at 50 yards, leaving him with no qualms about taking shots at deer-sized game at 100 yards. Larry recalls the time he spent on several large ranches in south Texas as a wildlife manager. There he often carried his Ruger Blackhawk for dispatching troublesome wild hogs. He enjoyed shooting the .44 Magnum handgun, but he was less than impressed with the factory loads available at the time. Unless he hit a 150- to 300-pound wild hog in the head or spine, the animals seldom went down with only one shot. He feels that the factory ammo now available from Winchester, Remington and Federal do a much better job. The Winchester Supreme Partition Gold is an excellent example of what Larry is talking about by way of ammunition for handgun hunting. For the popular .44

Magnum, Winchester offers a 250 grain hollow point, which leaves the muzzle of an 8-inch revolver barrel at about 1,200 f.p.s. and with 840 ft. lbs. of energy. Firing a single-shot handgun like the T/C Contender or Encore, the load will probably leave the muzzle of a 10-inch barrel at about 1,350 f.p.s. with 1,000 ft. lbs. or so of energy.

These ballistics may not seem as impressive as the 2,000-plus f.p.s. velocities cited for cartridges like the .308 Winchester, but modern technology has designed the Partition Gold bullet to ensure that it expands and transfers every ounce of energy to the target. Large .44 Magnum revolvers—i.e., the single-action Super Blackhawk and the double-action Redhawk, Colt Anaconda or Taurus Model 44—are all excellent 50- to 75-yard whitetail guns. In the hands of an expert handgunner, these revolvers stuffed with the Winchester Partition Gold ammunition can still take a big whitetail buck out to 100 yards.

As for revolvers, deer hunters should take a good look at the wheelguns chambered for the .454 Casull, a real powerhouse. When used with some ammo, it packs more energy at 100 yards than the .44 Magnum generates at the muzzle. Out of a 10-inch barreled revolver, such as Freedom Arms' Model 454, Winchester Partition Gold ammunition with a 260 grain hollow-pointed bullet produces a muzzle velocity of slightly over 1,800 f.p.s., which translates into 1,880 ft. lbs. of energy. Out at 100 yards, this bullet can drive home more than 1,300 ft. lbs. of energy. Another revolver chambered for the power-packed cartridge is the Taurus Model 454 "Raging Bull." Both guns fire five shots instead of the more common six-shot revolver capacity. Quick follow-up shots may be important to some hunters, but it seems that serious handgunners these days concentrate more on accuracy—putting that first and only shot right where it needs to go. That explains why such well-built single-shot handguns as the T/C Contender and Encore have become so popular. Some of this can be attributed to the range of calibers available, allowing hunters to select factory-loaded rounds capable of delivering the accuracy

and knockdown power needed to anchor a whitetail within reasonable hunting ranges.

I recall that on one early handgun hunt, I carried a mid-1980's version of the T/C Contender in .30/30 Winchester. That big single-shot sported a long 14-inch barrel and was topped with a 4x Redfield long eye relief handgun scope. The gun shot well with most factory loads, and off the bench I generally grouped inside 3 inches at 100 yards (which was pretty good for this "rifle" shooter). One thing that kept the .30/30 from being the kind of handgun hunting caliber it could have been was the factory ammo. Don't forget those millions of lever-action rifles

COMPLETE BOOK OF WHITETAIL HUNTING

chambered for this century-old cartridge. Because they featured tubular magazines, blunt-nosed ammo had to be used (a sharp-pointed bullet would have acted as a firing pin on the next cartridge). Recoil from a shot could, as a result, detonate a round in the magazine. That's why manufacturers offer factory loaded .30/30 rounds with either a flat-or round-nosed bullet. At one time, I handloaded every centerfire rifle or handgun I owned. Along with my new .30/30 Contender, I picked up a set of RCBS reloading dies. But instead of loading with the blunt-nosed bullets, I concentrated on the spire-pointed ones offered by Speer, Sierra and Hornady. Some of my more accurate loads for the break-open single-shot consisted of 125 and 130 grain bullets. My favorite proved to be the 130 grain Hornady spire-point. I don't remember the powder or charge used, but across the chronograph the bullet left the muzzle at almost 2,300 f.p.s., which calculates into 1,525 ft. lbs. of energy.

During my first season with the handgun, I took one of my best whitetails ever. I was hunting in northern Missouri, not far from the Iowa border, on the opening morning of the nine-day modern gun season. In addition to the .50 caliber muzzleloader I carried during this hunt, I also packed the long-barreled T/C pistol along with one of Uncle Mike's shoulder holster rigs. Shortly after daybreak, a wide-racked 10-pointer sauntered into the far end of the small field I was watching, then turned and walked straight toward my stand. As the deer passed within 30 or 40 yards, I held just to the rear of his front shoulder and squeezed off a shot. The 130 grain bullet drove home and the

Larry Weishuhn has become a big fan of hunting deer with a handgun. Here he practices with a big in-line muzzle-loading handgun which he later used to harvest several whitetails.

chambered for the .308 Winchester. With handloads consisting of Speer 130 grain spire-point bullets, I've tamed down the muzzle jump and, like the .30/30, have made it a lot more enjoyable to shoot than when feeding it factory 150 or 180 grain ammo. The load I now shoot leaves the muzzle at about 2,550 f.p.s. with around 1,875 ft. lbs. of energy. At 100 yards, the bullet can hit a whitetail with close to 1,400 ft. lbs. of energy. At 150, which is farther than I'll ever shoot at a deer with a handgun, it was still good for 1,100 ft. lbs. One of the earliest bolt-action handguns I ever played with was a used Remington XP-100 in .221 Fireball. I had picked it up during the

Tom Fegely dropped this Texas buck using a custom .309 JDJ single-shot pistol built on a Thompson/Center "Contender" frame.

250-pound buck charged for the other side of the clearing, piling up before it was halfway across.

As I remember, the load seemed mild—and fun—to shoot. Actually, its recoil and muzzle jump were quite tolerable. My son was 10 years old at the time, and he would often sit at the bench and put maybe 20 or 30 rounds through the big handgun. More recently, I've used one of the same models

late 1960s and often carried it for woodchucks, especially when hunting in areas where shots would be less than 100 yards. I missed more chucks than I hit, but I still enjoyed shooting that handgun. From the bench, it was deadly accurate. Several years later, I had the opportunity to shoot my second bolt-action handgun—a beautiful single-shot gun from Wichita Arms. A hunter was sighting in for an upcoming hunt with this 15-inch barreled .308 Winchester handgun, and when I expressed interest in it he offered to let me fire a few rounds. I was amazed at its accuracy—and its price tag. The pistol, scope, bases and rings had cost him more than $2,000! Today, Savage Arms offers a well-built, bolt-action big game handgun at a much friendlier price. In fact, for what that shooter forked out for his Wichita Arms single-shot alone, today's handgun hunter can own a Savage "Striker" bolt-action handgun, a good scope and mounts for a lot less.

Savage now sells this sharp-looking, accurate bolt-action in a variety of models, all available in a choice of .223 Remington, .22-250 Remington, .243 Winchester, 7mm-08 Remington, .260 Remington, and .308 Winchester. The standard model comes with a tough, black ambidextrous composite stock, while the "Super Striker" features an attractive laminated thumbhole stock (for right-handers only). The guns all feature a bolt that operates on the left side of the receiver, kicking its empty cartridge cases out the right side. All models are "repeaters" with an internal box magazine that holds three rounds. To tame the recoil and jump of the rifle cartridges for which this 14-inch barreled pistol is chambered, several versions are available with a ported muzzle. Scoped, and in the hands of a good shot, these big handguns—especially in 7mm-08, .260 Remington and .308 Winchester—should prove deadly at 200 yards against the whitetails.

Personally, I believe the .260 Remington has a great deal to offer whitetail handgunners. Remington now loads two different 140 grain bullets for the cartridge: a Core-Lokt spire-point and a Ballistic-Tip spire-point. Out of a 24-inch rifle barrel, the Ballistic-Tip leaves the muzzle at 2,890 f.p.s., with 2,226 ft. lbs. of energy. This and similar loads should leave the muzzle of the Savage Striker's 14-inch barrel at around 2,600 plus f.p.s., which translates into 2,100 ft. lbs. of energy. At this writing, not many factory loads are available for the .260 Remington. However, several bullet makers offer a good selection of .264-inch diameter bullets, allowing whitetail hunters to tailor their loads to handguns chambered for this round. Sierra and Hornady list bullet weights up to 160 grains, while Nosler and Speer offer theirs up to 140 grains.

Like a growing number of whitetail hunters, I enjoy pursuing deer with a handgun, although I will admit it's not my first choice. That's primarily because I have never considered myself a top handgun shot. In fact, with a good rest and an accurate, scope-sighted pistol in a hard-hitting caliber, I don't even attempt a shot much past 100 yards. I love it, though, when I make a good hit and the deer goes down within sight; but I also hate it when I've made a bad hit and can't find the wounded deer. The longer the range, the greater the chance of making a bad hit; hence, I don't take them. I have watched some excellent handgun shots topple silhouettes at 200 and 300 yards with large

caliber pistols. If you can hit 'em good enough to put 'em down with whatever you're shooting, I say, "Go for it!"

In selecting a handgun for hunting whitetails, first check your own state hunting regulations. In addition to prohibiting the use of centerfire rifles (for safety reasons) the .30/30, 7mm-08, .308 and .30/06 bottle-necked rifle cartridges are not allowed. Many Midwestern states, where long gun hunters are restricted to shooting shotguns with slugs or muzzleloading rifles, allow only certain "straight-walled" pistol cartridges such as the .44 Magnum.

Likewise, those who are intrigued by the challenge of taking a whitetail with a muzzleloading handgun should do some homework before heading out. Some

states allow the use of .44 caliber percussion revolvers, but none can produce the energy level required to do the job. Even the Ruger .45 caliber "Old Army" percussion revolver, stuffed with a maximum chamber-filling 35 grain charge of FFFg black powder behind a 190 grain conical bullet, is only good for about 260 ft. lbs. of energy. A better choice is one of the new 12- to 14-inch barreled in-line pistols loaded with saboted, jacketed hollow-point bullets of 240 to 260 grains and a maximum powder charge of 70 grains of FFFg black powder or Pyrodex "P." These guns and loads produce velocities of around 1,200 f.p.s. and energy levels of 825 ft. lbs., or about the same as factory-loaded .44 Magnum ammunition. ■

PART FOUR

Muzzleloading

WITH ■ *Jim Shockey, Canadian Outfitter & Writer*
■ *Dave Ehrig, Black Powder Hunter & Writer* ■ *Russell Markesbery, President of Markesbery Muzzle Loaders*

Daybreak came slowly for first-time whitetail hunter Deborah Bennett. It was opening morning of the November firearms deer season in Illinois, a day which she had anticipated for months. Early the previous spring, this "city girl" who had moved to the deer-rich river country of western Illinois suddenly developed a fascination for shooting and a strong desire to learn. She started with a .22 rifle and began learning the basics of gun safety, the need for a solid aim, and how accuracy was dependent on a slow trigger squeeze. She wanted to hunt deer mostly, so I volunteered to loan her one of several .50 caliber muzzleloaders in my gun rack. The one she finally settled on was as modern as a frontloading rifle can get. It was a custom "bolt-action" in-line ignition rifle designed and built by custom riflesmith Henry Ball (Greensboro, NC). It was built on a modern Howa centerfire rifle action and fitted with a top-quality McGowen barrel.

What really makes this rifle so unique is its ignition system. Like all in-line ignition rifles, it has a removable breech plug. Instead of using a nipple and percussion cap to provide fire for the powder charge, though, this state-of-the-art frontloader actually chambers a reusable, stainless steel ignition module primed with an even hotter No. 209 shotshell primer. More importantly, it is the first muzzleloader designed and built to handle modern smokeless powder loads with safety.

The load I found most accurate out of this "new millennium" muzzleloader was 35 grains of Alliant 2400 behind a saboted 260 grain .451-inch Speer jacketed hollow point. On previous hunts, I had taken several good whitetail bucks with this load all the way out to 210 yards without having to allow for excessive drop—because there isn't any! The load is good for just over 2,350 f.p.s. and more than 3,100 ft. lbs. of energy at the muzzle. While this is about twice almost 2,300 f.p.s. at the muzzle, with more than 2,600 lbs. of energy. Recoil is practically nonexistent.

Shortly after daybreak, Deborah caught her first glimpse of whitetails in the woods when a young buck chased a doe along the top of a nearby ridge. About an hour later, she heard something running up the backside of the point where she had taken a stand. Then, as she stood up to get a better look, a huge buck and doe passed within 10 yards, nearly running her over. She tried to get the deer in her Nikon scope, but it was turned all the way up to 9x. Both deer were gone in a flash, disappearing into the thick cover of a draw close by. Then, as she sat back behind a log she was using for a blind, a nice eight-pointer appeared, standing in one of the shooting lanes I had cut several weeks earlier. It was scarcely 50 yards away and offered a perfect shot. Slowly, Deborah eased the rifle up over the log, centered the scope on the buck's chest cavity and eased off the safety of the Howa action. At the crack of the shot, the whitetail buck dropped where it stood. And with that, the world had gained one more white-tailed deer hunter—and a muzzleloading fan as well.

Modern in-line ignition rifles are high in popularity because of their down-range knock-down power and sure-fire reputation in almost any weather.

the energy produced by any standard in-line percussion rifle and a 100 grain charge of Pyrodex "Select," recoil is considerably less. Still I managed to work up a lighter load for Deborah in anticipation of her first deer hunt. With only 30 grains of Winchester 571 ball powder behind a saboted Speer .45 caliber 225 grain jacketed hollow point, the rifle still prints inside of 1 1/2 inches at 100 yards. The load is still good for

COMPLETE BOOK OF WHITETAIL HUNTING

Muzzleloading simply isn't the same sport it was only 20 or 30 years ago. It has matured into a true hunting and performance-driven sport. Those whitetail hunters who now head for the deer woods with a frontloader thrown over their shoulders want all of the efficiency, accuracy and knockdown power a muzzleloader can muster. Whether or not there's actually smoke hanging in the air doesn't seem to matter any more. The rifle and load Deborah Bennett used to take her first whitetail may represent the final evolution of the muzzleloading rifle. One thing is for certain: the hot smokeless loads that perform so well with her in-line ignition rifle have done more than any other muzzleloading system ever offered in bridging the gap between the old-fashioned frontloaders and today's hypersonic, flat-shooting centerfire big game rifles. The same loads that shoot safely out of this exceptional rifle will completely destroy any other modern muzzleloader. And with the $2,500 to $3,500 price tag for one of Henry Ball's hot custom smokeless frontloaders, it's doubtful that you'll run into many in the deer woods. However, as this was written, Savage Arms Inc. (Westfield, MA) had tooled up to build several prototypes on Ball's design, with the intention of bringing the rifle to the market. Those muzzleloading hunters who don't have the cash for one of the custom versions, or who are not willing to wait until Savage introduces a commercial model, it's muzzleloading as usual. However, when time is taken to work up an accurate load for practically any other in-line percussion muzzleloading rifle, these guns will prove far superior to the older designs from the past.

One of the most respected muzzleloading big buck hunters today is

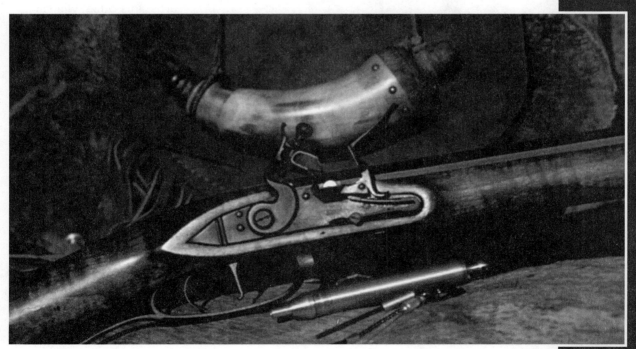

Canadian outfitter and outdoor writer Jim Shockey, who makes his home on Vancouver Island in British Columbia. But when it's time for big whitetails, this muzzleloading expert heads for Saskatchewan, where he also outfits trophy whitetail hunts. Before the whitetail seasons get rolling, Jim looks for any of the wild North American sheep, bears, elk or caribou to get in the sights or scope of his favorite Knight .50 caliber in-line ignition muzzleloader. Jim's philosophy is to shoot the same load for everything—from whitetails to Alaskan brown bears. His modern in-line ignition rifle consists of a 100 grain charge of Pyrodex "Select" behind a saboted all-copper Barnes Expander-MZ hollow-point bullet. This is an excellent choice for the hunter who wants to develop one muzzleloader load for hunting all kinds of big game. The bullet's deep, hollow-pointed nose ensures full expansion on game that weighs 100 to 1,000 pounds or more. It also encourages proper expansion once the big bullet begins to slow down at 150 yards (or longer) ranges. On the other hand, the bullet's all-copper construction prevents it from fragmenting when driven into a big game animal at near maximum velocity 20 or 30 yards distant. Whether a big whitetail stands at 50 yards or 150 yards, this bullet will still deliver enough wallop for a clean kill—provided, of course, the hunter was using a rifle capable of delivering the big hollow point accurately. Another bullet Jim Shockey likes is the saboted 300 grain Swift A-Frame bullets. Even though he occasionally changes from one bullet to the other, what-ever he shoots at the beginning of fall he stays with all season long. He knows exactly where to hold at 50 on up

to 200 yards, thanks to his off-season practice sessions.

I hunted with Jim the year he switched to the all-copper Barnes bullet. Until then, he'd been shooting twist. That is simply too slow to impart enough spin on the lengthy all-copper Barnes bullet for proper stabilization and accuracy. Knight rifles produced after 1988 all feature a one-turn-in-28

a saboted all-lead 310 grain bullet. But now he wanted something that offered better performance for a brown bear hunt he was planning a month after our Wyoming pronghorn hunt. I suggested the Barnes bullet, which I had used successfully on several elk, but Jim's rifle couldn't keep any two bullets within 8 inches of each other. Several impacted the 100-yard target sideways, indicating improper stabilization. When I inspected his Knight MK-85, it dawned on me that it was an early production rifle featuring a one-turn-in-32 inches rate of rifling

inches rate of twist, which does an excellent job of stabilizing the all-copper bullet designs. Following our pronghorn hunt, Jim switched to a new MK-85 and was soon shooting sub-two inch groups at 100 yards. He got his brown bear (plus several good whitetails later in the season) shooting the same bullet and powder charge.

Due to their all-copper construction, the Barnes Expander-MZ (and a similar bullet produced by Remington, known as the Premier Copper Solid) must be longer to achieve the same weight as a

Ultra-modern in-line ignition rifles like the Knight D.I.S.C. Rifle are more capable of printing better than 100-yard groups than are many out-of-the-box center-fire deer rifles.

jacketed lead-core bullet design. If you plan to shoot one of these bullets, concentrate on rifles with a one-turn-in-24 to 28 inches rate of rifling twist. Owners of rifles that are still available with a one-turn-in-32 or 38 inches rate, and who want to try these bullets on deer-sized game, should try the shorter 250 grain .50 caliber or 275 grain .54 caliber Expander-MZ bullets. For the .54 caliber muzzleloader, Barnes offers a lengthy 325 grain Expander-MZ as well, and Remington offers its Premier Copper Solid in 289 gains for both the .50 and .54 caliber bores.

With so many great saboted bullet choices available, I like to tailor my loads for whatever game species I'm going after. I wouldn't use the same 150 grain spire-point bullet fired from my favorite .270 Winchester centerfire when hunting everything from pronghorns to moose, and I wouldn't do the same with my muzzleloading rifles.

There is, after all, a bullet best suited for hunting nearly all different-sized game. One of my favorite saboted bullets for the in-line rifles I hunt most often with are the .45 caliber Speer 260 grain jacketed hollow-point designs. With a 100 grain charge of Pyrodex "Select," this bullet leaves the muzzle of a fast-twist, 24-inch .50 caliber barrel at about 1,625 f.p.s. with 1,550 ft. lbs. of energy. At 100 yards, the bullet hits with almost 1,200 ft. lbs. of knockdown energy. At 150 yards, the bullet is still good for around 900 ft. lbs. of punch. Not many .50 caliber one turn-in-24- to 32-inch barrels I've fired with a saboted .45 Speer bullet have failed to produce acceptable accuracy. Anyone looking for a reasonably priced sabot and bullet combination for hunting whitetails with a modern fast-twist muzzleloader ought to give this one a try. Over the years, I've taken about 50 deer and other deer-sized game animals with this bullet, and none have ever required a second shot.

Speer, Nosler, Hornady, Barnes, Swift and a few other bullet makers, along with some of the muzzleloading rifle makers, now offer a great selection of saboted bullets for the popular in-line ignition muzzleloading rifles. Deer hunters armed with muzzleloaders can choose from among saboted bullets as light as 180 grains all the way up to 400 grains and more for a .50 or .54 caliber big game rifle. For whitetails, bullets of 220 to 275 grains offer the best in the way of velocity, energy, trajectory and mild recoil.

Russ Markesbery (Markesbery Muzzle Loaders) suggests that hunters seeking the best possible accuracy from a bore with a faster twist should concentrate on those sabot and bullet combinations that include a bullet closest to actual bore size. For example, both .44 and .45 caliber bullets can be loaded into a .50 caliber bore, but they require different sabots. The smaller .429-.430-inch diameter .44 bullets call for heavier plastic sabots to make up the difference between bullet and bore than when loading with a slightly larger .451- .452-inch bullet and sabot. The sabot's thin plastic sleeves have a tendency to peel away from a .45 bullet faster than the heavier sleeves of a sabot made for the .44 bullet, hence they have less effect on downrange bullet flight and accuracy. "One of the worse combinations a hunter can shoot, accuracy-wise," claims Russ Markesbery, "is a .44 out of a .54 caliber bore. The sabot may stay with the bullet for several feet instead of inches."

Markesbery's "Outer-Line" rifles are built with a blend of modern and traditional features. A center-mounted exposed hammer swings in an arc, striking a nipple that threads into the breech plug at a 45-degree angle. Ignition is as fast as a true in-line percussion system, yet the rifle's design

Russ Markesbery

Noted muzzle-loading hunter Jim Shockey shows off a superb Saskatchewan buck taken at about 100 yards with a hard-hitting saboted bullet.

offers shooters a taste of traditional styling. Russ Markesbery realizes, however, that modern muzzleloading whitetail hunters want the most effective design available, offering their rifles with fast rates of rifling twist. Both the .50 and .54 caliber models come with fast one-turn-in 26 inches rate of twist, turning in the best performance with saboted bullets. The .45 caliber models come with a slightly faster one-in-20 inches—a real tack driver with saboted 180 or 200 grain .40 caliber handgun bullets. The .45 also handles big conical

"Maxi" bullets. Bullets of this type got their name due to the popularity of the "Maxi-Ball" (designed by Warren Center back in 1970 as the companion projectile for his newly introduced Thompson/Center Arms "Hawken" rifle). The rifle and bullet together were the most popular big game combo until the popularity of the modern in-line percussion rifles arose during the mid-1980s.

The Thompson/Center Hawken is still available today and remains a popular hunting rifle for shooters who like to cast a bit of history over their

The Remington Model 700ML displays the same basic lines, feel and features found on the company's highly respected line of bolt-action centerfire rifles.

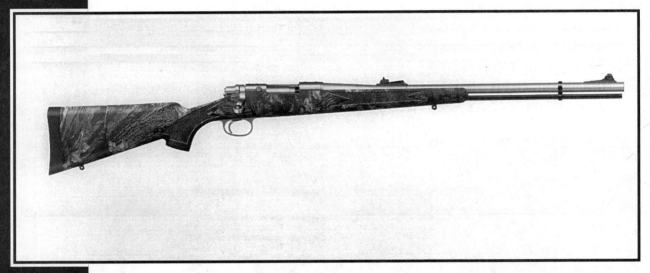

bullets of up to 400 grains with real authority; and when loaded with 80 to 100 grains of FFg black powder or Pyrodex, the often border-line .45 caliber rifles can become potent medicine for deer.

While saboted bullets are now the most widely used projectiles for hunting whitetails and other big game, there still remain a large number of muzzleloading hunters who prefer the heavy, hard-hitting conical bullets, known as

shoulder as they head out for whitetails. Today's version still features a relatively slow turn-in-48 inches rate of rifling twist, just as it did during the 1970s. The company has long touted the twist as being suitable for shooting loads comprised of either a bore-sized maxi-style bullet or a patched round ball. At best, this rate of rifling twist is something of a compromise, usually rewarding the shooter with merely acceptable accuracy with either projectile. A true bullet bore will feature rifling with a faster spin, whereas the round ball normally produces optimum accuracy with a considerably slower rate of twist. The most accurate elongated bullet rifles of the mid-1800s often featured rifling that spun as fast as one-turn-in-20 to 24 inches. Some were built to shoot a bullet nearly three times as long as its diameter. Most maxi-style bullets available to hunters today are about twice as long as their diameters, performing well out of most bores with rifling that spins with a one-turn-in 24 to 38 inches. As a rule, most of these bullets weigh about twice as much as a round ball for the same caliber bore; when loaded with a hefty powder charge, the big bullets hit with a wallop well beyond 100 yards. By comparison, the .490-inch soft lead ball shot out of .50 caliber bores weighs 177 grains. The .50 caliber Hornady Great Plains Bullet comes in two styles and weights. One is a 385 grain hollow-based, hollow-pointed bullet, and the other is a 410 grain solid-based, solid-nosed design. Another popular bore-sized lead .50 caliber bullet is the Thompson/Center Maxi-Hunter, which is available in 275 or 350 grain weights (the company also offers the same bullet design for the .54 caliber in 360 and 435 grains).

When shooting large, soft lead bullets of 400 grains or more, it takes a healthy powder charge to get them rolling at acceptable velocities. It also prevents big hunks of lead from nose-diving back to the ground once they've gone past 100 yards. Many .50 caliber

rifle shooters load up to 110 grains of FFg or Pyrodex behind bullets of 370 or 385 grains, leaving the muzzle at about 1,500 f.p.s. and generating approximately 1,900 ft. lbs. of energy. Once this much lead gets rolling along, it tends to maintain energy levels well down range. At 100 yards, these big .50 caliber bullets can still drive home with more than 1,400 ft. lbs. of killing power. Because of their weight, though, the bullets often take on the trajectory of a thrown brick. Sighted dead on at 100 yards, some of the heavier designs can drop more than 10 inches by the time the bullet reaches 150 yards.

Dave Ehrig

Dave Ehrig, a Pennsylvania muzzle-loading authority, won the title of Pennsylvania's "Mr. Black Powder"—and for a very good reason. For one thing, Dave is a die-hard muzzleloading hunter, which is a must for anyone in the state of Pennsylvania who intends to hunt during the muzzleloader-only season. Not only does the season take place in December during some of the worse weather of the year, it follows close on the heels of the general firearms season. In Pennsylvania, however, muzzleloading hunters are restricted to hunting ONLY with a patched, round ball projectile—and ONLY with a rifle of early flintlock design. Along with thousands of other whitetail hunters who head out under such handicaps, Dave Ehrig accepts the challenge in the hope of squeezing one more shot at a whitetail before the season ends. To achieve the best accuracy with a patched round ball, Dave is quick to recommend a bore with a rifling twist of one-in-60 to 72 inches. The grooves can then spin slow enough to grab the cloth patch, which in turn grips the soft lead sphere. Dave points out that the most accurate round ball barrels are cut with relatively deep grooves of .007" to .014" depth. This allows excess heavy patching somewhere to go once the tight ball and patch are forced through the muzzle.

In the hands of an ace shot like Dave Ehrig, a properly loaded, quality round ball rifle can be deadly accurate. In fact, the ball is still the most widely-used projectile for muzzleloading target competition. As a hunting projectile, though, the round ball has serious shortcomings, making it the least effective of all muzzleloading rifle projectiles Because it's a perfect sphere, the round ball quickly loses velocity and down range energy levels. At 100 yards a round ball will smack a whitetail with only one-third as much energy as was generated at the muzzle. Loaded in front of a 100 grain charge of FFg black powder, a 177 grain .490-inch round ball leaves the muzzle of a 28-inch .50 caliber barrel at about 2,000 f.p.s., with almost 1,600 ft. lbs. of energy. By the time the ball hits 100 yards, it has slowed down to less than 1,100 f.p.s., with only 450 ft. lbs. or so of remaining energy—hardly enough to take big game as large as a whitetail buck with consistency. That's not to say the patched

COMPLETE BOOK OF WHITETAIL HUNTING

round ball won't take whitetails cleanly. But anyone who accepts the challenge of hunting with a traditional projectile should be aware of its maximum effective range. For the light 128 grain ball —the kind shot out of most .45 caliber rifles—the range will likely be inside of 50 yards. Hefty loads behind a ball in a .50 caliber could stretch the range to 60 or 70 yards; and 100 or more grains of powder behind a 224 grain .530-inch ball should still have enough wallop to take a buck at 75 or 80 yards. Even then, a round ball will only occasionally pass all the way through a big deer, leaving an entrance wound that is probably the only wound on the deer. Should a hunter make a questionable hit, there normally is no exit wound, making it difficult to follow a blood trail.

In recent years most whitetail hunting opportunities have arisen from the establishment or expansion of muzzleloader seasons. The lure of more hunting time and the chance to harvest bonus game has caused many converts from modern gun and archery seasons to pick up a muzzleloader for the first time. As the ranks of muzzleloading hunters have grown, so have the whitetail herds in many states. To promote larger harvests, and to keep the herd in check, many game departments have relaxed the strict regulations governing legal muzzleloaders and loads. In most states, frontloading deer hunters today can head out with as traditional or as modern a muzzleloader as they wish to carry. That includes a choice of hunting projectiles, ignition systems, and even a scope in place of open sights. ■

Today's muzzle-loading hunter can hunt with either a patched round ball, a heavy lead bore-sized conical bullet, or a modern saboted bullet. He must, however, use a rifle designed to shoot each style of projectile.

PART FIVE

Chapter Three

Bowhunting

WITH ■ *John Sloan, Bowhunter & Writer*
■ *Will Primos, President, Primos Game Calls*
■ *Richard P. Smith, Whitetail Expert & Writer*

The concept of the bow has not changed much for a thousand or more years. A simple handle, two limbs and a string used to hurl an arrow for quite a distance. In various parts of the world—where the bow was a primary arm for protection, war or putting food on the table—early versions varied considerably in shape, length and in how they were used. And yet, they all operated in basically the same manner. Twentieth century archers had to hunt with this primitive design until the early 1970s, when the first "compound" bows began to appear on the market.

I bought my first compound in 1972. It was a strange-looking Allen compound produced by a small operation near St. Louis, Missouri. For limbs, the bow was built with nearly one-inch square solid fiberglass rods on each end of the handle, or riser. At the end of each limb was a metal bracket with a wheel mounted slightly off-center. A metal cable wound around each wheel and was attached to individual adjustments near each end of the riser. Stretched between the two wheels a bow string was attached to the ends of the cables. When the string was pulled, the heavy glass limbs flexed some, but most of the cast for the arrow came from the off-center "eccentric" wheels that rolled over in unison as the string returned. While the early compound design looked strange indeed, with all of its cables and adjustments, I was able to move up to a heavier bow by reducing the amount of pull needed to bring the string to full draw by some 30 percent. The arrows left the bow rest faster than from any of the more advanced recurve bows then available.

The Allen compound actually revolutionized bowhunting. Within a few years of its introduction, every major bow manufacturer in the country was producing a compound design under a licensing agreement with the Allen company. Old time recurve and long

bow shooters like Fred Bear didn't like the compound "contraptions," but they were smart enough to realize that here lay the future of bowhunting. Bear supposedly never hunted with a compound, but the company bearing his name has become one of the largest manufacturers of compound bows in the world.

One day in the spring of 1973 I remember entering an archery shop looking for an extra string in preparation for an upcoming Ontario black bear hunt. The shop owner exploded at the sight of my Allen bow and literally threw me and my mechanical contraption out the door. Four years later, I returned to that same shop, and of 100 or so bows on the racks, 80 to 90 were compounds. Archery had changed in a hurry! For the

past decade or two, there's been a resurgence in the use of "traditional" archery gear, i.e., hunting with either a long bow or recurve. A look at the market indicates, though, that the mainstay of bowhunting sales today is easily the compound. Companies offering compound designs along with a few recurves or long bows are well aware that more than 90 percent of their business comes from the purchase of compound models.

The ultra-modern Jennings compound I use today is completely different from the old Allen I owned nearly three decades ago. The bow is much more refined, with a machined metal alloy riser, super-strong carbon and graphite limbs, a unique one-cam design, a much smoother draw, and a

Bowhunter Brenda Valentine poses with a Mississippi buck she took with a single 30-yard shot. She used a razor sharp 100 grain 3-blade Savora "Contender" broadhead.

full 65 percent let-off. The latter not only enable me to shoot a much heavier poundage bow, I can now hold the arrow at full draw for a greater length of time as I improve my sight picture or steady my aim on a whitetail at 15, 20 or 30 yards. Arrow flight is so flat that I can shoot from 20 to 30 yards without changing sight pins.

Will Primos

These and other equipment improvements have made bowhunting more appealing to an ever-growing number of deer hunters. Becoming proficient with an older recurve type bow often meant shooting for 30 to 60 minutes a day year-round. The more forgiving nature of the modern compound allows modern bowhunters to practice an hour or so a week for a month or so before opening day of bow season—and still be able to place an arrow right where it needs to go once a whitetail steps within range. In recent years, compound development has been geared more toward faster arrow flight. Bows of 80 percent let-off have been around now for several years, and the hunting bow has gotten lighter and the overall length shorter, plus a fully tricked out bow (sights, quiver, stabilizer, etc.) with better balance. Today's modern compound is simply a better hunting tool.

Before acquiring my first compound during the later 1960s and early 1970s, I hunted with one of the faster recurves. It could throw a 30-inch long Port Oxford cedar arrow with a 125 grain Bear Razorhead broadhead off the rest at around 160 to 175 f.p.s. My old Allen compound upped arrow velocity to 190-200 f.p.s. The one-cam Jennings bow I'm shooting now, for example, casts an aluminum arrow at almost 250 f.p.s. Some of today's bows are capable of speeds approaching 340 f.p.s., or about twice the speed produced by the fastest recurve bows. Speed isn't everything, though. I would rather shoot a deadly accurate bow with arrow velocities of 225 to 260 f.p.s. than a model of questionable arrow flight with speeds exceeding 300 f.p.s. Still, speed can be important when placing a shot on a wary whitetail.

Experienced bowhunters like Will Primos now realize that whitetails can react merely to the sound of a bow as the hunter releases his string. All bows make some noise as the string slams forward, cams kick over, and the arrow is launched from the rest. Manufacturers have struggled to make compounds quieter with better cam designs, especially those models that have one cam on the lower limb and an idler wheel on the upper limb. Still, even with rubber or yarn silencers to deaden the "twang" of a taught string, compound bows can't help but make noise when the arrow is released, whereupon the survival instincts of the whitetail result in immediate reaction. Believe it or not, a whitetail standing 20 yards away can duck an arrow, even one flying as fast as 250 f.p.s.!

When a whitetail drops, it's not necessarily to duck an oncoming arrow. It's simply preparing to make a sudden getaway. A whitetail's first move in almost any emergency situation is a hard leap—one that makes it a lot easier, once the deer drops down, to put as much spring into its legs as possible. Thus, what may appear to the hunter as a buck ducking an arrow is nothing more than the sudden bending of the legs and relaxing of the leg muscles in preparation for an immediate exodus. The drop is usually enough so that an arrow intended for a lung hit will pass right over the deer's back. With a deer that is standing broadside, Will Primos recommends going for a heart shot low in the chest cavity, at the bottom rear line of the front leg. With a low heart shot, the arrow might even make a good double lung hit should the deer drop in reaction to the shot. If the deer doesn't react, and the hunter's shot is on target, the arrow should catch the heart and possibly even the bottom of one or both lungs. So when shooting at a deer that's quartering away from you, think about where the arrow will exit, then hold accordingly. A standing whitetail who picks up on the sudden slap of a compound will almost always drop. An arrow that's flying at 300 f.p.s. reaches the target much quicker than an arrow moving along at only 200 f.p.s. Thus, a faster arrow determines how much the deer drops before the arrow reaches it. Bear in mind, though, that a deer at 40 yards has more

time to react to a shot than a deer at 20 yards. It's all part of what makes bowhunting an exciting short range pursuit.

Most bowhunters have absolutely no business taking shots past 30 yards. They simply aren't good enough to put a broadhead tipped arrow through the vitals of a deer at that range with any consistency. Those who spend lots of time shooting realistic 3-D deer targets in the backyard and who keep their hits inside the 'kill zone" often aren't all that great at judging distances once they get into the woods—especially from a tree stand 20 feet off of the ground. With most bows being hunted with

Good tracking skills and the ability to read exactly where a whitetail has been hit play an important role in the recovery of downed animals.

today, a different sight pin is needed for shooting at 10, 20 or 30 yards. A broadhead tipped arrow flying at 225 to 250 f.p.s. drops a great deal from 10 to 30 yards, enough to completely miss the chest cavity of a whitetail—or worse yet, make a poor hit. A bow that's sighted to hit dead-on at 10 yards can hit as much as 12 to 14 inches low at 30 yards. Even with a bow equipped with a multi-pin sight set for the different yardages, a miscalculation of 5 or 10 yards can cause a miss or a poor hit. One of the best investments any bowhunter can make is an accurate rangefinder, one that can determine distances within one yard. Once a hunter goes into a new stand, it's a good idea to take readings on several nearby landmarks. That way, you'll know whether a buck is 18 yards away from that stump, or 22 yards from that big oak. In any event, never try to shoot beyond your ability to keep arrows within the heart and lung area. A miss or a poor hit could mean you'll never get a chance at that buck again.

Outdoor writer John Sloan feels that most bowhunters place their stands too high, increasing the angle of the shot. John, who is an experienced and successful bowhunter, rarely goes higher than 15 feet with most of his stands. He prefers a relatively low entrance wound, with the arrow angling just enough to exit low on the opposite side. Such hits produce the best blood trails and a much higher recovery rate of deer shot.

COMPLETE BOOK OF WHITETAIL HUNTING

I also prefer a quartering away shot, often waiting until the deer has completely passed before drawing my bow. Deer usually aren't in a big hurry when moving along at a natural gait, which gives me plenty of time. By letting the deer pass before drawing, there's a lot less chance of being spotted. While many bowhunters whistle, grunt or bleat to get a deer to stop, I let them keep walking as I release the shot. A walking deer, I've found, is less likely to "jump" the string (i.e., drop at the sound of the shot). Depending on the distance and speed of a deer, I may throw in a small lead, or hold dead on. One problem here is that instead of dropping at the sound of the bow being released, whitetails will often come to a dead stop. I've actually missed a few easy 15- to 20-yard shots because I shot in front of a target that was standing

still. It's all part of bowhunting.

A big razor-sharp broadhead does a lot of damage when it passes through internal organs, slicing and dicing as it goes through heart, lungs, even the liver. John Sloan believes that the higher the entrance wound, the lower the exit wound. The worst possible shot to him is the straight-down shot, where the exit hole punches through the rear portion of the brisket. When an arrow exits that low, it's often

Bowhunter John Sloan believes in practicing year-round, shooting his bow from elevated positions in order to duplicate shooting situations.

Here John Sloan practices shooting his bow at varying distances.

reason. They tend to stick with one brand or type, mostly because they fly out of the bow, killing what they hit. Ideally, a good broadhead should do both. Dozens of brands are available, with choices ranging from light-weights of 85 grains up to heavy weights of 170. There are fixed heavy blades that can be resharpened, or those with replaceable razor-blade type inserts. No single bowhunter can prescribe a broadhead for another; but they can always make recommendations based on their own experiences. Following are descriptions of the top-selling broadheads used by modern bowhunters.

By far the most widely used broadheads are the *insert type heads*, because they work well on whitetails. It only takes a few minutes to slip the razor-like blade inserts into the body of these heads, then thread the broadhead into the insert of an aluminum arrow shaft (or the ferrule type tip of a carbon shaft). Such broadheads allow shooters to practice with the same broadheads they'll be using during the hunt; then before heading out to the stand, replace the insert type blades with new ones. With blades of this type, there's no excuse for a hunter carrying broadheads in his quiver that aren't sharp enough to do the job. Like it or not, shooting a deer with an arrow means that the animal must die from

easily plugged by bits and pieces of internal organs cut away by the broad-head. Little if any blood can flow from a plugged exit hole, and when an entrance wound is high, the chest cavity usually won't contain enough blood to flow from the wound site. Unfortunately, many of these hits are lethal and the deer die, but they aren't recovered because of a poor blood trail—or the complete lack of one.

Most bowhunters have a favorite broadhead, but not always for the same

COMPLETE BOOK OF WHITETAIL HUNTING

loss of blood; i.e., it must bleed to death. It takes a good sharp edge to punch through hair, skin and muscle and still have enough power to slice vital organs and blood vessels. Start out with a dull edge, or one of questionable sharpness, and it's quite likely the job won't get done.

A growing number of bowhunters now install "overdraw" attachments to their bows. The idea is to move the rest closer to the string, allowing the hunter to shoot a shorter, lighter arrow. Again, the lighter the arrow, the faster and flatter it will fly. Likewise, more archers now hunt with the newer carbon arrow shafts, which are also lighter and faster than aluminum ones. To keep the arrows

from getting "nose heavy," broadhead weights are now made lighter. During the '60s and early '70s, most recurve archers opted for a massive cutting edge and heads ranging from 125 to 150 grains. Today, the average weight of the more popular broadheads weigh between 100 and 125 grains. Many shooters now rely on heads as light as 80 or 90 grains.

In their zest for more speed, bow-hunters should never forget what a broadhead must do when it hits a deer. A broadhead that's too lightly constructed can easily break apart upon impacting a heavy rib bone, shedding the razor insert blades before they ever get into the chest cavity. There also has to

Illinois has earned a deserved reputation as a bowhunting hot spot. These two monsters were taken on a hunt in western Illinois.

be enough cutting edge to ensure a quick, humane kill. Most three- or four-bladed 100 to 125 grain insert type broadheads—sold under the brand names of Satellite, Wasp, Savora, Thunderhead and others—will certainly do the job. Some states dictate a minimum cutting width, so hunters should check this before choosing an ultra-light broadhead that could be illegal.

Today's broadheads, which are made with such precision, require less "tuning" than designs from the past. When enough time is taken to assemble the insert type points properly, the broadheads will be well-balanced. One side is not heavier than another, nor is any blade non-concentric with the other blades, either condition enough to cause an arrow to fly wild. Still, for some odd reason, arrows cast from some bows tend to fly truer when the blades

of each arrow are set at identical angles. This probably has something to do with how the blades of the point and the fletching of the arrow catch the air in flight, either working with or against each other. I prefer shooting an aluminum arrow with a metal insert held in place by heat-type cements. I simply heat the tip over the stove or with a propane burner until the cement begins to liquefy, then I turn the broadhead and insert inside the hollow shaft, positioning the blades exactly the way I want them. In five or six minutes, I can have the blades of every broadhead positioned in exactly the same spot.

Since the later 1980s quite a few bowhunters have switched to the so-called *mechanical broadheads*. Actually, there's nothing mechanical about them. They simply feature blades that fold forward, the sharp cutting edge fitting

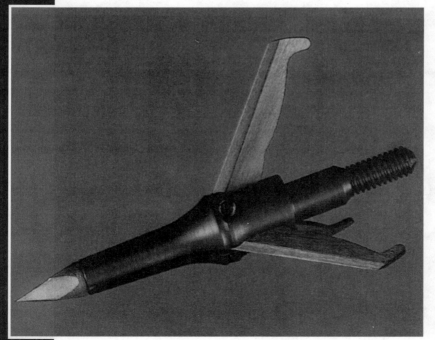

into slots in the body of the broadhead. A tiny rubber O-ring slides up over the blades and holds them in a closed position. When shot into a game animal, a flared edge on the tip of each blade causes the blades to fold back into the open position, exposing the sharp cutting edges. Most bowhunters who've gone this route generally comment on how well the points fly—"practically the same as practice field tips." As far as I'm concerned, though, the jury is still out on these heads. I've been on hunts where deer have required lots of follow-up shots.

Hunters who accept the challenge of taking whitetails with a bow and arrow must accept the fact that, sooner or later, they will most likely make a hit that's less than perfect. A lot of factors come into play in determining where an arrow will hit, including wind drift, brush deflection, excessive drop (due to incorrect estimates), poor release, excitement, or simply not enough practice. By the time a bowhunter hits the field, he or she should already know where the "kill zone" is located—that area just to the rear of, and partially covered by, the front shoulder. That doesn't mean an arrow shot through the sweet spot automatically means the deer will go down within a reasonably short distance, or that an errant arrow means there's no hope of finding the wounded deer.

Richard P. Smith, an experienced whitetail hunter and outdoor writer, claims that the quantity and color of hair and blood can serve as important clues in determining where a deer has been hit. He acknowledges that often an exit wound can yield more hair than an entry wound; also, that the hair from the exit hole of an arrow is often different than the strands left from where the shot entered. Hair varies in length, color and overall characteristics from one part of a deer's body to another. With hairs 2 1/2 to 3 inches long, mostly gray with a short brown section—plus a black tip on

the entry side and whitish-gray hairs that are black-tipped on the exit side—it usually means the arrow hit somewhere in the chest area at least halfway up and made its exit above the belly line on the opposite side. Or it could be that an arrow caught the whitetail at a good angle. Whether or not it passed through the heart and lungs is usually determined by observing blood on the ground and how much it has covered the arrow (assuming it passed completely through the deer).

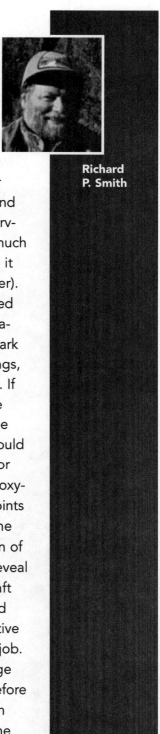

Richard P. Smith

Blood that's light in color and filled with tiny air bubbles is a good indication that the broadhead found its mark and passed through one or both lungs, depending on the angle of the shot. If hair left from the shot indicates the angle of the shot was good, but the blood trail is bright red in color, it could mean a shot has caught the heart or one of the major arteries filled with oxygen-rich blood. As Richard Smith points out, dark red blood is commonly the sign of a liver or gut hit. Examination of the recovered arrow will generally reveal more details. If the broadhead, shaft and fletching are covered with food particles from the stomach or digestive tract, it could mean a long tracking job. Smith is quick, though, to encourage hunters to wait a couple of hours before following up on gut-shot deer. Often lethal hits cannot be claimed until the wounded whitetail has time to hole up and lay down. Unless a hunter actually sees a deer go down within sight of the stand, it's wise to let a wounded deer go an hour or two before pursuing the blood trail. Too often, mortally-wounded deer are pushed so hard they no longer leave a blood trail, only to die unrecovered.

Today's bows and bowhunting equipment have been designed and built to proved hunters with years of trouble-free, performance-minded service. The variety of compound bow models—sights, rests, quivers, stabilizers, arrows, broadheads, releases and arrow holders—is nothing short of astounding. When selecting a new bow and all the goodies needed to fully trick it out, however, listen to the advice of veteran bowhunters and the experts at a good archery pro shop. Few if any will steer you wrong.

Most bowhunters today use a modern compound with a 60 to 70 pound pull and a 65 percent let-off. The bow will most likely be fitted with one of the "center-shot" rests or arrow launchers, practically eliminating arrow shaft contact with the bow and rest. Also required is a quality sight featuring fiber-optic pins for better sighting in low light conditions, a quiver that holds enough arrows for a day's hunt (usually four to six), string silencers, a stabilizer for better balance, or a combination stabilizer and torque tamer that balances the bow and helps eliminate torque or jump when the string is released.

DAMN! I just described my own bow. ∎

Hunting With The Crossbow

Chapter Three

One of the most heated debates among archers concerns whether or not the crossbow should be allowed during the various archery seasons held across the country. Many archers feel it would give the crossbow-toting hunters too great an advantage. They would sit in a stand with their bow strings cocked back, arrow in place and all set for action. It would be too simple, they say, for hunters to simply raise their crossbows, take aim and send their arrows flying. Everyone knows that a crossbow is lethal at unbelievably long ranges—or is it? Ottie Snyder, Executive Director of the American Crossbow Federation, claims that:

"Those victims of the crossbow myth who [go out and] purchase a crossbow and think they have a .30-06 that won't make any noise are going to be disappointed the first time they shoot it. A 150-pound draw-weight compound crossbow will deliver about the same performance as a 65 to 70 pound compound bow."

Snyder goes on to point out why a crossbow of more than double the draw-weight of a quality compound bow will only turn in equal performance.

"It's all in the 'power stroke,' or the distance the string pushes the arrow before it leaves the bow, or crossbow. With a compound bow set up for a 28- or 30-inch draw length, the arrow is actually pushed by the string for 22 to 24 inches."

With most crossbows, the 'power stroke' is considerably shorter, 10 to 12 inches with most models currently available, such as the Horton Hunter Express SL. This 165 pound draw-weight horizontal bow will cast a 20-inch Easton XX75 Horton "Lightning Strike" bolt (arrow) tipped with a 125 grain Horton TRI-LOC blade insert broadhead at a little under 300 f.p.s. I've shot one of the Horton compound Hunter Express SL crossbows many times and have been extremely impressed by its accuracy. The bow is equipped with a 4x Horton crossbow scope featuring five horizontal crosshairs. With the main or primary crosshair sighted to print the arrow dead on at 15 yards, the corresponding four crosshairs put the arrow into the point of aim at 20, 30, 35 and 38 yards, or close enough to the point of aim for hunting purposes. Even this high-tech crossbow is far from being a 100-yard hunting tool. At most, I'd shoot at a whitetail at about 40 yards, or only about 10 yards farther than I would with my compound bow. And that's only because of the crossbow's scope, which provides better sighting.

Ottie Snyder's home state of Ohio is one of only a few that permit the use of a crossbow during the regular archery seasons. Most other states issue special permits to hunters who have physical handicaps or impairments of some kind. With so many states facing the need for bigger harvests in order to manage the ever-growing whitetail population, it seems odd that they would prohibit the use of a hunting tool that allows more hunters to participate. Let's face it, some hunters will never become good bow shots, and they'll never take up bowhunting for that reason. Indeed, there are already a lot of archers out there slinging arrows who have no business trying to take a deer with a bow. A precision-made crossbow will give these hunters an option that allows them to harvest deer more cleanly. Isn't that the whole idea of deer hunting?

"No bowhunter has lost a day of the season." Ottie Snyder insists, "or seen the bag limit reduced as a result of crossbow hunting opportunity. Chevys and Fords still kill more deer in Ohio than all the crossbow hunters and vertical bowhunters put together!"

Isn't it time we put the crossbow myth behind us and start to enjoy hunting the white-tailed deer? Whether most vertical bowhunters like it or not, crossbow hunting will eventually catch hold throughout the country. After all, when enough hunters demand a season, one is usually established. Isn't that how archers got their seasons in the first place?

Whitetail Hunting: Which Style Is Right For You?

WITH ■ *Tom Fegely, Outdoor Writer & Photographer* ■ *John Sloan, Bowhunter & Outdoor Writer* ■ *Richard P. Smith, Whitetail Expert & Writer* ■ *Jim Shockey, Outdoor Writer & Canadian Outfitter* ■ *Russ Markesbery, President, Markesbery Muzzle Loaders, Inc.*

With high winds whipping the tree tops back and forth, sitting in the portable climbing tree stand was like being a bull rider at the rodeo. The sudden midday change in the weather and stronger than expected winds caused Russ Markesbery to rethink his plans for the afternoon and evening. It was early in the muzzleloader season, and Russ had located plenty of buck sign. He had hunted that morning along a promising rub line that followed a trail running along the length of a ridge, leading from a bedding area to a feeding area. He had seen several does and fawns but not bucks, and as much as he wanted to stick with the spot, gut instinct told him that the deer wouldn't be traveling the high ground in such strong winds.

Reluctantly, he climbed down from the swaying tree, removed the stand, and started back to his pickup. After all, he still had the rest of the afternoon. But after thinking about his decision a few minutes, he changed his mind. While scouting the area a few days prior to the hunt, he had located the beginnings of a scrape line along a lower valley bottom. At this time of the year, Russ knew he'd be better off hunting from an elevated stand rather than slipping quietly through the deer woods, looking for deer among the heavy underbrush. The rut was just around the corner and the bucks were really on the move, so the hunter who positioned his stand in the right location stood a great chance of getting a shot.

As he eased along the small creek that flowed down the valley, it became clear to Russ that he had made the right decision. The buck activity had picked up, and every 50 to 100 yards he would come across a new, fresh scrape. When he discovered one that was easily twice the size of any other he had seen, he knew he had found the right place to hunt. A perfectly straight oak without any limbs for the first 25 feet was perfectly situated to cover the scrape and a nearby trail from only 40 yards away. Within minutes, Russ was in position with his two-piece climber from Trophy Whitetail Products (Anderson SC), with a great view of the scrape, trail, valley and side of the ridge opposite his stand site.

He didn't have long to wait. Barely half an hour after positioning the stand some 20 feet up the tree, an eight-point buck eased along the side of the ridge, within easy range of the .50 caliber Markesbery "Brown Bear" rifle Russ used for the hunt. Just as he was trying to make up his mind whether or not to take the deer, a flicker of movement down the valley caught his attention. He watched as an even bigger nine-pointer slowly emerged from the lower

foliage and headed right for the scrape. Russ followed the deer in his scope, and when the animal offered a broadside shot at about 50 yards, he eased back on the trigger. At the roar of the muzzleloader, the buck dropped in its tracks as the saboted, all-copper 250 grain hollow-point bullet punched squarely through the chest cavity.

Like millions of other hunters across the U.S. and Canada, Russ Markesbery has discovered that the special muzzleloader seasons now offer the serious whitetail hunter some of the finest opportunities to harvest a good buck. This is especially true where a liberal season structure schedules an early muzzleloader hunt prior to the state's general firearms season, as is the case in Markesbery's home state of Kentucky.

Many such seasons are held during the pre-rut, when bucks tend to be on the move and become quite visible. Since the only other hunting pressure the deer may have experienced was from bowhunters, in most areas the whitetails didn't even know they were being hunted.

The lofty wooden platform I had built hastily one afternoon a week or so prior to the opener of the Illinois bow season consisted of a three-by-three foot piece of heavy plywood. It was nailed down to two two-by-fours that spanned the forked trunk of a huge old wild cherry tree. It was located in a grown-up fencerow that led from a wooded ridge to a tangle of creek bottom cover several hundred yards away.

It was the third week of October and the white oak acorns were falling so heavily on the ridge that they often sounded like rain whenever a gentle breeze stirred the upper limbs of the ancient oaks.

On one side of the brushy fencerow was a standing corn field, and on the other a harvested soybean field. Along each side of the fencerow was a well-used trail leading from the creek bottom bedding to where the whitetail gorged themselves on the succulent mast crop. I had hunted the same stand for nearly a week without ever spotting a single deer—but that was about to change. Just as the sun touched the top of a distant wooded ridge, an old doe and

Many experts agree that a tree stand hung almost anywhere in prime white-tail country will ultimately produce shots at deer. But learning to read sign accurately can increase the odds of placing a stand where it will be most productive.

a single fawn stepped out of the lower cover and onto the edge of the cornfield. Slowly, they walked in my direction, staying between the last row of corn and the fencerow. Then, about 50 yards out, the doe stepped into the corn and the fawn followed. My heart sank as I watched the tops of their ears ease past my stand only 25 yards away. At least five or six rows of corn lay between us, robbing me of a shot.

I stood with my bow ready, arrow on the string. As the doe reached the edge of the hardwoods, I was about to hang my bow back on a small branch when a sudden movement almost directly behind me caused me to look down. Right there in the open, not 20 yards away, stood a button buck. The deer was busy watching the doe and her fawn and had no idea I was anywhere near. The bow was still in my left hand, so I eased around on the wooden platform, slowly pulled the string back to full draw, took aim and let fly. The arrow found its mark, and the young buck walked less than 75 yards before going down out in the open field. I had just taken the trophy of a lifetime.

It was only my first bow kill, taken in the fall of my 14th year. The bow was a Ben Pearson "Colt" recurve with a 45-pound pull. I had bought it with money saved by putting up hay for local farmers during the summer. I was shooting Port Oxford cedar arrows, tipped with Bear "Razorhead" broadheads. The year was 1964—the first season I ever picked up a bow—and the young button buck was the first

whitetail I had ever shot at with a bow. That early success definitely made me a lifelong bowhunter. Each time I draw back on a whitetail, or even think about doing so, somewhere in the back of my mind is that hunt years ago that set the stage for future bowhunts.

As outdoor writer John Sloan maintains, "Bowhunting isn't for everyone. It is not a panacea for replacing the lost thrill of the hunt. I have been flinging arrows for many years, but I still thrill at a well-placed rifle shot and the smell of black powder. Bowhunting may be my favorite form of hunting, but I'm not sure that's true. I think my favorite form is whatever type of equipment I'm using at the time. Not true—bowhunting is my favorite!"

John openly admits that he doesn't feel any greater satisfaction when he takes a whitetail with a bow than he does with a modern gun or muzzleloader. What he has come to appreciate most about bowhunting is that it has taught him a great deal more about the whitetails he hunts. Pursuing them has forced John to "watch" whitetails more carefully, to learn more about their habits, movements and behavior. This knowledge enables John to harvest deer in greater numbers with his short-range equipment. From studying the deer, John has become a much more educated hunter, hence a better one Now, whenever he takes a good buck with a modern centerfire rifle or muzzleloader, he credits much of his success to the fact that he bowhunts. "I like to shoot a bow." John adds. "I have targets in my yard year-round. When I step out the door in the morning and zip six arrows into a three-inch ring at 15 to 30 yards, I find that very satisfying."

Bowhunting whitetails does require a stronger commitment than hunting deer with a muzzleloader or some other type of modern firearm—a rifle, shotgun or handgun. Being prepared to bowhunt means having spent enough time with the bow on the range to put shots consistently inside the "kill zone" of the chest cavity. Many centerfire rifle hunters I know buy a single 20-round box of ammo and shoot about half the box in a week or two prior to the general firearms season. They want to make sure their favorite 30-30 or .30-06 is still dead on, so they can hunt the rest of the season with the other half-box of cartridges. A lot of muzzleloader hunters don't shoot much more than that, either. To become proficient enough with a bow to attempt taking a whitetail nearly always requires hundreds, or even thousands, of practice shots to hone the archer's shooting ability, and to ensure that the bow, arrows, sights, broadheads, rest and type of release are all working together for the best possible results.

Hunting whitetails with a bow is a close-range endeavor. Many experienced bowhunters question the ethics of any bow-

hunter who continually attempts shots at deer with bow and arrow at ranges of 50 yards or more. I enjoy shooting a bow throughout most of the year, and I can easily keep most of my hits inside of six inches (dead center of the chest cavity) at distances exceeding 40 yards and often at 50 yards. Still, I've established 30 yards as my personal maximum effective range. When presented with a clear broadside shot out to that distance, I am extremely confident that I can put an arrow exactly where it needs to go. Once the distance exceeds 30

Bowhunting whitetails means getting close to the target, and that calls for well-honed hunting skills. The ability to place a broadhead tipped arrow right where it needs to go means spending lots of time on the practice range.

yards, though, I begin to doubt my own ability, which means I shouldn't try taking that shot. Another problem is how to pinpoint the exact range past 30 yards. A misjudgment at that distance by as little as 5 yards can cause an arrow to hit seven or eight inches low or high, resulting in a poor hit and a lost deer. Most hunters can reasonably judge distances out to 25 or 30 yards; but once past that, most will be off five or more yards out to 50 yards. From 50 to 100 yards, most hunters will misjudge distances by 10 to 20 yards. While such miscalculations are not considered a problem with a modern gun or muzzleloader at such distances, they are with a bow.

Because of the close-range nature of bowhunting, a hunter must also be prepared to spend long hours in the stand, waiting for that perfect shot. It's not uncommon to hunt two or three mornings and afternoons each week for one or two months straight before ever getting a shot. In today's fast-paced world, most whitetail hunters simply don't have that kind of patience— or time. Still, as John Sloan pointed out earlier, bowhunting is a great way to spend time in the woods, observe deer, and learn from what can be seen. Whitetail hunters who have honed their hunting skills to the point where they can regularly harvest whitetails with a bow are often the same hunters who are equally successful with a muzzleloader or a modern gun.

My good friend, outdoor writer Richard P. Smith, is definitely patient enough to stay put in one spot. I've hunted with him on numerous occasions and remember many times when he stayed with the same stand from

Late muzzleloader hunts can extend the season, but that often means hunting wary deer during cold, snowy weather.

daylight to dark in mighty nasty weather. But Richard, being an adaptable whitetail hunter, has developed his own personal hunting techniques, one of which he refers to as "mobile stand hunting."

Richard hails from the upper peninsula of Michigan, where modern gun and muzzleloader hunters were not allowed to hunt from elevated stands until the 1998 season. As ridiculous as this may sound, the game department there once contended that it was safer for all hunters to be on the ground firing at the same level, rather than shooting at deer from an elevated stand with their rifles pointed downward. This particular game department might know a thing or two about wildlife management, but it apparently knows beans about bullet flight!

When forced to hunt on the ground, a hunter is faced with several obstacles. First, how far can a hunter spot a deer from a ground location? In some cover, the distance can be relatively short. Second, when hunting from the ground a hunter's scent is more easily detected by the sensitive noses of whitetails. A hunter's scent at ground level tends to hang closer to the ground and is more

easily picked up by deer traveling down wind. A hunter who stays all day in one spot will leave a lot more human scent on the ground than the hunter who walks into an elevated stand and climbs up 20 feet or so. It is this last element which prompted Richard Smith to develop his hunting tactics using a mobile stand. They help prevent the deer from

To take full advantage of the rut, outdoor writer Gary Clancy feels the hunter must master the art of calling deer with both rattling antlers and a grunt call.

patterning the hunter before he can single out a buck's movements in time to get a shot.

Richard recalls one hunt in which the effectiveness of his technique was obvious:

"An out-of-state hunt prevented me from scouting the area for fresh activity before the season opened. When I arrived at my hot spot on opening day—the same place where I had shot two bucks on previous hunts—there was snow on the ground and little or no sign of fresh activity. The area was located in a wooded flat, and on the way in I noticed fresh tracks in the snow. With that, I backtracked to the side of the ridge and took a ground stand where I could still see the bottom flat, while at the same time covering some of the ridge. I spent the entire day there and saw just three deer. First, a doe and fawn passed by along the crest of the ridge, about 100 yards away. Even if it had been a buck, I wouldn't have had a shot opportunity because of the heavy brush. I thought about moving closer to where I had seen the deer, but decided not to. Half an hour later, a young buck followed the same route. Just before dark, I heard another deer walking in the crunchy snow. I tried grunting and rattling, but got no response."

Richard went on to describe how, the next morning, he posted about 100 yards west of where he had spent the previous day. The new stand allowed him to watch the travel route used by the last deer he had seen, which meant he could no longer watch the lower flat. Nothing moved that morning, and when the wind shifted in mid-day, he relocated near the head of a small valley that ran down to a swamp. Several days later, Richard returned to the same area, this time moving to high ground on the opposite side of his first stand. Shortly after daylight, he spotted another young buck—the same yearling he had seen on opening day. After noting where the deer had gone, Richard moved to the upper end of a small valley and took a stand there until midday.

After spotting four more deer, Richard decided to check out the same flat where he had first hunted during the season opener, and there he discovered new buck activity consisting of four or five freshly made scrapes, including one big scrape near where he had begun the season. Since the area was crisscrossed with large tracts, Richard took a new stand where he could watch as much of the area as possible. At about 3:30 that afternoon, a hot doe made an appearance with a mature 4 1/2- or 5 1/2-year-old buck right on her heels. Seconds later, one well-placed shot from Richard's scoped .30-06 rifle dropped the big horned eight-pointer.

Richard maintained that if he had simply stayed with his original stand, he might not have seen the buck he eventually harvested. He had, after all, hunted the same area for three days from seven different stand locations. By moving around, he was able to keep within 300 yards from the spot where he had spent the season opener. His movements, as a result, caused the deer to miss Richard's pattern. That's how this veteran deer hunter developed his own successful hunting style. His ability to read sign and determine when to move came from a lifetime of hunting whitetails, as opposed to the hunter who simply walks into the deer woods, plops down anywhere, then moves repeatedly without any reason other than the fact that he hadn't seen any deer at the last spot.

Jim Shockey, a Canadian outfitter from Vancouver Island, British Columbia, does most of his whitetail hunting in Saskatchewan. He too is a successful whitetail expert who has learned to be flexible and adaptable when pursuing

a big buck. At times, he figures, there's no better way to hunt whitetails than to take a stand and stick with it until the deer you're after shows up. Jim is also quick to point out , though, that sometimes a hunter must get out of his stand and go looking for the buck. "There are those days," he allows, "when a hunter greatly improves his chances of seeing deer by climbing down and taking the hunt to the deer. When the conditions are just right, even the clumsiest hunter has a much better chance of closing with a buck. Hell, on the right day, a hunter can drive a bulldozer through the woods and still be able to sneak up on a buck . . . well, almost."

Jim Shockey's favorite still-hunting conditions are those windy days that

Jim Shockey prefers "still hunting" over other whitetail hunting tactics, but he realizes this is not for every hunter.

play havoc with a whitetail's senses—and nerves. When a stiff breeze rattles the treetops and lower brush, it become increasingly difficult for a whitetail to pick out a slow-moving hunter. Shifting, swirling winds can dissipate human scent to the point where it is undetectable, or at least makes it next to impossible for a deer to determine exactly the direction from which it comes. More than once, Jim has had whitetails pick up his scent and run straight at him. He feels the deer were confused by the swirling air currents and had no idea of his location. Still, even on very windy days, his key to successful still-hunting remains the same: "Move slowly . . . very, very slowly."

"Still hunting," Jim contends, "is like making a day-long stalk on an animal you haven't seen, and may well not even be there. It's a great test of a hunter's self-discipline. I know I may have blown an opportunity I might not get again. Very often, the deer are not where you think they are." Jim also points out that simply believing deer are ahead and hunting them slowly are important ingredients to still-hunting success. Experienced still hunters soon recognize the terrain and cover that tend to hold deer, along with cover and landforms through which deer might slip undetected. As a professional outdoor writer, Jim is the first to admit that knowledge about deer-hunting is not learned solely from magazine articles or books; it must also be developed from practical experience.

Of all the different ways whitetails can be hunted, the classic deer drive is by far the mot sociable event. Other than a guided hunt, most all other whitetail hunting becomes more of a one-on-one pursuit. A deer drive can consist of as few as two or three drivers and two or three standers, or it can be as many as a dozen or more of each. The size, density and terrain of the cover involved in the drive usually dictate how many hunters are needed to push whitetails from their covers, and how many standers will be needed to cover all the exit points. The key to a successful drive is good organization and participants who are willing to listen. A line of drivers who cannot keep abreast will often leave huge holes in the bush through which deer can easily escape. Likewise, standers who do not remain where they are posted can leave exit routes uncovered as well.

Whitetail hunter Tom Fegely of Pennsylvania is another outdoor writer who hunts in six or more states each fall. He goes after deer with a bow, a muzzle-loader, or with a variety of modern firearms. Tom has learned that by using all three types of arms, he can stretch his deer season from September until early February, or from the earliest scheduled bow seasons to the end of those long southern gun seasons. Back in the early to mid-1960s an advertisement featured a hunter adorned half in brightly-checkered red clothing and half in camouflage. He packed a centerfire rifle in one hand and a bow and quiver full of arrows in the other. The ad was paid for by one of the major archery companies, but its aim

COMPLETE BOOK OF WHITETAIL HUNTING

was to promote the longer, more liberal archery deer seasons at the time. Tom Fegely points out that if someone were to run a similar ad today, they'd have to figure out how to get a frontloader thrown over that hunter's shoulder.

Across the country, muzzleloading has become a bona fide third season opportunity, one that continues to pull new participants from both the ranks of modern gunhunters and ardent bowhunters alike. In a way, muzzleloading has become something of a happy middle ground. On one side there are the hard-core bowhunters who would never dream of picking up a long-range centerfire to hunt deer. On the other hand, there are gun hunters who would never throw so much as a sharpened stick at a deer. But hunters from both sides of the fence will readily embrace the muzzleloader seasons as a way of extending the amount of time they can spend pursuing whitetails. The smart hunter is the one who has learned to become a "Three-Season Hunter," one who enjoys whitetail hunting through the fall months.

Deer hunters evolve into a particular style of whitetail hunting for various reasons. These may include the challenge, serenity and company of the deer camp; but primarily it's because they have adopted a certain way of hunting with success. Killing deer becomes secondary to hunting deer; but even so, there has to be some suc-

cess or hunters will lose interest. Each hunter must determine his own style of hunting, one that best suits his expectations with the promise of success. Even as a growing number of hunters turn to other seasons with which to extend the time spent in the deer woods, so the wise hunter will rely on more than merely one tactic or technique. After all, when you're after a wise old buck, it's good to have an extra trick or two up your sleeve! ∎

Tom Fegely's deer hunts keep him afield for three months or longer. Hunting the late seasons successfully often means being prepared to hunt in some nasty weather. (Betty Lou Fegely photo)

Chapter Five

Stand Hunting (Or Patience Has Its Rewards)

WITH ■ *John Sloan, Bowhunter & Outdoor Writer* ■ *Richard P. Smith, Writer & Authority on Whitetails* ■ *David Hale (Knight & Hale Game Calls)* ■ *Mark Drury (M.A.D. Calls)*

It was opening day of Minnesota's deer season for firearms. I had spent most of the morning packing a portable tree-stand on my back while scouting for a hot spot to hunt the next morning. A stiff breeze and sub-zero temperatures created a chill that went right to the bone. I had been in the area a few days, braving the cold and trying to get in some last-minute bowhunting before the firearms season opened. I finally settled on hunting the edge of a long, narrow cornfield that ran the length of a high ridge.

The field was nearly a half-mile in length, but it averaged only 200 yards in width. I had decided on a spot for my stand where the harvested field narrowed to about 100 yards. Hundreds of tracks in the freshly fallen snow cover indicated this was a well-used crossover from one side of the wooded ridge to the other. That final afternoon of bowhunting convinced me that I had made the right choice. Several extremely

good 130 to 150 class bucks crossed just out of bow range. They'd have been easy pickings for the scope-sighted in-line percussion .50 caliber muzzleloader I'd be packing for the rest of the hunt.

The temperatures plummeted to -18 degrees that night, and as I headed up the side of the ridge the next morning in the pre-dawn darkness, the windchill factor was close to -40 degrees. Since I knew I was in for a cold day in the stand, I had carried in some extra wool clothing. As it happened, I didn't fire a shot all day, but I was able to stay with the stand long enough to observe more than 50 deer crossing within muzzle-loader range of my portable tree stand. By the time the sun settled below the western horizon, I was so cold it was all I could do to climb down from the 20-foot high platform.

The next morning I was back on stand long before the sun had bright-ened the snow-covered landscape. It was every bit as cold as the previous day, and the weather was already having an affect on the whitetails. They were in the field all morning long, pawing through the snow cover to find remnants of corn left in the field. Shortly after mid-morning, a half-dozen shots sounded from the bottom of the ridge at my back. A few minute later, nine deer appeared along the edge of the field about 100 yards to my left. One was a tall, handsome eight-pointer scoring well into the 130s. It stood looking across the field for several minutes, then headed with the other deer for the lower side of the sloped field across the way. There the whitetails milled around in a shallow pocket. I aligned the crosshairs of my scope on the buck, but then I noticed that all the deer were looking back across the field. I leaned forward until I could see the spot where the deer had first appeared. A huge ten-pointer had stepped into the field and was bounding through the deep snow toward the others. I followed him with the scope, and the moment he stopped on the other side I centered the crosshairs slightly to the rear of the shoulder and squeezed off a shot. The saboted, jacketed hollow point bullet struck pay dirt and the big buck nose-dived into the fresh snow.

Credit for taking that deer belonged as much to my comfortable, well-placed tree stand as did the accuracy of the rifle and load I used. Had I tried to cover the field from the ground, I would

most likely have been detected by the other deer already in the area. The ensuing commotion of the startled whitetails could have easily ruined the hunt. Also, the deer that had suddenly appeared along the edge of the field came in from behind me, downwind of my stand. Because it was 20 feet off the ground, my scent was too far above the deer as they made their way up the side

The author displays the rewards of a long, cold wait, made possible only by a comfortable tree stand placed in the right spot.

of the steep ridge. The elevated stand also allowed me to look down into the shallow depression on the opposite side of the field. Had I been sitting—or even standing—next to that same oak, I'd never have seen those deer once they reached the opposite side.

Equally important was the comfort of my stand. Without the padded seat, the back rest and the "easy chair" design of my Trophy Whitetail Products climbing stand, I probably would never have stayed with the stand as long as I

did. If statistics were available indicating the numbers of whitetails harvested using each hunting method, I daresay that just as many (if not more) deer are taken from stands than all other methods combined. It is by far the favored technique of hunters wherever whitetails are found and hunted.

Richard P. Smith, an outdoor writer from Marquette, Michigan, happened to be on that same Minnesota hunt described above. He has hunted whitetails from the north country of Michigan and Canada to the swamps of Georgia and Alabama and the vast cornfields and agricultural lands of the Midwest. Every season finds Richard hunting whitetails— and he does so primarily from a stand. "More than 95% of the whitetails I've shot over the years with gun and bow" he comments, "have been killed while on stand. Most of my deer hunting, in fact, has been spent waiting for whitetails to come to me, not because I enjoy that method the most, but because I have been consistently successful that way."

Smith firmly believes that most hunters prefer to ambush whitetails from an elevated stand because their chances of being scented or seen by the deer are greatly reduced. Being above ground level is another important advantage. As long as a hunter and his stand are downwind of a whitetail, the chances of a deer detecting the hunter before the hunter sees the deer are greatly reduced. In some situations, a man's scent originating from an elevated hunting position can actually catch air currents that drift well above a deer's sensitive nostrils. For these and other reasons, dozens of manufacturers now cater to the hunter's need to get off of the ground, thanks to a tremendous selection of commercially available stands. The more common varieties are as follows:

FIXED POSITION STAND

These stands are often referred to as "chain-on" (or "lock-on") types, which the hunter attaches to a tree by encircling it with a chain, heavy webbed nylon strap, or flat metal band and attaching it to each side of the stand. Stands of this type consist of a platform on which to stand, a seat of varying degrees of comfort and whatever form of chain, strap, rope or band a hunter uses to attach his stand to a tree. Some feature a second strap that is wrapped around the tree trunk and then tightened to make the standing platform more stable. Others include a T-shaped arrangement that fits through a hole in the back of the stand, then screws into

the trunk of the tree. This makes the stand more solid and less likely to shift back and forth whenever the hunter changes position.

The advantages of a fixed (or lock-on) stand include affordability, versatility, portability, and ease of concealment. Without having a lot of costly components, these stands are economical to produce and sell at affordable prices. Most of these stands can be attached

Chain-on type stands are securely attached to the tree to form a solid and safe platform from which to hunt. The shooting rail used by this hunter can steady those long range shots effectively.

the most popular being screw-in type steps. A few of these steps placed low to the ground will enable the hunter to reach the lower limbs of a tree, from which he can then climb to the desired height. The strap-on ladders have become quite popular, but many land owners, along with several state and federal agencies, prohibit the use of these screw-in steps because of the damage they can do to the trees.

CLIMBING STANDS

As the name suggests, these stands are used to climb to whatever height a hunter desires. Stands of this type generally consist of two parts: a standing platform and an upper portion that commonly doubles as a seat. To start, the hunter slips each foot into webbed loops attached to the top of the standing platform. Using the climber portion of the stand to support his weight, the hunter's feet are then raised and the bottom half of the stand is repositioned slightly higher on the tree. The hunter then stands upright, repositions the climber portion of the stand and repeats the motion until the desired height has been reached.

Although a variety of climbing stands is available, almost all operate in basi-

A small hoist eliminates a lot of the work in putting a tree stand in place.

to any straight portion of a tree, and they can be used almost anywhere. Moreover, they weigh only 8 to 12 pounds, so they are easy to pack into remote hunting spots. Being relatively compact, these stands are easily hidden among the tree limbs, making it easier to position a stand wherever surrounding cover helps camouflage the hunter.

Among the disadvantages of a fixed stand is that the hunter must also pack something to help him reach the stand,

COMPLETE BOOK OF WHITETAIL HUNTING

cally the same manner. Some of the more popular models feature comfortable seats and backrests, plus arms that resemble lofty lounge chairs. Many of these climbers are built so that the hunter faces the tree, which is fine when hunting with a gun. The tree makes a handy rest for taking long shots with rifle, shotgun, handgun or muzzleloader. Unfortunately, though, this same design makes it nearly impossible to hunt from a stand with a bow. As a result, more and more manufacturers are now building their stands with seats that can be positioned to face the tree or in the opposite direction. This setup can be extremely comfortable when hunting with gun or bow.

Another advantage of the self-climbing stand is that no screw or strap-on steps are needed. When winds shift, or the sun is in one's eyes, the stand can be easily moved around to the other side of the tree. The disadvantages of a climbing stand are its weight and bulk, not to mention the noise that's generated as one actually climbs a tree and its limited use in some parts of the country. Many of these climbing stands weight 20 pounds or more, so packing a two-piece climber is often like carrying in two stands. While most require little effort to use, they make plenty of noise when shinnying up the side of an oak, especially when deer are close to the stand site. Finally, it takes a particular kind of

tree when using a climbing stand—one without any limbs below the stand, and one that's relatively straight. In some parts of the country, trees like this simply don't exist, and when found, may not be in the best locations for hunting.

LADDER STANDS

Among the easier and quicker stands to erect is the simple ladder-type stand. Most consist of three or four ladder

Good camouflage can make motionless hunters nearly invisible.

sections that slip together to create a standing or sitting platform 10, 12, or 15 feet off the ground. Some of the more elaborate ladder stands can even include a standing rail around the platform, and perhaps a comfortable bench-style seat. Nearly all ladder-style stands can be slipped together in only a few minutes, leaned up against a tree, then attached to the tree by running a chain or strap around the trunk and cinching in tight until the platform is solid. The whole process can be completed in ten minutes or less. The major drawback with this type of stand is its weight. Most tip the scales at 30 pounds or less, while others with larger, more

spacious standing platforms, plus a leaning rail and a comfortable seat, can weigh upwards of 70 or 80 pounds. The stands are bulky, too, and may require two hunters to pack in. Once in place, though, they are the easiest to climb into and the most comfortable during those long waits for the buck of one's dreams to show up. These elaborate stands are also difficult to camouflage and can be quite expensive.

TRIPOD STANDS

Not all elevated stands are true "tree stands." The tripod stand is exactly what the name implies: a standing or sitting platform that is held off the

ground by three tripod legs. These stands earned much of their popularity in the brush country of south Texas where there are few trees, and those that do exist are usually not big enough to support a stand. Sitting 10 to 15 feet from the ground, a tripod stand allows hunters to watch thick brush for spotting deer as they work through openings in the heavy cover. Some designs, meant solely for rifle hunters, are built with comfortable seats and shooting rests on all sides. Some even boast roomy standing platforms, allowing bowhunters plenty of room to draw and get off a shot.

Tripod stands are great in those cases where the hunter can drive in, erect the stands, and leave them out all season. Erecting them can also be noisy and time-consuming. They're not exactly portable either; but on the other hand, they can be placed almost anywhere and are easy to climb into.

PERMANENT STANDS

Before the introduction of commercial portable tree stands, most hunters who wanted to get up off the ground simply built crude platforms above the ground. Many hunters still prefer permanent stands over one of the portable arrangements described above. Permanent stands can range anywhere from a simple section of 2x6 wedged into the crotch of a forked tree to an elaborate, enclosed mini-condominium atop poles, complete with gas heat, windows, a shooting bench, and maybe even a small refrigerator. Most permanent stands fall somewhere in between.

GROUND BLINDS OR STANDS

Not all stands are elevated. Many whitetails are taken each year from blinds located at ground level, or close to it. These blinds can range from a pile of rotting logs to a carefully constructed

Tripod stands have become quite popular in areas where the trees are too small to allow use of tree-mounted stands.

accustomed to its presence. Other than when they are downwind of the hunter's position, the deer have no idea that a hunter is in the area. In many parts of the country a ground blind can be set up where no suitable trees exist for installing elevated stands. In fact, elevated stands were still illegal during Michigan's firearms deer season until 1988, forcing some 900,000 gun hunters to do so only from ground level.

Nearly 20 years ago, during the first half of Illinois' split firearms season, I used an old, long abandoned barn to take one of my most prized whitetails. For several years, one of the local farmers had been telling me that each year on

brush blind that hides hunters from the whitetails' sharp eyes, or perhaps it could be a commercially manufactured, portable and camouflaged blind. Such arrangements offer several advantages. Faced with building a ground blind, a hunter can make it as roomy as he likes; and should wet weather arrive, a hastily-built, lean-to roof can be quickly erected. Also, should a hunter elect to use an old rock pile, clump of brush or an abandoned building as a stand or blind, the deer will have already become

opening morning he spotted at least one good buck slipping down a long, wooded fencerow that led to a tangle of brush and saplings on what had been the farmer's barn lot. He figured those old bucks would hole up in the thick cover until the three-day hunt was over, then return as soon as the army of orange-coated hunters had left. Anyway, that old farmer's stories got my attention, so I decided to check out his barn lot. Only a few doe and fawn tracks were evident along the outside edges, so I hung a stand back in the big timber several days before the season opener.

The more I thought about what that farmer kept insisting, though, the more it made sense. Come opening morning, I sat in the loft of the old barn, and each time a shot sounded from the woods nearby the more I thought I had screwed up. A few moments later, I spotted some movement along one of the fencerows and discovered a huge eight-pointer with nearly a two-foot spread.

I watched the deer make its way along the fencerow, careful not to step too far into the open soybean field. The deer stopped about 50 yards short of the farmer's lane in order to study the area, then made a hard charge for the cover of the barn lot. Once in thick cover, the deer settled down. He was now standing 25 yards from the old barn when I dumped him with a single shot from my self-built .50 caliber custom muzzleloader. Not only had several old bales of hay made one of the more comfortable stands I've ever sat in, but the open loft door had provided a window to the entire barn lot.

Through the years, I've taken a number of good whitetail bucks from a wide variety of blinds. Several were simply bulldozed piles of old tree trunks left over from the time the farm fields were enlarged. High points or rocky outcroppings over-looking a small wooded valley or

flat also make excellent stand locations. Just because an area has no trees suitable for hanging a tree stand, or because the landowner doesn't allow tree stands on his property, don't give up on what appears to be promising country. There's nothing wrong with hunting from the ground, especially if you can conceal yourself properly or have found a natural landform that provides some kind of advantage.

Stand placement is critical in getting clear shots. This bowhunter studies the terrain near a hot spot with great care, looking for just the right tree in the right location.

Whenever possible, I rely on a well-designed, roomy and safe tree stand. I like staying above the animals, especially when bowhunting whitetails. My favorites are the chain-on or lock-on type stands, because they can be hung in almost any kind of tree. All my stands are fitted with a set of shoulder-carrying straps, allowing me to slip one of the stands onto my back while I do my scouting and stand-hanging. I usually carry 10 or 12 screw-in steps in a small cloth bag, plus a small folding saw for trimming branches, an extra cinch strap, and a few screw-in hooks for hanging my bow, rifle, rattling horns, calls, jacket, fanny pack, and so on. I always make sure to carry a 20- to 25-foot pull up

rope or string as well. Other than the weight of my bow or gun, everything I need to put a stand into a tree and be ready to hunt weighs less than 20 to 25 pounds.

In my opinion, the best time to hunt from a stand is the day you hang it—provided, of course, the time of the season and the winds are right. Remember, that stand wasn't there yesterday, so any deer who might be using the location have no idea it exists. The element of surprise is always best on the day the stand is hung. Usually, I'll hunt the stand that morning or afternoon, then leave it for four to six days before returning—unless the spot is so hot that I can't resist going back in a day or so. Once I get 10 or 15 stands hung, especially when bowhunting, I try to hunt the same stand only once or twice during the course of a week. Deer will pattern the hunter sooner than the hunter can pattern the deer.

Tennessee bowhunter and outdoor writer John Sloan states, "I own fifteen portable stands and one ladder stand. When the season really gets rolling, I'll have thirteen of the fifteen portables in the woods. I always keep two in reserve for sudden discoveries." John's mix of portable stands includes a variety of fixed position stands and self-climbers. In addition to hunting in his home state, he pursues whitetails in several other states each fall, including Nebraska, Illinois, Mississippi and Alabama. On each trip, John takes along several stands of each type, his criteria being that they are all solid, roomy, comfortable and safe. He refuses to hunt out of anything that doesn't offer these qualities. A good example is a stand he was given by a new tree stand manufacturer several years ago for testing. John hung the stand, climbed into it and immediately decided it wasn't up to snuff. He quickly climbed out of the stand, unfastened it from the tree and proceeded to take the stand down. Once on the ground, he pitched the new stand into a 250-foot deep creek bottom where it remains.

When pressured to pick his favorite type of stand, John Sloan opts for a two-piece climber when he already knows which tree he'll hunt from, or when he plans to hunt on a wildlife management area where screw-in steps are prohibited. He also feels that a hunter will gain a lot more acceptance from landowners when he uses a climber that won't damage good hardwood or pine timber. John has no qualms, however, about slipping in and hanging a

Bowhunting writer John Sloan believes in practicing from a stand and wearing the same clothing he'll be hunting in (Except for the shoes!).

Mark Drury

David Hale

fixed-position stand in an area where the trees have too many limbs for a climbing stand. Whenever possible, he'll rely on a strap-on climbing pole or ladder instead of screw-in steps. John is the first to argue that screw-in steps do little if any real damage to timber, but he feels that any climbing device that doesn't penetrate the bark of a tree generally results in better relations with landowners.

Mark Drury, who hunts primarily in Missouri, Illinois and Iowa, finds that the oaks there are heavily limbed from five or six feet off the ground all the way to the top. Self-climbing stands are therefore completely out of the picture. The only choice in that case is one of the fixed position stands. A few screw-in steps near the bottom of the trunk, or several sections of a strap-on ladder or climbing pole, enable a hunter to reach the first limb. Often he can then climb the rest of the way to the stand position. Another advantage of a heavily-limbed tree is the camouflage it provides hunters in the stand. David Hale spends most of October, November and December sitting in a tree stand some 15, 20 or 25 feet off the ground. When selecting a stand, he insists on the following requirements:

1. *The stand must be quiet, allowing him to move into shooting position quickly without making any sounds that could give him away.*

2. *He must be able to hang a*

stand entirely by himself, since he most often hunts entirely alone.

3. *He needs a stand with a seat for those long waits in the stand.*

4. *He prefers the added strength of a chain for fastening the stand to the tree, if for no reason other than peace of mind.*

5. *The stand must have a platform large enough for comfort and security when the hunter moves into a better shooting position.*

TREE STAND SAFETY

All hunters, when selecting a stand, should first list the five or six most important features they need and want before looking at different stands. By taking this list with you, you're more apt to walk out of the store with a stand that best meets your needs. No matter what features you deem important, though, always look for quality construction. Don't forget, you're going to be spending a lot of time in that stand. Tree stand safety actually begins before you ever set foot on an elevated platform. First, make sure that your stand and climbing equipment are in top condition before heading into the woods. Are your safety harnesses strong enough? Will they snap under your weight? Have you found the right tree for the stand? Here are a few important safety tips:

1. *Always wear a safety belt or harness when hunting from an elevated stand. Leave only enough slack in the line to sit or stand comfortably.*

2. *Before heading into the deer woods with a new stand, hang the*

COMPLETE BOOK OF WHITETAIL HUNTING

stand in a tree in the backyard and check its sturdiness. Note how solidly it mounts to the tree. Has it been correctly assembled? Do all this with the stand at two feet off of the ground. Should something go wrong, the fall at that height won't hurt as bad.

3. Make sure the screw-in steps are turned in all the way, with the back of the step making contact with the tree trunk. Don't leave an inch or two of space between the back of the step and the tree. When placing your weight on the step, there should be some flex. How much is controlled by the space remaining between the back of the step and the tree.

4. Never leave screw-in steps in a tree from one season to the next. Adverse temperature changes through the course of a year can weaken the steps. Also, the wood around the threads can deteriorate to the point where any sudden weight on the steps could cause it to pull away from the tree.

5. When using screw-in steps, it's better to use more than enough. It's easier to reach steps at two-foot intervals than at four-foot intervals, especially when climbing into a stand in the pre-dawn darkness.

6. Take your time when climbing into a stand. Take extra precautions when the steps or rungs of a ladder are icy, or when the soles of your boots are covered with frost or mud.

7. When relying on limbs to climb into a stand, make sure they are large enough to support your weight. NEVER trust a dead limb. And NEVER hang a stand in a dead tree.

8. When choosing a tree for your stand, make sure it is large enough in diameter to prevent shaking every time you move.

9. Use good judgment during periods of high winds. If your stand is set in a large old oak that's still rock solid, that's one thing. But if the tree is really rocking, stay out of it.

When positioning a stand in a tree, it should be placed where existing limbs and branches help to break the hunter's outline. But be sure to trim anything that might prevent a clear shot.

Different hunters have different ideas of just what is the "ideal" height for a treestand. I've hunted out of pre-hung stands as low as 10 feet and as high as 35 feet. Most stands used for bowhunting are generally placed under 20 feet. A stand any higher can result in a more radical shot angle, making the "kill zone" smaller (see the section on bowhunting in Chapter 3). On the other hand, a centerfire rifle hunter seeking to cover as much territory as possible with a flat-shooting scoped rifle may prefer his stand as high as possible. Bowhunter John Sloan rarely hunts above 15 feet. Not that he's afraid of heights; he simply finds that going higher is usually more of a handicap than a benefit. As a rule, he lets the surrounding cover dictate how high to place a stand. The hunter who places his stand well above existing cover may be costing himself a deer by making it more difficult to see an approaching whitetail—especially when shooting an arrow back through the lower canopy.

Richard Smith claims that the average line of sight for a whitetail is less than six feet. Of course, this figure increases the farther apart the hunter is from the deer. While a hunter standing

A body harness-type safety strap ensures that the bowhunter won't slip and fall from his lofty perch.

10. *Always use a pull-up rope to haul your gun or bow to the stand.*

11. *Check permanent stands each year to ensure that all boards and nails are safe and solid.*

12. *When hunting alone, be sure to let someone know where you'll be hunting and approximately what time you expect to leave the woods.*

13. *Never sleep in your stand. At the first signs of drowsiness, climb down and hunt from the ground—or head back to camp and catch up on your rest there.*

COMPLETE BOOK OF WHITETAIL HUNTING

10 feet up a tree may get by with almost imperceptible movements when a whitetail is less than 20 yards away, it's a good bet that the sharp eyes of a veteran buck will quickly pick up the same movement when he is standing 50 yards away. Even so, Smith feels that hunters who are 15 feet or more off the ground, and who keep their movements to a bare minimum, will seldom be detected. This is especially true for hunters who have enough savvy to position their stands where the tree trunk and other nearby limbs serve as additional camouflage.

Hunters should always take care not to be silhouetted against an open sky or an expanse of some kind. Without some cover to blend into, every little movement becomes exaggerated. This can present a problem when hunting the edges of a field, for example. In such situations, the hunter will usually discover that he is less likely to be detected if the stand is positioned back from the edge at least five or ten yards. One thing is for certain: whitetails lift their heads up more today than they did 30 or 40 years ago. The reason, put simply, is that we've educated them to look up. The portable tree stand industry didn't get much of a start until the early 1970s, and even then only a few manufacturers catered to the growing number of deer hunters in the country. During the 1960s and early 70s, the deer herds were just beginning to grow

along with the hunting opportunities. During the mid-1960s, Illinois and a few other states issued fewer than 10,000 archery tags per years. Today, the state sells close to 200,000 archery deer tags. That means there are a lot more bowhunters sitting in trees, taking shots and missing. It doesn't take a whitetail long to realize that the Devil himself lives in the trees. Even if a deer is only spooked by the sudden movement of a human sitting in a tree stand, or it picks up human scent as it passes downwind

This hunter may have a solid stand in a great location, but he should be wearing a safety belt or harness.

of a stand, the deer learns to look up occasionally. Several hunters have shared with me their accounts of hunts in which the old does walked around looking up into the trees instead of watching where they were headed.

Jim Shockey, Canadian outfitter and outdoor writer, rarely experiences such problems when hunting from a tree stand, primarily because he hardly ever hunts from an elevated platform. He does most of his hunting from the ground and actually finds most any type of stand-hunting just plain boring! As he states, "I have to say that no one doubts the effectiveness of stand-hunting. Many times it's the only way to take a certain buck, or to hunt a certain area.

Sometimes the weather is the determining factor. If it's wrong for still hunting, even the most stealthful hunter would be wise to turn monkey!"

Shockey's favored method of taking big Saskatchewan bucks is to still-hunt as soon as there's snow on the ground. He enjoys finding the tracks of a good buck, getting on them and sticking with the trail until a buck is standing in front of him, or he has accidentally pushed the deer out of its cover. Jim knows that once he still hunts into the heart of a big buck's domain, it's a sure bet the buck will know about it. He feels the hunter will either kill the buck or it will escape. In the latter case, it's a sure thing that a record-book class buck won't be hanging out in the same cover the next day—or the next week. Jim's the first to admit that still-hunting can ruin a stand hunting location, and with that in mind he never still hunts in areas where he intends to stand-hunt. On those occasions when the promise of taking a nice buck means stand-hunting, he usually avoids taking to the woods with a tree stand strapped to his back. Instead, he prefers natural ground blinds or stands—places to which deer have already become accustomed. Since Jim is not a bowhunter, he has enjoyed his greatest success when he locates his stand as far from a deer's expected travel route as possible, yet still be within the effective 150-yard

range of his modern, scope-sighted in-line percussion muzzleloading rifle. Staying far to one side of a whitetail's normal travel route greatly reduces Jim's chances of being detected by the deer, and it allows him to slip back into the stand more often without being patterned by whitetails.

Jim does a lot of rattling while on stand. He likes it when he can observe a lot of ground simply by turning his head. Among his favorite setups is one where he locates several big hay bales close to well-used whitetail cover. Even though the bales may sit in an open hay field, Shockey feels they provide more than adequate cover, especially when he has a reasonably good idea from

Often a few upper branches need to be trimmed so hunters can have an open shot.

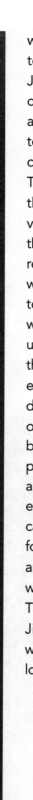

which direction a buck is most likely to approach his stand. The one factor Jim always pays heed to is the direction of the wind, so he invariably selects a stand site that's downwind. He likes to wait until the final weeks of Saskatchewan's long whitetail season to hunt. That's when snow is nearly always on the ground, making the deer more visible. Also, most other hunters by then have left the field, so he has the remaining big bucks all to himself. But waiting until the tail end of November to hunt also means facing some of the worst weather of the season. It's not uncommon for Jim to head out when the temperature is -25 degrees or colder and the wind chill factor drops to -50 degrees or -60 degrees. When headed out to a stand during weather this brutal, Shockey often shoulders a back pack that weighs as much as 60 pounds and contains plenty of extra cold-weather clothing and footwear, rattling horns, calls, enough food to last the day, optics for studying deer at long distances, and anything else that will enable him to stick with his stand from daybreak to dark. That kind of persistence has rewarded Jim Shockey with more record-book whitetail bucks than any other muzzle-loading hunter in the world.

Stand hunters—especially bowhunters—who are consistently successful know at the beginning of each season that they will probably spend a lot of time in their stands before they ever get that golden opportunity. For several seasons I bowhunted three or four mornings or evenings each week for the entire season without ever unleashing an arrow. Still, I've learned to enjoy every minute I spend in the stand, observing everything that goes on around me, watching does and bucks as they go about their daily lives without a clue that I'm watching them from a treestand only 10 or 20 yards away. Indeed, some of my most rewarding seasons were those during which I failed to take a buck with my bow. By the same token, some of my least rewarding seasons where those when I filled my tag too early to enjoy being in the woods and in the stand. For me, there has never been a bad season, for each time I come away a richer man because I know more about the whitetail simply by being in its presence.

As David Hale once told me, "Logging long hours in the stand is the main ingredient to taking a really good buck." No one has ever made a more truthful statement about hunting whitetails. ■

Still Hunting: How To Stalk Like A Pro

WITH ■ *Kurt von Besser, President, Atsko/Sno-Seal, Inc.* ■ *Jim Shockey, Canadian Outfitter & Writer* ■ *Bill Vaznis, Expert Bowhunter & Writer*

Snow had fallen through the night and into the morning, covering the ground with a solid coat of the fluffy white stuff. Outdoor writer Bill Vaznis sat in his truck debating on whether or not to head out. Poor visibility caused by strong winds that swirled the steady flow of snow, combined with a weather forecast calling for still more by nightfall, made it doubtful that any deer would be spotted that day. On the other hand, the regular bow season was about to end and the rut was in full swing. With that in mind, Bill grabbed his bow and headed for the woods. He comes from the old school that says you hunt whenever you get the chance.

Luck was with him. He hadn't gone 200 yards when he cut a fresh deer track in the snow. The track was big and headed for a well-known bedding area. Bill rationalized that only a buck would be on the move in such weather, prowling for an estrous doe. And so he followed, slowly, keeping an ever watchful eye ahead and on each side of the track as he eased along quietly through the white ground cover. Soon he came to a place where the buck had apparently rousted a group of does and fawns from their beds. The doe must have been bred already, because the buck track continued on—and so did the hunter. The whitetail's stiff-legged gait gradually became clearer, and Bill knew he was getting closer.

Suddenly, there stood the buck, lowering its head to munch on a patch of snow-laden golden rod.

As the deer's head disappeared into the weedy growth once again, Bill dropped to one knee and brought his compound bow to full draw. He held on the 20-yard target and then released. At the sound of the bow launching the arrow, the deer jerked its head upright. But it was too late. The razor-tipped aluminum shaft was already on its way, striking the deer exactly where the hunter had aimed. As the deer charged off through the underbrush, the tip of the aluminum arrow caught the tiny trunks of saplings, making a "tic .. tic .. tic" rhythm. Bill stood listening until the sound was muffled by falling snow. He walked over to where the deer had been standing and found blood everywhere. Knowing the deer had been hit good, and with the snow still coming down heavily, Bill decided to follow the trail immediately, before it was lost. He didn't have to go far. The eight-pointer had gone only 100 yards before piling up. What a great way to end the bow season!

Bill Vaznis is one of the most persistent and successful still hunters I know. Through the years, he has taken good bucks all over the country with bow, modern gun and muzzleloader—most of them from the ground. Actually, it's almost impossible to get Bill to spend any time at all in a tree stand. When he's not slipping quietly through the woods, you might find him taking a stand atop an old bulldoze pile, along a steep creek bank, or a high ridge point overlooking a good travel route. Jim Shockey, a highly respected Canadian outfitter and outdoor writer, is another very successful big buck hunter who prefers still-hunting or stalking over stand-hunting. There are times, though, when he is forced to throw in the towel and use a stand—but only when conditions or situations dictate his best chances

COMPLETE BOOK OF WHITETAIL HUNTING

of success are from an elevated stand. Otherwise, he almost always chooses still-hunting. In fact, some of his most prized whitetails have been taken while on foot. "If you are in good deer country," he claims, "you can wait in one spot and eventually a deer will walk by. It's guaranteed. You don't even have to be at a major deer crossing if you're prepared to wait in your stand long enough!"

Jim lives on Vancouver Island, British Columbia, and hunts whitetails in Saskatchewan. The more than a thousand miles separating his home from his favorite deer hunting spots is the main reason why he doesn't do any pre-season scouting. Instead, he prefers to still hunt, reading the sign as he goes. More often than not, he bases the entire hunting season on what he sees in the first couple of days. He likes to wait until the last two weeks of the Saskatchewan season, when snow is still likely to cover the ground. He loves to follow a big track through the snow and also because he can better see their dark brown forms against the white backdrop.

Jim's favorite times to still hunt for whitetails are when it's windy, raining or snowing lightly. Whitetails then are much more vulnerable. Their senses of sight, hearing and smell are diminished, giving stealthy hunters an edge. Still, hunters are warned to make every move with care. "To effectively still hunt," Jim points out, "a hunter must move without appearing to move, and the only way to do this is to move slowly. Even when the trees are swaying in the wind, or it's raining, going slow is the key— and that applies to every movement, not just a hunter's gait. Many hunters may move their legs slowly, but they also flip their heads this way and that looking for deer. A deer will pick up this

A successful still hunter must have enough stealth to slip within bow range of a wary whitetail. He therefore relies on the right kind of "quiet" clothing.

An experi-
enced still
hunter relies
on a good pair
of binoculars
to cover the
terrain instead
of his legs.

motion, and it won't wait around to find out what's making the motion."

Jim also recognizes that too often hunters grab for their binoculars and ram them up to their eyes the instant they spot a movement in the bush. This is definitely a no-no for ground level hunters trying to ease close enough to shoot a whitetail. If a hunter moves slowly and quietly enough to slip up on a deer to the point where he can sense its movement, then he's done every-thing right. The deer shouldn't even know he's there. So, what's the hurry? Instead of yanking the glasses to his eyes, the successful still hunter should slowly bring the binoculars up, maybe stopping several times in the process. If a hunter must hurry to lift his binoculars, it's a good bet the deer has already

been spooked. When that happens, there really is no hurry—that deer is already out of there!

"It would be difficult for me to trans-late how slowly a hunter should move into miles per hour," Jim Shockey comments. "Every situation calls for different reactions. If I sense there's a buck close by—meaning within several hundred yards—I might take only two very slow steps each minute or so, then stand still for a moment. In a full day I might travel a distance of only a few hundred yards. If I do it right, and the wind favors me, that should be enough. It means that I've penetrated directly to the point where the buck has led me. If he was there, I should have a crack at him. If not, it's no big deal. At least I know that I didn't bust in and spook him out. Besides, I may get another chance at him another day."

Hunters who are consistently successful, such as Bill Vaznis and Jim Shockey, realize that the rewards of a long, slow day in the deer woods can hinge on a hunter's clothing. Still hunters should avoid hard-shelled, tightly woven materials that make noisy scratching sounds whenever a twig or branch rubs against it. Some outdoor clothing is so noisy it makes a swishing sound as the hunter walks. Anyone dressed like that is unlikely to get close to a wary whitetail. Jim Shockey prefers outer clothing made of ultra-modern fleece-type materials or the old favorite: Wool. When snaking through tight quarters with saplings, branches and other brush, these materials allow a hunter to make light contact without those telltale scratching sounds that can alert the sensitive ears of a whitetail.

Bill Vaznis occasionally hunts during the firearms and muzzleloader seasons, but more than likely this multi-state hunter will be found in the deer woods with a bow in his hand. During the early part of the season, when there is still some foliage on the trees, most of the shots he takes are generally under 25 yards, but when the woods turn barren his average shot is closer to 40 yards. He believes in good camo, too, taking time each morning to paint his face and hands with camouflage. Bill owns

John Sloan mixes some ground level stand hunting with still hunting when easing through a promising area.

clothing in a variety of camo patterns and likes the new designs from Realtree and Mossy Oak, both of which incorporate bold limbs and leaves. He always wears a pattern appropriate for the time of the season, often shifting from brown-colored camo to one that includes several gray colorations as the deer season stretches into winter. That's when the snow camouflages take over. Often Vaznis will wear snow camo pants to match the ground cover and a gray pattern camo top to match the tree trunks. The more a hunter blends with the surroundings, he feels, the better his chances of getting close enough for a shot.

I recall one season in particular. I was hunting in northern Missouri and couldn't buy a buck. During the bow season, I had arrowed a big doe for the freezer on the first day of the season, and I saw plenty of antlerless deer and small bucks through five more weeks of bowhunting, but not one good buck ever showed. I then hunted the entire nine-day modern gun season without seeing anything worth shooting. As my nine-day muzzleloading season in December approached the downhill side, I still hadn't seen a shooter buck. Up to that point, I had toughed it out, hunting from treestands. With only three days left to hunt, I decided that if the bucks weren't going to come to me, I'd have to go to them. It was time to abandon the tree stands and hit the woods on foot.

Just before the opening of the muzzleloader season in early December,

the area had been blanketed by four or five inches of snow. During most of the hunt the temperature had risen to the upper 40s in the afternoon, and on the seventh morning of the season, as I headed into the dim light of dawn, the thermometer was in the mid-30s. Conditions were ideal for a day in the woods, so I planned my moves from one known deer hangout to another. Instead of the snail's pace preferred by Jim Shockey, I put plenty of ground behind me for the first quarter of a mile. Then, as I approached a grassy clearing I knew was a bedding area, I slowed to almost a crawl. It took an hour to cover the next 100 yards.

Using my Nikon 10x25 binoculars, I scrutinized the cover below, spotting several does as they moved into a deep draw and bedded down. Nothing with horns moved below, however, and as soon as I passed through the prime cover, I hotfooted it to another and slowly worked through it. Again, I saw not one buck. By mid-afternoon I had eased through a half-dozen promising pieces of deer cover. I had seen plenty of does and a few small bucks, but none that I wanted to shoot.

A bad weather front was moving in and the overcast skies got darker and darker. Still, the winds were mild and temperatures hovered around 40. The melting snow had turned the leafy ground cover into a soft, quiet carpet, allowing me to sneak through the woods as quietly as I ever had. Even when I was covering ground quickly to get from one piece of cover to another, rarely did I make a giveaway sound. It was while I was making such a move that I spotted a big deer feeding along the far end of a picked cornfield. Through my binoculars, I quickly determined it was a good ten-pointer. I could also make out a ridge of bulldozed tree trunks and brush less than 100 yards from the deer. A shallow creek skirting the edge of the field along my side would, I knew, provide plenty of cover as I moved some 400 yards to the other end. The wind was in my favor as I eased into the creek, and soon I was looking at the deer from his end of the field. My goal now was to reach the bulldoze pile, which required moving slowly through relatively open timber. I watched the buck's head carefully. When it was down and turned in the other direction, I would make my move, slipping from tree to tree. Once I reached a predetermined spot, I would stop until after the deer had lifted its head and returned to feeding. It took 40 minutes to cover less than 100 yards. Finally, after easing my way up the backside of the old bulldoze pile, I lay my scope-sighted .50 caliber in-line rifle across a handy log rest, took aim on the ten-pointer, eased off the safety and squeezed off the shot. The saboted 260 grain .45 caliber jacketed hollow-point flew true for almost 100 yards, catching the buck perfectly behind the shoulder. The big deer never knew what hit him and went down on the spot.

Larry Weishuhn slowly eases his way up a small stream searching the banks for whitetails.

Over the years I've probably taken as many good bucks while moving on the ground as I have sitting in a tree stand. While the tactics I used that morning were similar to those used by Bill Vaznis and Jim Shockey, I actually considered all three techniques as different styles of hunting. Vaznis clearly relied on tracking to put his buck on the ground, whereas the tactics I used to take my muzzle-

When slipping through heavy cover, a hunter should always be prepared for a quick shot at a fleeing whitetail.

TRACKING

As Bill Vaznis once explained to me, "Sexing a set of deer tracks is more an art form than a science. While it can occasionally be done by looking at a single track, it is the overall pattern in the snow, mud or soft earth that usually tells me whether the track (or tracks) were made by a buck or doe." He went on to say that does are more apt to avoid the issue than a buck, especially a big, dominant one. When a hunter sees narrowly spaced tracks meandering around through the cover, it's often some does and fawns nipping a bud here and there as they feed on the move. On the other hand, a buck's stride is longer, wider and seemingly more purposeful. During the rut, the buck tends to have one thing in mind: Go directly from one area frequented by does to another until he finds one in heat. He's often so caught up in the process that he won't even stop to urinate, allowing his urine to dribble while on the move.

Bill Vaznis also points out that a mature buck's track is much larger than that of even a big doe. Hunters primarily look for 1 1/2- to 2 1/2-year old bucks, and the tracks of a young buck may well be the same size as a track left by a 4

loader buck were more appropriately "spot and stalk." And the techniques described by Jim Shockey in hunting his Canadian monsters were clearly "still hunting" in its purest art form. The one thing we all have in common is that we stayed on the ground and kept moving. In essence, this type of hunting is a combination of all three techniques: tracking, stalking and still hunting. To be truly proficient at hunting on the ground and on the move, the whitetail hunter must learn to practice the following:

1/2- to 6 1/2-year old doe. Size is not always the determining factor. A buck has a tendency to drag his feet, though, probably because he's lost stamina during the rut. With three or four inches of snow on the ground, drag marks left by a buck become quite evident. But once the snow reaches six or so inches, nearly all deer will leave drag marks. In deep snow, Bill advises hunters to look for an indication of a buck's size by its rack. When looking for estrous does, bucks regularly sniff the tracks they come across. When they do, the tips of the main beams often make an imprint in the snow, providing attentive hunters with some idea of a buck's tip to tip spread. Unless pressured, bucks with wide racks will commonly skirt around stands of heavy brush, while does may often walk right through the thickest growth.

When Jim Shockey follows a big buck's tracks into thick cover, he knows he won't get through the tangle without making some noise, so he usually touches his rattling horns together lightly, enough to simulate two bucks sparring. Then, as he proceeds through the heavy cover, he will occasionally take the horns and rake the limbs. Once on the other side he'll put the rattling horns away and stand still for a while before continuing his quiet pursuit. When following a track in the snow, Jim doesn't always follow directly. He knows that a wise old buck, especially one that may have had close encounters with hunters, will occasionally stop to check its back trail. To counteract this, Jim walks on one side or another of the track while still keeping it in sight. It's a tactic that has rewarded this buck-wise hunter with several nice record book bucks.

STALKING

Out West, where the whitetail cover is often restricted to small strips of heavy cover along creeks and streams, "stalking" is a commonly used tactic enabling hunters to get within shooting range of whitetails. Many hunters simply drive to a high point in their pickups and glass until they see a good buck feeding in a hay field or moving from one stand of cover to another. Then they seek cover, enough to start moving in on the deer, or at least to move where a buck on the move might be intercepted.

Stalking can be an important part of a successful tracking job or a long day of still-hunting. Once the deer has been spotted, the hunter must then move closer for the shot, sometimes at high risk of being spotted by a deer. A tired hunter may also take unnecessary chances in his attempts to get close enough for a quick shot. Once the deer is in sight, though, the hunter has an advantage. He can, for instance, see which direction the deer is looking. If it's looking in the hunter's direction, the things to do is *FREEZE*. Don't move a muscle, even if you're standing out in sparse cover. Often deer can't distinguish a human form if it's not moving. Stand perfectly still. Then, after the deer has scrutinized the hunter for what may seem an eternity, the deer will usually return to feeding, scraping, walking, or what have you. But if you're standing out in a wide open field and the deer spots you, the hunt can be considered over, at least for the moment.

The clue is: Be sure to use all available cover for concealment, even more so once you sense the deer can no longer see you and continues to move along at a very slow pace. Just because the deer isn't visible doesn't mean it can't see your legs or feet, which are obviously at different levels than your eyes. A deer may not immediately recognize a flicker of movement in the brush as that of a hunter, but a wary old buck won't stick around to see what materializes.

STILL HUNTING

Other than moving along at a snail's pace, wearing "quiet" clothing, blending into the environment, and watching the woods ahead and to each side as you ease through the deer woods, the still hunter has only one other concern: *The wind*. More hunters are detected by a whitetail's sensitive nose than by its keen eyesight. Like most ardent still hunters, Jim Shockey always hunts into the winds, or at least into a crosswind. He'll often slip through good cover at an angle, then cut back in the opposite direction at a reverse angle, the same as tacking a sailing ship in order to keep the wind at his advantage. It's inevitable, however, that in some situations it's necessary for him to proceed with the wind at his back. Rather than worrying about it, though, Jim knows that he still has a good chance of spotting a buck off to one side or another of the course taken. He can even recall

When buck activity is at its peak during the final weeks of the pre-rut, a still hunter who throws in a little calling can often force some action.

times when a deer, having winded him, will move back in his direction, now and then offering a rare shot opportunity.

"I try not to worry about the wind too much," he explains. "In fact, the wind can be a still hunter's best friend, especially when it's fairly strong. A stiff breeze all but neutralizes one of a deer's most important senses: His *hearing*. When the wind is blowing, a hunter's footsteps are camouflaged by the sounds of the trees rocking back and forth, of brush rattling and leaves rustling. A good 10 or 20 m.p.h. breeze breaks up the molecular concentration of a human scent, making it difficult for a deer to know exactly where the odor is coming from. Shifting and swirling winds can carry a man's scent in different directions, too, and a deer who has picked up a hunter's scent somewhere off to the right might well run back to the left—right where you're standing!"

Kurt von Besser (president of Atsko/Sno-Seal Inc.) believes that many hunters begin their hunt with one strike already against them: the camouflage clothes they're wearing. Kurt claims that the manufacturers apply special brighteners on their materials before the camo patterns are printed on the cloth. To compound the problem, the dyes themselves contain brighteners, as do most of the water repellent treatments used on their outdoor clothing. Their goal is to produce a better-looking, more salable product. Washing will reduce or even eliminate some or all of the

brighteners, but nearly all regular laundry detergents—whether scented or non-scented—contain special ultraviolet brighteners for a cleaner, brighter wash. This may be what a hunter wants to wear at home, work or play—but it's the last thing you should wear when hunting whitetails.

Some whitetail biologists claim that a whitetail's eyes are as much as one hundred times more sensitive to ultraviolet light or light reflection than those of a human. Contrary to what many believe, whitetails are not exactly "color blind." Their eyes, however, have many more "rods" as they do "cones." The latter are largely responsible for color recep-

Kurt von Besser

Jim Shockey's slow-moving still hunting tactics are often just another day in the woods, but sometimes they result in an outstanding trophy buck.

that has been improperly washed, may shine like a new dime to a deer. This is especially bad news for ground level hunters who need to blend in with their surroundings as much as possible.

Kurt von Besser's company was among the first to offer products that eliminated the ultraviolet glow caused by brighteners used in the making of a hunter's camouflaged clothing. His "U-V-Killer" is a specially formulated spray that kills the ultraviolet reflection of new materials and dyes. Atsko's "Sport-Wash" is a laundry detergent designed to keep camouflaged clothing free of ultraviolet. To be truly effective, new camouflage clothing should be thoroughly sprayed with U-V-Killer, then washed with Sport-Wash.

tion and interpretation, while the rods are the black-and-white receptors which gather light, including ultraviolet wavelengths. Whitetails are thus creatures of low light conditions, moving mostly in late evening, at night, or in the dim light of daybreak. As creatures of their environment, survival depends on good eyesight at the same time when a human can hardly see his hand in front of his face. Since deer can easily pick up on the ultraviolet portion of the light spectrum, that means hunters who wear newly camouflaged clothing, or clothing

There are those who scoff at the idea of a whitetail being able to pick up on the ultraviolet light spectrum, much less the thought that, in the deer's eyes, a camo-clad hunter glows in the dark! For years, I was one of them. But when I began studying the eyesight of a deer and began paying more attention to how I laundered my clothing, I started using products like those listed above and elsewhere. As a result, I have witnessed a noticeable decline in how many times deer have spotted me for no apparent reason. ∎

Deer Drives That Work

WITH ■ *David Hale, Co-Founder, Knight & Hale Game Calls* ■ *Marvin Briegel, Nebraska's Drive King*

Chapter Seven

As far as Iowa deer drives go, ours wasn't much. I had dropped off four hunters along the abandoned bed of a long-forgotten railroad track. The hunters were spaced out several hundred yards apart, thereby covering the major points and draws that dropped down from about 40 acres of timber. I guessed that these natural landforms would funnel any deer pushed from the wooded lot down to where my hunters were positioned.

It was the fourth afternoon of a five-day hunt in early December and the deer had simply failed to move. I was guiding a group of five hunters from Georgia who had yet to take a deer. All could have dropped does, but they had made the long trip to the Midwest for a shot at one of the big racked whitetails for which this area is famous. One of the hunters had tried a long shot on a nice eight-pointer with a shotgun and slug, but he failed to connect. After that, he borrowed one of my scoped in-line ignition muzzleloaders. When I mentioned that we ought to undertake a drive, four of the five hunters jumped at the suggestion. The lone abstainer felt that he was getting close to a good buck and decided to return to his stand.

Once the hunters were in place, my two companions and I drove around to the other side of the timber. With the wind now at our backs, we decided to use it to our advantage. Instead of simply busting through the wooded area and pushing the whitetails out physically, we elected to zig-zag back and forth as we worked back toward the four hunters. That way, the wind would blow our scent to any deer bedded down among one of many small draws or on an isolated knoll. Our gentle push was barely half through when shots rang out on the other side of the ridgetop. Two separate two-shot volleys were fired with shotguns followed by a single crack, which I recognized as my muzzleloader. Just as I topped the rise, three more shots roared on my right. A minute later, a huge buck nearly ran me over as it doubled back into the cover we had just pushed. Had I been packing a gun, I could have tagged one of the best-looking whitetails I'd ever seen in the woods.

Marvin Briegel

From the time I posted the standers until the sound of the last shot, this entire drive took less than 30 minutes. As I eased down to the old railroad bed with the other two drivers, I saw that three of the four hunters had taken nice bucks, and the fourth had missed the monster who had cut back past me. In extremely short order, we had turned an unproductive hunt into a successful one simply by putting some pressure on deer that had stopped moving on their own—at least, not during daylight hours. Before the hunt wound down the following evening, we managed to get one of the other hunters a beautiful ten-pointer using similar tactics.

I had learned to use the wind to my advantage from Marv Briegel, an old friend who farms some of the finest Nebraska whitetail cover I've ever run across. When it comes to conducting deer drives on the 1,500 or so acres he owns along the Republican River in southern Nebraska, Marv was something of a wizard. I've never hunted with anyone who knows more about how deer respond to pressure than this gentleman farmer. The very first time I stepped foot on Marv's place was a day I'll never forget. It was in early December on the third day of the

Nebraska muzzleloader season, and the weather was much warmer than usual. In fact, afternoon highs were reaching 70 degrees, and the deer were moving mostly at night, offering only brief opportunities during the first light of morning and the last light of evening. For the first couple of days, I had hunted another large farm several miles from Briegel's place. I had spotted several good bucks then, but they were far out of muzzleloader range. On that third day of the hunt, a friend introduced me to Marv Briegel, who immediately took me for a ride in the back of his pickup through hundreds of acres of brush that rimmed the edges of the fields he farmed. During the drive, I was amazed at the number of deer we saw. In less than ten minutes, I had spotted no less than 30 whitetails as they scurried along through the brush.

As we eased down a road along the river, Marv nosed the front of his truck into a brush-hogged cut that paralleled one of his cross fences. He told me to take my muzzleloader and walk about halfway toward the edge of a field that sat 100 yards away. I immediately took a stand next to a big old cottonwood tree while Marv and a friend continued on down the field road, out of sight and hearing. I stood there in the quiet for only a few minutes before spotting a flicker of movement, followed by another, and then another. In an instant, the woods were alive with deer. Whitetails ran up to the fence and leaped over the top strand of barbed wire, one after another, all along its length. Suddenly,

I spotted a flash of antlers. The safety went off and I stood ready for the shot as a handsome 140 class ten-pointer stepped into the open. I had just brought the rifle up when several more bucks appeared along the far end of the fence line, barely 60 yards away. I quickly shifted my rifle in the direction of a real bruiser, but at that moment a large doe walked up and blocked the deer. The huge buck disappeared in a couple of bounds, but by the time I shifted back to the first buck, he too was gone. I stood there in amazement as several dozen more deer emerged from the thick river bottom brush, but not one good buck. About five minutes later, my friend and the landowner came walking out of the brush, about a hundred yards apart. They must have seen the look of astonishment on my face, because both men roared with laughter when they spotted me. I had just witnessed the most successful deer drive I had ever seen up to that time. In less than 15 minutes, those two men had pushed between 60 and 70 whitetails past my stand, all within 60 yards of where I stood. Although I failed to get a shot at either one of the bucks I had spotted, it was an experience I'll always cherish.

Several days later, the two drivers took me on another short drive less than half a mile away. I did manage then to take a good ten-pointer at about 100 yards with my modern in-line percussion rifle. What both of these

Nebraska's Marvin Briegel (right) organized a one-man drive to put this late-season ten-pointer in the author's sights at only 40 yards.

drives had in common was someone in charge who knew the lay of the land, and where deer would most likely exit their cover once a little pressure was placed on the other end. Instead of relying on a lot of whooping and hollering, both drives had elected to push the drivers' scent at the deer and the waiting hunter.

During the brief three- and four-day shotgun and muzzleloader seasons in my home state of Illinois, drives are very popular. Here, as in many states, more than 50% of all harvested whitetails are taken on opening day of the season. Many hunters now know that staying on stand can be an important key in hanging their tag on a deer. When the whitetails suddenly feel the pressure of so many hunters in the woods, they often keep on the move all day long, which makes a hunter's chances of getting a shot equally as good at noon as at 8 a.m. or 4 p.m. Come late evening, however, the deer seem to find holes into which they disappear. After an opening-day flurry of activity, hunters who seek deer are often forced to get out and push whitetails from their pockets of heavy cover.

The preferred method of taking deer in Iowa tends to be large-scale drives. I witnessed one such during the mid-1990s involving 50 or so hunters. I was living in northern Missouri then and working in nearby Centerville, Iowa. Driving to my office one morning, I had crossed the state line only a few miles

when I came upon a drive still in the planning stage alongside the road. At least 20 or 25 pickups and rundown automobiles lined the side of the road. As I eased past, I recognized a few of the hunters and pulled over to ask if I could observe the outcome of the drive. Across the hood of the "command vehicle" I noted several large aerial photos of the area. Two hunters were in charge of the drive, one to lead the drivers and the other to ensure that the standers were stationed where they should be. After 15 minutes of discussion, it was decided that most of the standers would be placed along the far edge of a deer cover, about 1.5 miles away. Several others were positioned strategically along the side of

the area where the deer were most likely to exit when pushed from cover. About half of the hunters followed in their vehicles as one of the leaders led the way. The remaining hunters were then called together by the driver commander, who began assigning starting points for the long drive. Twenty minutes later, all the men were in position. At the blast of a small horn, the long line of drivers stepped off the country road and drove into a mixture of timber, fields, pasture and brush. For the next 15 minutes, shots rang out sporadically from both sides of the drive as both standers and drivers took occasional shots at deer moving back and forth between the two lines of hunters. As I drove around one side of the area on a

Hunters look over a topographical map in preparation for a drive. Lots of planning goes into a successful deer drive.

Mature older bucks, like this Illinois monster (taken by the author during a drive), will often break away from the does and take a completely different course from other deer who've been pushed from heavy cover.

gravel road bordering the drive, I came upon one of the standers who'd been posted alongside the cover. He was dragging out a nice ten-pointer.

From a high point I could now see out across a fairly open pasture where most of the drivers, with their fluorescent orange vests, jackets and hats highlighted the barren December landscape. I was quite impressed that, with more than half the distance covered, these hunters had stayed in line. Shots continued to ring out as I drove around to a back road bordering the far side of the hunt area. There I came upon the vehicles driven by the standers. I sat there for a good 20 minutes before the first driver stepped out onto the road.

Amazingly, nearly all the hunters emerged from the cover in a span of only five minutes, which I found remarkable for a drive of this magnitude. In all, some 18 whitetails were harvested during a drive that took considerably more time to plan and coordinate than it did to orchestrate the drive itself.

Unless such large drives are well-planned and coordinated, they often result in disaster and a waste of time. But this drive—and the two smaller ones already discussed—proved to be productive methods for harvesting whitetails. When drives become as large as the 50-man operation I observed in Iowa a few seasons back, pressure on the whitetails makes it almost impossible to hunt deer from a stand or by still hunting in that location for days or even weeks afterwards, especially if you are hoping to hang your tag on a good buck. In Iowa, stand hunting and still hunting continue to take a back seat to drives. When pushing cover two or three times a day throughout the season, organized drives usually return to the same stands of cover every two or three days, pushing out still more deer. This is especially true where other groups are driving nearby stands of cover as well. Party hunting is allowed in Iowa, which means all hunters can keep hunting until all tags are filled.

Personally, I prefer much smaller drives. Instead of tackling 1,000 or 1,500 acres with large numbers of drivers and standers, I enjoy higher success rates when pushing out 40 acres or less at a time, relying on four or five standers and the same number of drivers. Short drives are much easier to coordinate and to make certain the standers are where they should be. It's a lot easier to keep four or five drivers in line for a 15-minute push than a drive that takes two or three times as long. "The way to keep from pushing deer off your property" Marv Briegel advises, "is to keep drives small. Don't try to push the entire area. I always try to keep pushing my drives in from the property boundaries toward the center of the property, but stopping before I reach that point."

Marv is truly a master of this tactic. During a four- or five-day hunt he will lead at least one or often two drives a day on his 1,500 acre tract. Rarely will any of his drives push more than 100 acres of the flat river bottom cover. And hardly ever do his drives take more than 30 minutes, some of which may be spent pulling out a downed buck. Should a drive fail to produce a good buck, his hunters take stands along the opposite corner of the property in preparation for the afternoon hunt. Generally, several deer—those that were pushed into that area by one of Marv's short drives—become quite visible as they head back to the cover from which they were rousted earlier.

Located nearly in the center of this farm is a 50- or 60-acre tract of nearly impenetrable brush, which the landowner jokingly refers to as "The Jungle." This refuge of sorts is rarely driven; and if it is, it's usually on the last day of the hunt. That's where most of the deer head when pushed from the farm's outer fringes. During a drive there several years ago with outdoor writers Monte Burch and Wade Bourne, I noticed that quite a few deer had cut across a 100-acre cornfield to reach "The Jungle," rather than stick with the brush that bordered the edge of the field. The next day, I positioned myself along the fence at the edge of "The Jungle" opposite the area driven by Marv and another hunter. Close to 100 deer came across that field, most jumping the fence just 30 yards away, including several 130 class eight- and ten-pointers. Because I was intent on tagging at least a 140 buck, I never took a shot. But several of the deer had spotted me and snorted loudly as they shifted into high gear and headed for the safety of the thick brush. Their response spooked a few deer standing far out into the field, including a nice ten-pointer. That afternoon, Marv and I erected a tripod stand (made by Warren & Sweat) next to a cottonwood tree, and two days later we tried the same drive. This time I dropped that nice buck at less than 40 yards with a single shot from my .50 caliber muzzleloader.

For those who are blessed with thousands of acres in which to hunt, large scale drives with large numbers of hunters are a good way to get plenty of shots at whitetails. But if you're limited to hunting a few hundred acres of prime habitat, go softly. Take it easy and push

Small drives
that concentrate
on woodlots,
drainages,
brush patches
or other small
parcels of cover
are often the
most successful
because they
are the easiest
to control.

on a dozen or so drivers to get the deer stirring, this highly successful whitetail hunter prefers hunting with just one or two others, encouraging them to disturb the hunt area gently with their presence. "In most cases," Hale declares, "the hunter's scent will drive the animals from their beds in a state of alarm—but not panic. The deer are then able to travel in their natural gate—trotting or walking, but not running." David refers to this kind of drive as the "soft method" drive. His drive also differs from other approaches in that he often posts the stander. Instead of taking a stand out ahead of the drivers, the designated shooter is often positioned toward the rear or far side where the walking hunter(s) will be still hunting slowly through the drive area.

only small thickets, brushy draws or other similar cover. In doing so, you won't be running all your deer onto a neighbor's property where other hunters may take that big buck you've been after.

David Hale, (Knight & Hales Game Calls) agrees that a well-organized drive is one of the most productive tactics for taking post-rut bucks. But David's approach to driving whitetails is a little different from others. Instead of relying

His reason for positioning the shooter this way, instead of ahead of the other hunters, is due to the well-known trait of big bucks who like to circle back around a hunter, usually through a pocket of cover. Does, fawns and even younger bucks will often run ahead of the other deer on the move. A mature buck usually won't go with the crowds, though, but will often try to sneak downwind in an effort to get behind the drivers. A hunter who covers a suspected escape route may thus get a crack at a big buck no one has seen.

David Hale recalls one particular hunt that persuaded him where and how to position his standers. One day, when a friend grew tired and decided to stay behind instead of joining a drive, Hale learned a valuable lesson. He and several other buddies had jut started a push through some good deer cover when two shots rang out back where they had left their buddy. Thinking something may have happened to his friend, David returned to the stand. As he approached, his friend yelled at Hale to take a look at the huge buck he had just shot. Sure enough, there on the ground lay a magnificent ten-point buck that had slipped back around behind the drivers.

With this incident planted solidly in the back of his mind, Hale planned the next drive a few days later, but this time one of the hunters would cover the rear flank. The day of the drive was so cold, however, that the drive was called off. David and several others knew of several areas where he and his fellow hunters could make three or four short drives, rotating the pushing and standing. It was the final day of the season and their last chance to hang a tag on a whitetail buck.

On the first drive, David was the designated shooter. Taking a stand next to a big hickory tree (to break up his outline), he watched as his two companions entered the cover several hundred yards upwind of his position. He listened to the fading sounds of his hunting partners as they walked over the crunchy, leaf-covered ground until he could no longer hear their footsteps. Suddenly, he heard the unmistakable sounds of a deer moving through the same leaf

Big mature bucks don't hesitate to cut across wide-open country when driven from heavy cover. Knowing the terrain and where deer are most apt to cross open fields can give a stander the upper hand.

instantly. "In seconds, I knew the buck was mine," David recalls, "and that my strategy was as sound as the buck's antlers. The pride of holding that magnificent ten-pointer is one of the greatest feelings I have ever experienced."

Hale's "soft method" of driving has since become a basic tactic of this whitetail hunting wizard. He has also discovered that during the post-rut period, such drives can be equally effective when hunting with a bow. The only real difference is that, when bowhunting, he must occasionally take time out to set up a portable tree stand in order to get off the ground. But not always. If there is good ground cover, David will bowhunt right from the ground, waiting for a big buck to slip past hunters as they push through a pocket of heavy cover.

Smart older whitetails will try to move back through a line of drivers. As a result, drivers often get all the action.

cover, and it was coming closer with each step. Hale easily found the buck in the scope of his rifle, but there was too much brush between him and the deer, and no way to slip a bullet through the tangle of limbs and branches. Quickly David reached for his grunt tube and blew several soft "grr-nnnts." At the last note, the buck turned and began trotting toward Hale. As the deer entered a small opening in the heavy cover, Hale fired and the buck hit the ground

Successful deer drives nearly always have certain factors in common. The following list of "must do's" explains what it takes to force a whitetail into gun or bow range.

1 *Knowledge of the Hunt Area.* This is extremely important. If a hunter planning a drive has never set foot on the property, or has never studied the terrain as shown on an aerial map, there is little hope that his standers will be in the right spot, nor will his drivers be able to push through the best cover. There's obviously more to a successful deer drive than lining up a bunch of waiting hunters and having a line of pushers run deer toward them. In theory, that's how it works, but in reality the deer may have other ideas. Standers must be posted where natural land-forms, such as small creeks, draws, wooded points, fencerows and road-ways tend to funnel their movements. Those who make a push must know the topography to prevent following the wrong lay of the land, only to emerge somewhere entirely different than where they should have.

2 *Standers Must Stay Exactly Where They Are Supposed To Be.* There is nothing more frustrating than for several drivers to spot a good buck and work together in pushing it toward where the standers are supposed to be posted, only to find that they've moved 100 yards one way or another in order to get a better view—or a more comfort-able place to sit. A designated stander must stay exactly where he is posted. The drive coordinator knows the area well and he assigned that spot to his stander for a reason: to intercept deer movement. So, stay put!

3 *Drivers Must Work Together and Stay Aligned.* Doing so will push more deer to designated standers than a line of pushers who are poorly organized. Most drives unfortunately almost always include one driver who thinks he's a track star. He's the guy who gets to the other end of the push in half the time everyone else does. Not only does he stand a chance of blundering into a deer that may have been headed for a stander, but his absence on the line can leave a huge hole through which deer can escape. Also, because he is located somewhere between the other drivers and standers, he is likely to be in the middle of the fire zone. No one knows exactly where he is, which could be a dangerous situation. If your group includes one of these track stars, put him somewhere along the outside edges of the drive. That way, even if he gets ahead of the other drivers, he may even do some good. Often a forward driver can prevent deer from breaking outside the area being pushed. When that happens, the wayward driver may even get off a shot.

4 *A Well-Organized Drive Can Have Only One Boss.* A good organizer will listen to what the hunters have to say, especially if they know the area as well or better than he does. But when it comes to making stander and driver assignments—i.e., who will be where, what are the beginning and ending points, etc.—too many chiefs could ruin the drive. A leader for both standers and drivers in a large-scale drive is often a good idea. Still, one person needs to coordinate the entire drive.

5 *Never Bite Off More Than You Can Chew.* This is great advice when planning a deer drive. Always keep in mind that the larger a piece of cover is to be driven, the more drivers and standers it takes to do so effectively. If standers are not guarding all known travel or escape routes, or if drivers are spread out so far they can't keep sight of one another, then you are probably wasting your time. Whitetails cannot be pushed in a straight line for long distances. They are not cattle, and they'll look for every hole possible to break away out of gunshot, or at least the area being driven. It is better to push a large tract with two or three shorter drives than to attempt doing it all at once.

6 *Safety Always Comes First.* In most cases, drive members are gun-toting hunters who are busy compressing whitetails between them. I've witnessed 30-minute drives during which more than 150 shotgun slugs were fired. That's a lot of lead in the air during a very short period. Lots of fluorescent orange jackets make more sense during a deer drive than when whitetail are hunted in any other way. Hunters need to know where the standers are situated and exactly which direction the drivers are coming.

Driving whitetails isn't for every hunter. Many prefer the solitude of hunting alone, either from a stand or while still hunting. Conversely, some hunting parties may not be big enough to conduct a drive properly. But there is no denying that, when done right, a good deer drive will produce whitetails. ∎

Hunting The Pre-Rut

WITH ■ *Sam Collora, President, Mrs. Doe Pee's Buck Lures* ■ *John Burgeson, President, Wildlife Research Center* ■ *Dick Idol, Whitetail Expert* ■ *Eddie Salter, Hunter Specialties Pro-Staffer* ■ *Terry Rohm, Marketing Director, Wellington Products*

Iowa bowhunters, who take their whitetail hunting seriously, live for the month of November. As the rut approaches, big horned bucks with swollen necks suddenly become more visible as they move from woodlot to woodlot or from bushy draw to bushy draw in search of does in estrous. Mid-November marks the height of the rut in the Hawkeye State, giving bowhunters all the action to themselves for the entire month (the general gun seasons don't take place until early December).

Sam Collora, president of a small company (Mrs. Doe Pee's Buck Lures in Mt. Pleasant, IA), is one of those bowhunters. To him, there is no bad time to be in a tree stand, and the three-month-long archery season gives him plenty of opportunity. Still, he knows that there is no better time to be in the deer woods than the two weeks prior to the height of the rut. Like so many dedicated big buck hunters, Sam usually delays his hunting start until the last week of

October, or even the first week or two of November, when he knows that bucks tend to be extremely active.

Early one afternoon in mid-October 1996, a friend of Sam's dropped by to pick up his hunting clothes, which he had left hanging in the exhaust room of Sam's deer urine collection area. Collora decided it would be a good day to get away from work and kick off his hunting season. It was a beautiful fall day, one which had started out cool and crisp, but had warmed into the low 60s by early afternoon. A light but steady breeze was blowing from the south, so Sam decided to hunt from a stand he'd left hanging from the last season. On several of his hunts late in the previous season, he had spotted a nice 140 class buck several times from that stand, once even letting the deer pass within easy bow range without releasing an arrow. Sam had his sights set on tagging a much bigger buck he was sure inhabited the same cover.

Chapter Eight

Sam Collora

Sam Collora is extremely scent conscious. In addition to working hard to keep himself "scent free," he also believes in using natural scents to attract deer and to cover his own human odor. He and several of his hunting buddies have found that if they hang their hunting clothes in the exhaust room of Sam's deer urine

collection area, they will smell like deer. So when he travels to a hunt area, Sam always packs his clothing in an almost airtight rubber snap-top container. Then, once he reaches the hunt area, he slips into his camouflage clothes. Recalling his first afternoon of hunting in October 1996, Sam comments: "I put

my Scent-Lok suit, my outer clothes and my rubber boots in a Rubbermaid container as soon as I took them out of the exhaust room, and they stayed in the box until I got to the edge of the woods. I slipped them on and tied a drag rag to my ankle. I put a few drops of our "Doe-in-Estrous" scent on the rag. I put only a small amount of scent on to start out, and add more as I walk toward my stand, so a buck will track me in the direction I've walked."

This particular afternoon, Sam went out of his way to cut across two or three travel routes. The loop he took added a few hundred yards to his walk into the stand. When he finally reached the location, he walked past the stand for another 20 yards. He then untied the drag rag and hung it about three feet off the ground within easy bow range of the portable platform that was positioned only 14 feet or so off the ground. The stand was located along a well-used travel route between the deer's bedding and feeding area. On his final approach to the stand, Sam had spooked a doe. While the deer had not scented him, the hunter and deer held a ten-minute stare-down before the old doe bounded off. Sam climbed into the stand, figuring that he probably wouldn't see another deer for the rest of the evening. But he didn't really care. It was a great evening to be out, and Sam found it relaxing just to sit in the stand and enjoy the peace and quiet.

"I was soaking up the evening," he recounts, "when all of a sudden I noticed this huge buck straight down-wind from me. He was about 75 to 100 yards away, in a direction I didn't expect a deer to come from. When I saw him, the first thought that entered my mind was, *This is the biggest buck I've ever had a shot at!* It was a weird sensation. I knew he was a Boone and Crockett buck, and that's what I was after. But I had no idea beyond that. His huge body made his rack look smaller than it was."

About 30 yards from Sam's stand, the buck turned to his left and looked out across a fence. That's when the bow-hunter got his first good look at the rack. The sight rattled him and he tried desperately to maintain his composure. He avoided looking at the deer's head, fearing the buck might take off. Slowly, Sam drew his compound bow to full draw, but he still didn't have a clear shot. The big whitetail began smelling the ground where Sam had pulled the drag rag, and once again he stared off into the brush, as if looking for the hot doe he knew must be nearby. Fortunately, the deer didn't leave, but instead headed for one of the shooting lanes Collora had cut the previous year. Just before the buck

reached the opening in the under-brush, Sam brought his bow to full draw, and as the deer stepped across the open lane, the archer centered the sight pin on the front shoulder. Then Sam released and the arrow was on its way. It impacted farther forward than Sam Collora would have liked, but the tremendous 14-pointer staggered only 150 yards before going down for the count. Sam had just arrowed the high-est grossing typical Pope and Young record book buck ever taken. The magnificent whitetail gross scored 223

This muzzle-loading hunter proved success-ful during the first stages of the pre-rut by setting up along the edge of a feed area.

points, and by the time deductions were made for a few abnormal points and differences in point/beam lengths and circumferences, the huge deer still netted 193 3/8. "I truly feel like I didn't

do anything other hunters wouldn't have done," Sam insisted. "I was in the right place at the right time. I didn't do anything special—but something special sure happened to me!."

I have a confession to make. As an outdoor writer who spends a good deal of time writing about whitetail hunting, I receive a lot of promotional lures and

scents. At times, I use some of this largesse freely. One of my favorite tactics is to fill a small spray bottle with deer urine. Then, as I walk to my stand location, I mist the air in front of my feet lightly with the scent. If it's a long walk, I'll wait until I'm within 100 yards of the stand before spraying. This natural "deer" smell tends to overpower whatever amount of human odor may be on my boots. During an early November hunt in Iowa a few years back, I used this tactic while making my way to a stand that was situated along the crest of a long, narrow wooded ridge. The deer often used the ridge to avoid exposing themselves in the open fields. Along each side of the wooded rise were a number of rubs and scrapes. To keep from walking the full length of the ridge, I cut in from the bottom, about where I guessed my stand would be located. Just before reaching the top of the ridge, I began misting the ground where I walked. When I topped out, I was about 60 yards off the track, so I kept spraying the ground until I reached the stand.

About an hour after climbing onto the platform shortly before nightfall, I heard a loud crashing noise below where I had topped the ridge. White antlers suddenly appeared, coming fast up the side of the ridge exactly where I had made the climb. The buck overshot

COMPLETE BOOK OF WHITETAIL HUNTING

the top of the ridge and was 30 yards down the other side before it stopped. The deer ran back over the ridge top in the opposite direction, then stopped somewhere out of sight. I quickly pulled a grunt tube from my jacket front and grunted softly several times, meanwhile reaching up for my bow. I was just in time. A big eight-pointer came charging right in, stopped broadside and presented me with an easy 18-yard shot. That deer may have been a far cry from the Iowa bruiser taken by Sam Collora, but it was still a really good Pope and Young buck.

Like Sam and most other serious bowhunters, I believe the best time to pattern and take a good buck is during the period known as the "pre-rut," or the period whitetail expert Dick Idol refers to as the "pre-breeding" period. "Without a doubt, the pre-breeding period is my favorite time in which to hunt a big buck," Dick says. "Like the rut preparation period that precedes it, the pre-breeding period features regular, predictable buck travel; but now the odds are starting to swing toward the hunter, because daytime activity is on the rise."

According to Dick, the pre-breeding—or pre-rut—period in most parts of North America lasts three to four weeks. In more northern latitudes, this magical period usually starts in early to mid-October and ends the first or second week of November. Farther south, especially in south Texas and Mexico, the pre-breeding period tends to kick in about a month later. "The beginning date of the pre-breeding period is not precise," Dick points out, "at least where evidence of sign is concerned. Its beginning is predictable, however, to within a week or so. What is most significant is the fact that the buck's priority has switched from food to does. He continues to feed, of course, but more of his time, thoughts and travel are directed toward the opposite sex."

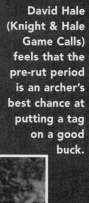

David Hale (Knight & Hale Game Calls) feels that the pre-rut period is an archer's best chance at putting a tag on a good buck.

each buck's priority instinctively switches to the does.

Buck activity usually picks up dramatically as the pre-breeding period progresses. Most evident is the increased distance a buck will travel each day in his search for a receptive doe. While the does may be several weeks from entering estrous, the bucks are ready now. The drive to breed causes them to spend much of their time on the go. Bucks that once remained well within the confines of a specific tract of cover now show up miles from where they spent the summer and early fall. "The average buck during the rut-preparation period travels one to two miles in a 24-hour period," Dick Idol states, "but the same buck in the pre-breeding period will cover 8 to 10 miles each day if deer densities are high —and as much as 15 to 20 miles if densities are extremely low.

During this period, otherwise nocturnal older class bucks now and then break off their normal routines and provide the patient hunter with a rare shot at a true trophy of a lifetime. While most of these deer still travel under the cloak of darkness, the excitement of an oncoming breeding period, or rut, can cause an old monarch to linger longer than usual during the first dim light of dawn, even earlier in the evening. As Dick Idol points out, the frequency of

The reason why it's hard to pinpoint the exact day the pre-breeding period kicks in, Dick explains, is the slow transition that can take a week or ten days. Decreasing daylight triggers a change in a whitetail buck's personality and priorities. As the days grow shorter, the buck's system automatically receives a dose of testosterone, the male hormone, which travels into the bloodstream via the testicles. The amount of testosterone emitted increases each day during the transition period, so that scrape-checking escalates toward the end of the pre-breeding period. Competition is a big factor. Bucks want to monitor the most active scrapes as often as possible, because they sense a hot doe may choose a particular buck at any moment. Whether the scrape checking occurs at various time around the clock or is confined strictly to the dark hours is affected by the amount of hunting pressure.

John Burgeson

John Burgeson, founder of Wildlife Research Center, Inc., feels that scrapes provide hunters with excellent opportunities for hunting big bucks. He also points out that while bucks do make a lot of scrapes, they don't visit them all on a daily basis. What makes it even harder to hunt over a scrape (or scrape line) is the fact that most of this activity takes place at night, when deer movement is greatest. Does urinate in the scrapes during late evening or during the pre-dawn darkness, and that's when the bucks will most likely check them. Often the trick is to locate a scrape that's been hit harder than others in the area, one that is being worked more and where the deer tend to spend more time. This knowledge increases a

hunter's chances of being in his stand when a buck decides to check the scrape for activity.

John Burgeson's Wildlife Research Center is one of several companies that market a device that drips doe-in-heat urine into a scrape on a timed basis. Called the "Ultimate Scrape Dripper," it is designed to drop only during daylight hours. As daytime temperatures begin to rise, this dripper activates, periodically releasing a drop of urine into the scrape. In the evening, as temperatures begin to drop, the device shuts down automatically. The scent is applied only

The first step toward the successful use of hunting scents is the elimination of human odor on clothing, equipment, and the hunter's body. Sprays like "Scent Killer" (Wildlife Research Center) make the job easier.

during daylight hours because that's when a buck is most likely to begin checking the scrape. Burgeson recommends that hunters should hang one of his drippers five or six feet above a scrape for several days before hunting the area. This will give a buck time to make the scrape part of his normal travel route without increasing the odds of the hunter contaminating the area with human odor.

"One of the best ways to get a feel for where a buck makes his scrapes," John advises, "is to get out and do a lot of scouting. Keep your eyes open for places where scrapes tend to appear. Bucks like to establish scrapes in border areas. Often scrapes are found in fairly thick areas near more open areas. I consider a border area to be one where there's a change in the type or density of vegetation and trees."

John states further that where hunters have located scrapes, bucks tend to return to the same general areas year after year. When looking for active scrapes, these spots are great places to begin looking each season. And where there are lots of scrapes, hunters should concentrate on those that appear to be the most heavily used. These are often located in more dense cover, away from other lesser scrapes.

Where lots of other buck sign appears, but there's little evidence of scrape activity, many hunters now use a "mock" scrape. John Burgeson advises hunters in that event to pick a location similar to where you'd usually find natural scrapes. Pick a spot with a small tree next to it, with a few branches extending out to where the mock scrape will be located. Overhanging branches should be five to six feet above ground level. Once the spot is located, all leaves and other ground cover must be scraped away and the dirt disturbed in much the same manner as a buck when making a real scrape. To prevent contaminating the area with human odor, hunters should wear rubber boots and rubber gloves. Once the area has been cleared and the dirt scraped to look as if it had been pawed with front hooves, the freshly disturbed soil should be treated with deer urine. Burgeson recommends hanging one of the drippers directly over the man-made scrape. Over the years, I've made hundreds of such scrapes and found that, when located in the right spot, they attract deer as well as the real thing. Many of the scrapes I make, however, are the real thing. When scouting, I usually wear a camouflaged vest with a large game bag on the back containing a dripper and hand tools for making the scrape.

Before heading for the area where I plan to set up a mock scrape, I look for a stretch of cover—at least four or five miles away—where I can quickly find several natural whitetail scrapes. After breaking up the soil there, I'll scoop the dirt saturated with deer urine into a zip-lock bag. I then return to where I plan to make the mock scrape and mix the dirt from a real scrape with the freshly disturbed soil. By establishing such a scrape in accordance with my plan, I've found that mock scrapes are often more effective than the real things. One of my favorite places to gather dirt from scrapes made by whitetails is an old logging road that runs along the top of a wooded ridge for nearly a mile. Beginning around mid-October each fall, this road is covered with scrapes along its entire length. In less than a mile, I've discovered 40 to 50 scrapes.

Dick Idol classifies such scrapes as "boundary scrapes," claiming they offer the least promise for shooting a good buck. Such scrapes are commonly found along the fringes—a field edge, hedgerow, fence line, narrow corridor, or perhaps along the edge of an island of cover located in some open area. Dick

feels that scrapes of this type are made mostly at night and must be worked mostly at night. He further contends that "trail scrapes," which are made inside some types of cover in association with a trail of some sort, offer a better opportunity for getting a shot at a good buck. Since trail scrapes are often visited during daylight hours, they make a good bet for hunting.

Dick Idol also believes that trail scrapes can become what he refers to as "breeding area scrapes"—i.e., when large numbers of bucks use the same area. Breeding area scrapes are established and maintained regularly in those small areas where the most interaction between does and bucks is found. Here the odds are best that a buck will find a

John Sloan traveled from Tennessee to Iowa to take advantage of an early November pre-rut hunt. He was rewarded with this nice buck.

disturbing any deer in the breeding area, will enjoy some fantastic big buck action.

When trying to slip into an area undetected, human scent should be a hunter's primary concern. Sam Collora admits that he takes matters to an extreme by hanging his hunting clothes in the exhaust room where he collects real whitetail urine for his bottled buck lures. He handles his clothing carefully, packs it in an air-tight container prior to carrying it to the hunting area, and always wears rubber boots when headed into the deer woods. Not every hunter knows a friend who is in the deer scent business, nor anyone who has a "deer urine collection area." However, it's easy to get the same effect simply by spraying one's clothing with natural deer urine and storing it in a plastic snap-top box, or an over-sized, zip-lock plastic storage bag. The sprayed clothing, when allowed to remain in a sealed storage box or bag, will as a result be permeated with the natural scent while in the woods. Many deer hunting experts warn against spraying hunting clothes with a doe-in-heat type scent, however, because the smell could trigger an attack from a rutting buck.

Terry Rohm, marketing director for Wellington, which markets a line of scent-related products for deer hunters,

receptive doe when the time is right. Traveling bucks often target the same areas, which can become the center of deer activity. Scrapes here can develop into large, well-used barren spots that have been pawed into shallow depressions capable of holding water after a hard rain. Such scrapes are most evident during the end of the pre-breeding period, just before the rut kicks in. The hunter who locates such an area, and who can find a way to slip into a well-positioned stand without offers the following advice. "Before using scents, a hunter needs to first reduce his natural human body odor by bathing with one of the specially formulated unscented soaps developed especially for the deer hunter, and to wear clothing that has been washed with a similar product. Nothing made today will take it all away, but you can reduce human odors enough to keep from spooking every deer that passes downwind of your stand."

Terry is a highly successful bow-hunter who is very conscious of wind direction. He almost always passes on hunting from a prime stand location in favor of one that offers less promise but where the wind direction is positive for hunting. He is also quite conscious about which scent to use and warns against thinking that the mere use of a deer-hunting scent guarantees a buck will come running.

"Scents can be, and are, great tools for the hunter," Terry avows, "so long as he doesn't rely on them 100 percent. One way a deer communicates is by smell. Using the right scent at the right time is obviously an important factor in getting a shot as opposed to spending a pleasant morning or afternoon in the stand. Don't use a doe-estrous type scent too early in the fall. I've found it best to rely on a straight doe or buck urine

during the first week or two of bow season, and often on into the early stages of the pre-rut. As the rut approaches, and the bucks begin to get more active, I advocate switching over to doe-in-heat urine, generally pouring a few drops into a well-used scrape nearby. Buck urine seems to work well all season. During the season's early stages, bucks are often still traveling in groups. When they pick up on the smell of a newcomer, they come into the odor to get acquainted. As the rut approaches, the scent of another buck may trigger an urge within dominant bucks to challenge

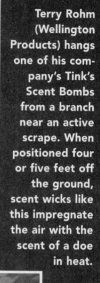

Terry Rohm (Wellington Products) hangs one of his company's Tink's Scent Bombs from a branch near an active scrape. When positioned four or five feet off the ground, scent wicks like this impregnate the air with the scent of a doe in heat.

the intruder. That's when I use what is commonly referred to as a *dominant buck* urine type scent."

Terry Rohm's best bow-killed buck was taken during a pre-rut hunt in Illinois. Even though the area was covered up

Terry Rohm

with big buck sign and the deer seemed to be uncommonly active, Terry had not spotted a single good buck after a week of sitting in well-positioned stands. Each day he watched small bucks enter the area following the mock scent trails, or responding to fresh scrapes doctored with a few drops of Tink's No. 69 Doe-in-Rut urine (made by Terry's company), plus a few deer who had responded to rattling and grunting. Not one good buck had passed within sight. Terry surmised that the big boys must be moving entirely at night. After a week had passed, he decided to hunt several more days in hopes of getting a shot at one of the big bucks he knew inhabited the area. The next two days were no more eventful than the entire previous week. Terry had a plane to catch the next morning, but he planned to hunt until eight o'clock or so before leaving his stand. It was a decision he'll never regret.

Eddie Salter

"The next morning looked to be a repeat of more than a week of hunting." he recalls. "By the time eight o'clock rolled around, I had watched several more small bucks, but nothing worth shooting. I knew it was time to get out of the stand, but something told me to stay, and my eyes began searching the area. Suddenly there

was a movement. It turned out to be the top of a sapling swaying back and forth. I raised my glasses and immediately made out the head of a deer sporting a good rack with nice, long tines. I knew immediately it was a shooter. I also immediately forgot about the time."

The buck continued to work on the sapling for another five minutes or so, then raised its head and looked in both directions. The next thing Terry knew, the deer was walking right toward a nearby scrape along a route that would take the deer past his stand at less than 20 yards. About 30 yards from the stand, the big deer walked behind a wall of brush and stopped. At almost the same moment, Terry raised his bow. The hunter knew the buck hadn't yet spotted him, but he couldn't help thinking the deer possessed "extra sensory perception." It knew something was not quite right. About a minute later, the deer continued walking, and at exactly 8:05 a.m. Terry Rohm arrowed the best buck of his bow-hunting career, one that grossed well into the 160s and netted right at 155 points.

Eddie Salter, a member of Hunter Specialties Pro-Staff, claims there is no better time to be in the deer woods than the two weeks prior to the start of the rut. In most parts of the country this magical period extends from the last week of October to mid-November. Like most dedicated bowhunters, he also prefers hunting the pre-rut. From a lifetime of hunting the whitetail, Eddie now realizes that the deer are simply more active during the week or two preceding the actual breeding period. "During the pre-rut," he explains, "all deer become very active—does, young bucks and even the dominant older bucks. While much of the increased movement takes place at night, the deer tend to still move more in early morning and early evening. Mature dominant bucks cover a lot of ground during this period, their presence announcing to the does, *'Hey, I'm available.'* Heightened buck activity excites the does to some degree and encourages things (the rut) to happen."

While most trophy hunters target mature 4 1/2- to 5 1/2- year-old bucks, Eddie Salter points out more opportunities exist at satellite 130 to 140 class 2 1/2- and 3 -year-old bucks. For most bowhunters, these are still great trophies. Hunters who are prepared to take a "good" buck rather than holding out for a Boone & Crockett class deer can expect a high degree of success during the pre-rut. As they enter their second and third years, these bucks become very aggressive and are often the ones who do the most fighting. They may not be a match for a huge 160 class 4 1/2-year-old buck living in the same habitat, but these young bucks are bent on establishing future dominance and territory. It's not uncommon for bucks of

this age class to cover a lot of miles every day, including some during daylight hours. This makes them more vulnerable than older, wiser bucks who are almost entirely nocturnal.

When he finds an abundance of rubs and scrapes, Eddie senses that somewhere close by is a good food source attracting a large number of deer to the area. This is especially true during the early stages of the pre-rut. To locate whatever food source is responsible for a concentration of sign, Eddie will walk about 10 to 15 yards from the center of

Rattling is a great way to get the attention of a buck during the pre-rut. Terry Rohm clashes a set of antlers together during an early pre-rut hunt.

the activity, then walk around the area in a big circle. If he doesn't find what he's looking for, he'll move out another 10 to 15 yards and circle the area again, and so on until he discovers a big white oak that's dropping acorns, a patch of honeysuckle that's been nibbled on heavily, a stand of sweet persimmons, or maybe a clover field, or a freshly harvested soybean field. Locating the

80 yards downwind of these areas. Probably more often than not, a buck won't run right up to a scrape and sniff it to see if a hot doe has used it. He doesn't have to. He can work downwind of active scrapes and sniff the breezes to see if there has been any activity. Not only will a hunter miss seeing bucks that are 75 to 100 yards back in the brush, but by placing a stand directly over

During the pre-rut, bucks are continuously on the move looking for receptive does. The use of a decoy is a great way to pull an otherwise suspicious buck in close for the shot.

deer's primary food source is a key reason why a hunter will most always find more rubs and scrapes where food sources are best. The food attracts the does—and the does attract the bucks.

"I believe that one of the biggest mistakes many hunters make," Salter warns, "is to set their stand so it directly overlooks an area of concentrated rubs and scrapes. I've found it much more productive to locate my stand 75 or

the scrapes the hunter increases the odds of being winded by any deer passing downwind."

Salter feels that hunters stand their best chances at getting a shot during the first two or three days after a stand has been hung. Many top-rated whitetail hunters claim a hunter should not hunt the same stand more than once or twice a week, but Eddie feels that if one takes care to avoid contaminating the area with human scent, or spooking deer, there is absolutely nothing wrong with hunting the same location day in and day out. But instead of relying on a single stand, he prefers to hang two stands, one somewhat on the east side of the area and another on the west side. This offers the flexibility of switching locations when the wind direction changes.

Eddie Salter is an Alabama native who now hunts all across the country each fall. He once harvested between 20 and 30 deer every season. In his home state, liberal bag limits allow him to take a deer a day during a 60-day season. He now hunts primarily for good bucks while relying still on tactics he once used to keep his freezer filled with venison. He is a firm believer in "making things happen," forcing the action by using a variety of calls to bring deer within bow range. "When calling during the pre-rut," he says, "I rely on several different deer sounds to make a buck think there's more than one deer up ahead. I like the multi-tone calls that allow me to go from the grunt of an old buck to that of a younger buck or the bleat of a doe simply by changing the amount of finger pressure on the reed. Throw in a small amount of rattling, and you'd better be ready for some action."

There's more to calling than making tones that duplicate those of a real whitetail. Most hunters, according to Eddie Salter, don't put enough "feeling" into their calling. The tones of their calls may be right, but the emotion is missing. There's no sense of urgency needed to prompt another whitetail's response. To add a greater sense of realism, vary the pitch of the calls, put a little quiver into a bleat, and keep the sequences from becoming too repetitive. Eddie is also one of the country's most respected turkey hunters. Long ago, he learned that decoys will often bring a gobbler into shotgun range. When calling whitetails, Eddie is also a firm believer in using a deer decoy (or two or three).

"When restricted to using just one decoy," he warns, "I'll stick with a doe decoy during the pre-rut. After all, that's what the bucks are looking for. Where decoys can be transported easily to the hunting area, or where they can be hidden in a nearby draw or brush, two or three decoys have an even greater draw. To give the setup even more realism, I'll drip a few drops of doe urine on the decoys. Never forget a whitetail's nose. When a buck comes in from downwind, sees the decoys but cannot detect the smell of deer, he may well become nervous and leave."

One tactic that has brought more than one good whitetail within bow range of Salter's stand has been a fawn bleat. Eddie admits that the call works better during the early part of the pre-rut than the days immediately preceding the beginning of the rut. He has also found it to be more effective in the South than in the North or upper Midwest. He rarely uses a fawn bleat when first getting into a stand in the morning, and never during an evening

in late October and early November—a time when not many general firearms seasons are open. Across the U.S. and in some Canadian provinces several early muzzleloading seasons provide whitetail hunters an opportunity to head out with a gun of older, frontloading design. The same pre-rut tactics covered here, especially the use of scents and calls, will produce deer during the early muzzleloader hunts as well. This is especially true when one of the seasons happens to take place during the two weeks directly preceding the start of the rut. As Dick Idol says, "Timing is one of the most critical elements of effective calling." He also notes that there's a relatively narrow window of prime time. During the rut-preparation period, which Idol classifies as the weeks prior to true pre-rut activity, he feels the bucks lack enough interest in breeding to respond to calling or rattling. The only exception is probably a fawn bleat, which will attract does. Dick also points out that later, during the actual rut or breeding period, the bigger and more dominant bucks are with their receptive does almost around the clock and are unlikely to respond. The prime window is the two- to three-week pre-breeding, or pre-rut period prior to the first does coming into estrous. The closer the start

Harold Knight (Knight & Hale Game Calls) is a highly successful pre-rut bowhunter who relies heavily on horn rattling and the use of a grunt tube to get big bucks like this one within range.

hunt. He often waits until he's ready to leave the stand around 9:00 or 9:30 after a full morning of hunting. Then he'll fill the air with fawn distress bleats, hoping to catch the attention of does in the area. Their maternal instincts often bring one or more running to the call, and right on their heels there's often a buck. Occasionally, a lone buck will slip in to check out the commotion.

Most of what has been covered in this chapter pertains to bowhunting of the actual rut, the more effective calling can be. Dick also recognizes that once the rut has wound down, during the post-rut, response to calls is generally low, unless buck competition is extremely high.

"Vital factors in any calling method," Dick states, "are an undetected approach and a proper setup. If a buck is tipped off to a hunter's presence, it's a near certainty he won't respond. Knowledge of bedding areas or where you think the buck will come from is necessary to get within a buck's hearing distance without disturbing him."

The ideal setup for Dick Idol is a favorable wind direction and adequate visibility. Nearly all bucks will respond on the downwind side. The hunter must choose a location where he can see about as far as a downwind buck can pick up his scent. This usually means clear visibility for 50 to 200 yards, depending on terrain, weather conditions and wind currents. Ideally, the downwind approach should offer plenty of cover for a responding buck. If the country is too open, a season-wise old buck may be reluctant to cross close enough for a hunter to spot him. "When does far outnumber bucks, competition is low. The result is fewer rubs and scrapes, less buck travel—and lower response to rattling and calling," claims Dick Idol.

The one thing that most whitetail hunting expert agree on is that the pre-rut is the period during which whitetail bucks tend to be the most responsive to calling. It's also the time during which scents, when used properly, can create enough curiosity to bring a buck in for an easy shot. When most serious trophy hunters are given the choice of hunting a week during the height of the rut, or the week just prior to the outset of the rut, they will opt for the pre-rut hunt. It's a time when you should be in the deer woods as well. ∎

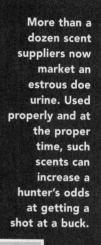

More than a dozen scent suppliers now market an estrous doe urine. Used properly and at the proper time, such scents can increase a hunter's odds at getting a shot at a buck.

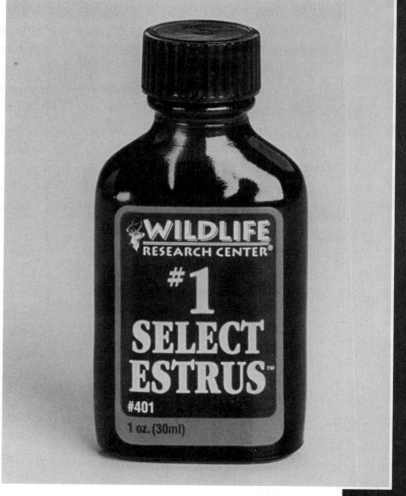

Chapter Nine

Calling Whitetails

WITH ■ *Brad Harris, Lohman Mfg.* ■ *Harold Knight, Knight & Hale Game Calls* ■ *David Hale, Knight & Hale Game Calls* ■ *Mark Drury, M.A.D. Calls* ■ *Stan Potts, Bowhunter & Wildlife Manager*

As a technique or tactic for hunting whitetails, calling is a relatively new method. To my knowledge, there exists no written record of early hunters relying on the imitation of whitetail vocalization to lure deer within shooting range, although it must have been done to some degree. Well before 1950, several call manufacturers offered "bleat" calls imitating the sounds of an adult doe or fawn, and the art of rattling was already a popular technique by the turn of the 20th century. As for today's widespread practice of calling deer, whitetail hunters have been actively pursuing that practice since the mid-1980s. Today, a dozen or so call makers offer a wide range of "grunt tubes," doe/fawn bleat calls, and a large selection of synthetic rattling horns, rattling bags and hand-operated rattling calls.

One of the first hunters I know who tried luring bucks within bow range by means of simulated buck grunts is Brad Harris (Lohman Manufacturing), a prominent manufacturer of calls for nearly all game species. Brad took notice of the guttural sounds made by bucks as they pursued hot does during the height of the rut, or as they followed their line of scrapes, or cruised the woods looking for female companionship. He discovered that by playing around with the plastic reed of a Lohman duck call—letting it flap more loosely—he could imitate these sounds quite accurately. When he blew the call, it usually got a buck's attention, often causing him to come looking for the upstart buck who had invaded his territory or space. Sometimes the result was a much better shot, especially with a bow.

Harold Knight and David Hale, who built their company (Knight & Hale Game Calls) around the fascination of calling deer and other game, were among the early believers in the use of deer calls. It was David Hale's early encounter with a vocal buck that did much to influence the future development of the now widely used Knight & Hale grunt tubes. It all began in October, 1971, when David was hunting the "Land Between The Lakes" in western Kentucky, not far from his home. He had placed his stand in a big oak along the edge of an open field. Some 20 yards behind his stand was a deep ravine that cut into the side of the ridge. David felt that deer, being basically lazy, would funnel around the upper end of the ravine rather than cutting across the deep draw. About 9:30 that morning, a big doe came running along, and David decided to shoot. He had never taken a deer with a bow and was anxious to get one under his belt, even if by today's standards he was ill-equipped. But seconds before he started to draw on the doe, a sound he had never heard before caused David to let up on the string and look in the direction from which the doe had

appeared. What he saw was a giant buck trailing the doe and grunting loudly as it came through the hardwoods. The buck ran right up to the doe, who was stand-

Brad Harris

ing only 20 yards from David's stand, then stopped, offering a perfect broadside shot. Unfortunately, due to an immediate case of buck fever, his arrow caught the buck near the hip. Eight hours and two miles later, David found the big nine-pointer. It was his first whitetail taken with a bow and his first Pope & Young buck. It was also the first buck he ever heard make the kind of sound David

Brad Harris (Lohman Game Calls) is credited for refining the use of a buck grunt call. His first calls were made by altering the reed of a duck call.

Harold
Knight

would later try to duplicate with a manufactured call.

Harold Knight had heard the sounds made by both does and bucks many times while bow and gun hunting, but he never tried "calling in" a buck until the early 1980s. It was then that the first

soon as he blew the first soft series of grunts, Harold saw the buck's head rise abruptly. The deer stood there for several minutes, looking in the direction from which he had heard the sounds. When the deer lowered its head to sniff the leafy ground cover once more, Harold repeated the call, whereupon the deer came trotting towards the hunter. The buck ran to within 30 yards of the stand, then stood staring past Harold's position, looking for the source of the grunts. A few minutes later, Harold eased the call to his lips and grunted softly once more. With that, the deer spun around and bolted. At the same moment, Harold heard the unmistakable sound of another deer approaching from behind him in a hurry. Before he could react and get his rifle up, a nice buck charged past in pursuit of the younger deer. It was gone in an instant.

Harold Knight (Knight & Hale Game Calls) feels that the pre-rut is probably the trophy buck hunter's best chance of taking a bragging-sized whitetail. A grunt tube is one of the best ways to entice deer within range.

commercial grunt calls hit the market. Like many other hunters, Harold had purchased one in hopes of upping the hunting odds in his favor. This woodswise hunter then spent considerable time tuning the call until it sounded more like the natural sounds he had heard in the woods. One cold November morning, Harold spotted a young buck standing about 75 yards from his stand. Having never used a grunt tube to call to a live buck, he decided now was the time. Almost as

Harold surmised that if the grunt sounds had lured in both bucks, perhaps he could get the attention of the bigger deer once more by calling on the grunt tube. Five or ten minutes passed, but nothing happened. Harold was beginning to feel that he had missed his opportunity to hang his tag on that buck when a movement down the ridge caught his attention. Sunlight was reflecting off a buck's antlers, and Harold instantly recog-

COMPLETE BOOK OF WHITETAIL HUNTING

nized it as the larger of the two deer. Each time the buck dropped its head or looked off in another direction, Knight would grunt softly on his call. Thirty minutes later, the buck was standing about 30 yards away. This time, Harold didn't hesitate. He dropped the nice ten-pointer where it stood with a single shot. It was the first buck he had ever called in.

Thanks to Brad Harris, David Hale, Harold Knight and several others who "pioneered" this device, we now know more about whitetail vocalization than ever before. Following are some of the more common sounds made by deer. Learning how to duplicate them can add greatly to a hunter's chances of taking a true trophy buck.

THE SNORT

Anyone who has spent even a short time in the deer woods is probably familiar with the snort of a whitetail. It's usually a tattletale signal that a deer has either spotted or scented a hunter and is most likely followed by a flash of white as the deer raises its tail and heads for less congested territory, covering as much ground as possible with each leap. When a deer "snorts" or "blows," as some hunters refer to the sound, the deer is actually clearing its nostrils of mucus, foreign matter and possibly the strong smell of whatever it may have been eating. The sudden reverse flow of air through the nostrils causes the fine hairs inside

Whitetail hunter Tom Dube sprays a mist of natural cover scent onto his clothing before attempting to call deer. Whitetails will instinctively move downwind from any source of calling.

the nasal passage to stand upright (which is what makes the whitetail's sense of smell so acute). When free of anything that might interfere with the sudden smell of danger, the deer's sensitive olfactory system can pinpoint the source of the odor with great accuracy. Some knowledgeable deer hunters will argue that variations of the snort signify a higher degree of alarm than others. Mostly, though, the snort is associated with danger. Few successful whitetail hunters who rely on calling ever use the high-pitched coughing sound in their repertoire.

THE GRUNT CALL

The guttural grunts made by a buck are by far the most popular calls used

Stan Potts

by today's whitetail hunter. If you asked a half-dozen successful callers to give you an accurate description of their sound, you'd probably get as many different responses. Most will liken the sound to the grunts of a pig (hence the name of the sound). The one thing that most successful callers will agree on is that whitetail bucks all have their own different kinds of grunts. Stan Potts, one of the country's most successful whitetail bowhunters, recognizes that bucks make grunts with varying sounds, tones or volumes at different times. Not all grunts are the same, nor do they mean the same thing to other deer. "One of the very best times to call deer," Stan advises, "is when a buck is running a scrape line. As he does so, the buck

will usually grunt softly every 30, 40 or 50 yards. While a hunter who spots a buck working scrapes should not be too aggressive, neither should he be afraid to call. When the calls are kept soft, often the buck will come in, mostly because he's curious. He wants to find out who the other buck is and where he fits into the pecking order."

When a buck pursues a doe in estrous, the grunts can be very excited, drawn out and extremely repetitive to the point of being nonstop. Many whitetail experts refer to this as the "tending grunt." Other somewhat non-descriptive grunts include inquisitive ones (*"Where are you?"*) and loud, aggressive ones challenging another buck's presence. Whitetail bucks can become quite vocal before and during the rut. Knowing when to make a particular grunt sound can be learned only through experience in the deer woods, or from experts who have mastered these calls.

FAWN BLEAT

Indians of the Northwest have long used the fawn bleat to hunt coastal blacktail deer, and the same call works equally well when used on whitetails. It is a fawn's distress call, which says, *"I need help!"* The call plays on the maternal instinct of does, and practically all adult female deer will respond to it. When the call is used during the rut to call in the does, rutting bucks may well be right on their heels. Harold Knight feels it's an excellent call to use during the early portions of the bow seasons, when late-born fawns are found almost always with the parental doe. Instinctively, deer tend to protect their young. The fawn bleat not only calls in the does, but often a buck will respond as well—perhaps out of curiosity, or maybe to make sure that all is okay.

DOE BLEAT AND GRUNT

Adult does also make a bleating call, but mot experts at calling whitetails use the sound only on certain occasions. Stan Potts feel that any natural, "non-alert" call can be a part of calling deer. Deer are extremely curious animals and will often come to investigate any call that doesn't signal danger. David Hale regularly uses a doe estrous bleat or grunt when calling for bucks. He has actually watched a doe make the sound and describes it as similar to a buck grunt, but pitched higher and slightly longer than the common buck grunt. David reports having seen a number of does investigate the sound and concludes they were most likely the dominant does of the area, checking out a subordinate doe who had broken the pecking order and became too vocal. This could be an excellent call to use once the rut

begins to wind down or during a weak secondary rut. During these times, many bucks have grown tired of locking horns with each other. Their stamina and physical condition is down, and the last thing they want is another fight. However, the sound of a hot doe grunting, especially in the vicinity of a scrape that is still active, could be more than a buck's willpower can resist.

Multi-toned calls, such as this one designed by Mark Drury (M.A.D. Calls) can nearly imitate a whitetail's entire vocabulary.

Calling"). One of his favorite times occurs when a strong high pressure front suddenly pushes into his favorite Midwestern hunting hot spots during early to mid-November. It kicks the rut into high gear and causes the bucks to become extremely active. During the peak activity periods of late afternoon and early evening he will periodically combine a series of grunts with some aggressive rattling. This technique is especially effective when he knows two or more bucks are in the vicinity of his stand. Even when several bucks are chasing a hot doe, Mark will continue calling to them. More than once he has excited the deer into staging a fight, and sooner or later one will show up to investigate the buck they keep hearing but haven't seen. This tactic has rewarded Mark with a number of rut-crazed Pope & Young trophies, including a huge drop-tine buck in Pike County (Illinois) which gross scored into the 190s.

At one time, whitetail hunting experts warned against random grunting. The farther a buck is from a hunter's stand, the more likely it would circle around downwind of the stand until it detected the hunter's scent. But many of those same experts now promote the periodic calling practiced by Mark

Brad Harris convinced this buck that another buck had strayed into his territory. Grunt calls are exceptionally effective during the last stages of the pre-rut, when buck activity is often at its peak.

WHEN TO CALL

Mark Drury (M.A.D. Calls) believes in using some form of calling during every stage of the deer season, whether early, pre-rut, rut or post rut. Like most hardcore big buck hunters, Mark favors that time of the season which encompasses the week before the rut begins and right on through the height of the rut. In his opinion, this is the period during which bucks are most responsive to aggressive calling (which Mark has coined "Power

COMPLETE BOOK OF WHITETAIL HUNTING

Drury. Both David Hale and Harold Knight warn against calling to a buck when its head is up and staring in the direction of a hunter's stand. These two uncommon for a deer to bolt after halting for a second or two. In that event, you've probably helped to make the deer more difficult to call the next time.

experienced callers wait until the buck lowers its head to smell the ground or to feed, or when its attention has been directed away from the stand. Once the deer is walking purposefully toward their location, they soften the volume of their calls, or stop altogether. Once the deer is within range—especially bow range—they remain quiet. Often when they want the deer to stop for a shot, they will give one last grunt or bleat. Once the deer is within 20 or 30 yards of the stand, though, you'd better be ready to shoot. Deer know that their kind don't live in trees, and it is not

Brad Harris has discovered that a few loud grunts can help eliminate long tracking jobs once a buck has been shot with an arrow. Almost as soon as the arrow finds its mark and passes through the vitals of a buck, Brad grabs his grunt tube and begins grunting as loud as he can at the fleeing, mortally wounded whitetail. Elk bowhunters have found that a loud bugle will sometimes stop a wounded bull from crashing into a deep canyon or brush thicket where recovery is considerably more difficult. Using loud grunts on an arrowed white-tail buck seem to have almost the same

Bowhunter Steve Stoltz got the attention of this big Illinois buck by lightly rattling the tips of his antlers together. Calling experts tend to agree that hunters must watch the buck and its actions carefully in determining whether to call aggressively or conservatively.

effect. A wounded deer, upon hearing the grunts, will sometimes stop within sight of the stand. The lucky hunter can then watch the deer topple over instead of having to follow a blood trail for hundreds of yards.

Simple, one-tone grunt tubes are now practically a thing of the

past. Most of the more popular calls can be easily adjusted by moving a small rubber O-ring along the length of the reed to shorten or lengthen that part of the reed which vibrates when the call is blown. The shorter the reed, the higher pitched the call. The longer the reed, the deeper the tone to reproduce the grunts of a mature whitetail buck. The length of the tube

extension has an effect on the sound of the call as well. The longer the tube, the deeper the grunt.

The Knight & Hale "EZ Grunter" is a two-tone call that's easy to use. To produce the deeper grunts of a buck, the caller simply extends the collapsible tube and blows into the call. Inhaling produces the much higher tones of a young buck or doe grunt. To produce a fawn bleat, the reed portion of the call is slipped from the tube and adjusted to produce a much higher tone. Another multi-tone call is the Power Punch call (M.A.D. Calls), which can easily reproduce all whitetail vocalization, from the fawn bleat to the doe estrous bleat (or grunt) to the various buck grunts. The tones are changed by applying pressure to a button that causes contact with the reed. The more

COMPLETE BOOK OF WHITETAIL HUNTING

pressure applied to the button, the higher the pitch.

Nothing that's been written on the subject can teach a hunter how to make any one of the whitetail calls correctly. Videos and audio cassette tapes are among the best methods for learning how to make these sounds, either through the recorded sounds of live deer or taped calls made by experienced callers. Another way to learn is to attend a calling seminar presented by a knowledgeable hunter who has actually used calling as a technique for taking good bucks. The best way, of course, is to learn from the deer in the wild. Always listen when they are near, and store their sounds in your memory.

RATTLING

Horn rattling (or more appropriately, antler rattling) is nothing new. Hunters in whitetail lands have been doing it for years, especially in the thick brush country of central and south Texas. Whitetail hunter Murry Burnham (Marble Falls, Texas) is a legend in antler-rattling who would no more think about hunting south Texas whitetails without his rattling horns than he would without his rifle. More and more, serious big buck hunters now swear by the effectiveness of clashing a set of antlers together in order to lure a monster buck.

For years, hunters north of the Mason-Dixon line considered rattling a waste of time. Many felt that bucks simply wouldn't respond to horn rattling, primarily because of the often lopsided buck-to-doe ratio. In many parts of the Midwest, there can be as many as 10 to 20 does per mature bucks. Even knowledgeable whitetail hunters concluded that, with so many does available, bucks wouldn't respond to rattling. But not anymore. Truth is, rattling is nearly always a more productive way to call bucks where the ratio is nearly 50-50. On a number of large Texas ranches where the quality of deer is now being so closely managed, the regular (and often mandatory) harvesting of does has gotten the ratio close to the magical 1:1. With so much competition for does, bucks in that region have responded amazingly well to calling, especially rattling. In regions where the ratio is far from ideal, innovative hunters have learned that the greatest success is achieved when rattling and calling are combined. Experts like Brad Harris, Harold Knight, David Hale, Mark Drury and Stan Potts all rely on a few grunt calls mixed in with the rattle. Each has developed his own personal pattern of sorts when using the grunt tube and rattle, which indicates there really is no right way or wrong way to rattle and call. "Deer are a lot like schoolboys," claims David Hale. "When a fight breaks out, they want to watch. They want to see who the champion will be. This applies to everything from a button buck to the head honcho!"

Whenever possible, Hale like to rattle when hunting with a partner. Several days before the actual hunt, he'll hang tree stands in the area where he intends to call. Then he and his partner will slip into the area as quietly as possible. The partner will climb into the stand and David will remain on the ground (or vice versa). To David, rattling is most effective when the caller is on the ground. There he can not only clash the horns together, he can also smack the ground, rustle the leaves, and rake nearby tree trunks with antlers to simulate the other sounds made by two big bucks in battle. Also, with stands that have been carefully located, the caller can often stay hidden, whereas the hunter in the stand has a commanding view of the area. David keeps his rattling sequences short, though, and relies more on a grunt tube to bring bucks in close for a shot.

Like most whitetail hunters, David Hale often finds himself hunting alone —and not always on the ground, especially when bowhunting in heavy cover. At such times, he uses stand locations where there's little control over a buck's movement. In other words, he hunts from stands where deer have a harder time circling around downwind of his location in order to catch his scent. When hunting alone, David tries to keep his rattling sequences to less than a minute.

Rattling techniques vary greatly. Many feel that the rattling sequence should begin by first tinkling the tips of the antlers together lightly, then building up to more aggressive rattling. Others like to bring the horns together immediately with as much force as they can muster to get the attention of any buck within hearing distance. When it

comes to hunting a week or so prior to the rut and during the rut itself, I feel that a pair of 200-pound bucks will rarely "tinkle" their antler tips together. It's a question of territory. Which buck will breed the does, and who will dominate? I know that during the early bow seasons, when the rut is a month or more off, bucks will very often get into sparring matches in preparation for the oncoming breeding season. This is especially true among younger 1.5 or 2.5-year-old bucks. At such times, I'll often touch the tips of my rattling horns together lightly, hoping to catch the attention of any bucks within the vicinity of my stand.

When rattling aggressively during the rut, I'll usually hear a buck before I see it. Often the deer will come charging in, looking for a fight. Remember, this could be the dominant buck of the group, or at least one of the larger bucks who aspires to be the dominant one. When a deer hears the sounds of two other bucks fighting, it likely triggers a defense mechanism that results in running off the intruders. On the other hand, when rattling lightly during early October, or even the early November pre-rut period in the Midwest, the bucks will often come slipping in very quietly, like ghosts.

When responding to either vocal calling or rattling, the natural instinct for whitetails is to circle downwind in an attempt to smell what they hear. This is especially true in open terrain where deer can see for quite a distance. When they can't identify the deer they think

COMPLETE BOOK OF WHITETAIL HUNTING

they are hearing, they'll do their darndest to get downwind. The wise whitetail hunter will always play the air currents when hunting, and that is especially important when calling. Mark Drury, a seasoned big buck hunter with a number of impressive trophies, has duped many of them by combining rattling and grunting. Doing so, he knows, can be deadly on big bucks, especially at the beginning of the rut. The one thing he always heeds, though, is the direction of the wind.

During one bowhunt in Illinois several season back, Mark located a heavily used, narrow corridor of oaks and hardwoods near the end of a harvested cornfield. The area was laced with tracks and beaten down with trails running from one end of the field into a large tract of timber. With so many rubs and scrapes scattered along the length of this corridor, Mark knew the spot was an ideal location to take a good buck——except for one factor. The best stand locations were totally wrong for the southwesterly winds that dominated the first week of hunting. Nevertheless, Mark hung his stand and left the area alone until a high pressure front pushed in from the northwest, bringing with it northwesterly

winds and the first real chill of the bow season. It was early November and the deer were just beginning to show signs of rutting—the perfect time to rattle and call.

After climbing into the stand, Mark rattled for a few minutes, then grunted loudly on his grunt tube four or five times before settling back to watch

In wide-open country, hunters may find that some aggressive use of both rattling antlers and grunt calls are needed to get the attention of a whitetail.

John Sloan rattled in this fine Illinois buck to within easy muzzle-loader range during the mid-November peak of the rut.

Mark's stand only 11 yards away, whereupon Mark placed an arrow through the rib cage. The Pope & Young buck went less than 100 yards before it collapsed.

When calling to whitetails with either rattling antlers or vocal calls, it's usually the younger bucks who respond first. Often a big buck may be close by, but not within hearing distance. Unfortunately, the curiosity of younger bucks may take them downwind of a stand. Once alerted by the hunter's scent, the hunt will more than likely come to a halt for the time being. There's no doubt when a deer has picked up a human scent. Generally, the whitetail comes to an abrupt stop, its head immediately goes up with its nose high in the air. At that point, it's only a matter of seconds before the whitetail charges off. Stopping a buck at this point by calling it is not a good idea. Most experts feel that calling to a startled buck only tends to educate them. Instead, wait until the deer is completely out of sight, then rattle aggressively for 30 to 40 seconds, following up with a few loud grunts and wait another minute before rattling aggressively

daylight come in. He called once more at first light and had just hung up the rattling horns when he spotted a good eight-pointer working toward his stand, coming from the direction of the corn-field. Occasionally, the deer would look up, searching for the source of the rattling and grunting. The deer passed by again for about a minute. It's not uncommon for larger, more dominant bucks to chase off younger ones, and the sound of fleeing deer could actually become a productive part of a hunter's calling. On the other hand, should a dominant old doe get downwind of a hunter's location and pick up his scent, she will blow, snort, stomp her feet and raise a real ruckus, which means the hunt is probably over for the rest of the day. Every deer in the woods instinctively heeds the warnings of an older doe.

The market is filled with synthetic rattling horns, rattling bags filled with hardwood dowl rods, and other hand-operated calls that do a fair job of imitating the sounds of deer antlers clashing together. Still, most deer hunting experts—even those who work for companies that market synthetic antlers and rattling calls—tend to prefer the real thing. "Get a good set of horns that *sound* like a set of horns," says Harold Knight. Of course, he is talking about a set of horns picked up after the bucks have shed their antlers each winter. Thousands of hunters in every state now spend time afield looking for shed antlers. And while those from record book class bucks are often as highly prized as the antlers of a harvested book class buck, the small 120 to 140 class antlers can often be purchased at a reasonable price. Several can usually be found at deer classic shows and flea markets.

Nothing that's manufactured can duplicate exactly the sounds of real deer antlers. When buying a set of antlers for rattling, or choosing some from antlers you've already acquired, use only those which are sound and solid. If an antler is old and chalky looking, or covered with age cracks, it will most likely have a "dead" or dull sound. Fresh sheds—those which have been kept inside—will have a clearer, solid resonation when smacked together. Some hunters feel that by soaking older horns in water it will put new life in them. If there is any truth to this, it's at best a short term remedy. Try to use only good, solid sheds, and keep them out of the weather when not being used. With the proper care and storage, a good set of rattling horns can last up to 20 years or more.

One of my favorite set of whitetail rattling horns came from an old mule deer mount. While the mount itself was in poor condition, the horns of the 20-inch spread 4x4 were as sound as the day the deer was shot. The rack set up high, and when the bases were cut from the skull plate with a hacksaw the long lower portion of the main beam provided a nice, comfortable grip. The horns had a great sound, too. Real horns don't have to be a matched set. Some hunters even prefer using antlers from the same side, figuring they can interlock the tines better. Whether you find a matched set, or use mismatched antlers—or even antlers from the same side—it's advisable to saw off the brow tines. Otherwise, sooner or later you'll run one of these into a hand or scrape some skin from a knuckle. Either way, it can be painful. ∎

Chapter Ten

Understanding And Hunting The Rut

WITH ■ *Larry Weishuhn, Deer Biologist & Writer* ■ *Dick Idol, Whitetail Expert* ■ *Will Primos, President, Primos Game Calls* ■ *Mark Drury, President, M.A.D. Calls* ■ *Harold Knight & David Hale, Co-Founders, Knight & Hale Game Calls*

For the second day of the Kentucky deer season, things were going too slow for Harold Knight. All morning long he had heard only five or six rifle shots, far less than he should have that early in the season. He knew the woods were filled with deer hunters and that there should be much more action. Apparently the deer weren't moving as well as they should. Once, after he had climbed into his stand, a small group of deer had walked by in the dim light of pre-dawn. Otherwise, the November woods were uncommonly quiet.

Harold had chosen his stand location because of its commanding view of a small wooded valley and ridge side. He felt the area offered a natural funnel that would eventually bring deer within sight of his stand. The fact that the ground was literally covered with acorns, which he knew the deer were heavily feeding on, also played a big role in his decision to hunt this spot. Harold knew from experience that

during the peak of the rut, whitetails are usually quite active and constantly on the move. A stand location like the one he had chosen for the morning hunt afforded a good view of a well-used travel corridor. A patient hunter with the willpower to stick with his site for a long period should be rewarded with a nice buck. Fortunately, Harold's wait wasn't as long as he had feared.

The lack of whitetail movement had caused Harold to consider changing tactics. He knew the area well and where the deer normally fed and bedded. More than once he had still-hunted there trying to intercept the movements of whitetail bucks. On this particular day he was pondering where to start searching for a buck when a sudden movement along the far ridge caught his attention. Grabbing a pair of compact binoculars, Harold glassed what he'd been waiting for—a good buck. It was about 100 yards away, well within range of his scoped .30/06 rifle. But it was hidden by hundreds of limbs and tiny twigs, making it next to impossible to shoot a 150 grain bullet through the thick underbrush. He could only watch through his scope as the buck reacted to Harold's grunt tube. The buck paid no attention and kept looking in the same direction. Knight immediately filled the air with four or five short series of grunts, much louder than the first. The buck stopped abruptly, its head upright, and stared in the hunter's direction. Harold blew another short three grunt series, and suddenly the buck began trotting toward Harold's stand. Maybe this was going to be a better deer than he had thought! Now the whitetail had cleared the thick tangle of limbs, whereupon Harold slipped off the safety of his .30/06 bolt-action centerfire rifle, took aim and eased back on the trigger.

Within seconds, he had collected another trophy whitetail buck, thanks in large part to his ability to understand the whitetail's travel patterns and the patience required to stick with a stand long enough to put a good buck in his sights.

Whitetail bucks and does often spend lots of time on the move when the rut is in full swing. Being aware of this, Harold Knight had gambled the success of his mid-November rifle season on that trait. The payoff was a nice, heavy-horned 8-pointer. On the other hand, his partner, David Hale, prefers to concentrate on another trait of mature bucks: he heads for the thick cover those deer seem to prefer. "Personally, I think most hunters take the wrong approach when hunting mature bucks," Hale says, "especially when hunting the peak rut period."

Like many experienced hunters, Harold Knight knows that bucks often ignore scrapes when chasing after does during the peak of the rut, but he still likes to see them wherever he's hunting.

David feels that during the height of the rut, most does enter estrous. Too often, he explains, hunters spend too much time hunting from stands affording a long field of view. While such tactics may help the experienced hunter intercept a good buck, Hale prefers an area where he knows the bigger, older bucks hang out. "I locate these areas before the hunt and watch where the does are located," he points out. "I call these areas 'doe pockets.' I learned long ago that dominant bucks almost always do the majority of the actual breeding with the does. I have seen a dominant buck lying in his bed watching a subordinate buck chase his does. The old rascal knew the doe would never submit to a subordinate buck. I also believe a doe will gravitate to a dominant buck once she has become receptive. This is nature's way of keeping the species strong. A dominant buck knows who is king, so why should he expose himself when he doesn't have to? That's why I hunt the heaviest cover with the most does!"

David prefers to hunt the fringes of heavy cover. Years of hunting experience have taught him how hard it is to gain close proximity to a mature, dominant buck who lives in a stand of heavy cover. It's almost impossible to penetrate those big buck haunts without alerting the resident buck. When selecting a stand site, David pays special attention to the prevailing winds. Until the wind is ideal for setting up a stand, he won't start hunting. He normally uses a light, portable stand, one that enables him to

position the stand without making a commotion. He also like to make the stand as comfortable as possible, preparing for lengthy stays while hunting a mature buck. He packs in rain gear, snacks, water and a relief bottle. That way, he can spend the entire day in the stand while the rut is in full swing. At this time of the season, a hunter is as likely to see a shooter buck at noon as in the first or last light of the day.

While on his stand, David relies on two basic methods of hunting. First, he scans the hunting areas carefully with his eyes and binoculars early in the morning. If nothing is spotted, he turns to periodic "long range" calling with one of his company's grunt tubes. His calls are short but aggressive, which he feels represents the sounds of an aggressive buck tending his doe. David's favorite sequence consists of five to ten loud "grr-uuu-nnnts" in a very assertive manner. He normally grunts on the tube, waits two or three seconds, then makes several more grunts with the same short pauses between each one. One reason why this calling method works so well, David feels, is that many mature bucks have been pushed out of their favorite stands of cover. When returning to these haunts, the sound of another buck tending a doe drives the old buck out of his mind.

Larry Weishuhn, one of the world's most respected whitetail authorities, worked for many years as a biologist with the Texas Parks and Wildlife Department before becoming a consulting

COMPLETE BOOK OF WHITETAIL HUNTING

whitetail biologist for several large private Texas ranches and other privately held tracts of whitetail habitat across the South. While Larry obviously possesses the background to look at things with a scientific eye, he has also spent a lifetime studying the whitetail with a variety of firearms. "The primary purpose of the doe in the whitetail population," he insists, "is to produce fawns and thus help perpetuate the species. Most does will breed for the first time when they are about 18 to 20 months old. In some instances where doe fawns are eating highly nutritious diets, however, they will sometimes breed when they are only six months of age. On well-managed ranches where forage is plentiful, as much as 60 to 70 percent of these six-month-old fawns may have bred for the first time. Most does continue to breed and bear fawns throughout their lives."

Larry knows of one marked doe that produced fawns each year for 15 years, and another who continued to produce fawns up until the time of her death at the age of 19! It's easy to understand how one doe can be responsible for so many offspring. Then, too, each doe offspring produces fawns of her own, and they in turn produce still more. Mathematically, the number of offspring that can be credited to a single doe is astounding, adding up to hundreds of deer in short order. Hunting bucks only can throw a deer herd way out of balance and disrupt the length of the rut.

Larry has learned a great deal about whitetails from managing deer populations on large ranches surrounded by high fences. While some of these tracts covered thousands of acres, the deer were still somewhat confined and their population levels controlled. In these areas where the range of mature bucks

Whitetail expert and biologist Larry Weishuhn claims that on some Texas ranches a hunter could see 40 or more bucks during a single day while the rut is at its peak.

learned to eat all they needed under the cover of darkness. Mature buck could fulfill their breeding capacity at night as well.

On several ranches, Larry was able to study a number of bucks as they grew from fawns to maturity. Up until the time they were three year olds, they could be found and observed with ease. During the rut, these bucks chased lots of does and became quite visible. But as they approached their fourth fall season, these same bucks seemed to have completely disappeared. Despite numerous hunters on the property, once the antler development on these deer was complete and the velvet stripped off, they were not observed at all during daylight hours. The only time Larry could locate them was between the hours of 1:00 and 3:30 a.m., and then only with a spotlight.

With the permission of the local game warden, Larry spent an exorbitant amount of time late at night with a powerful spotlight trying to determine what the deer were up to under cover of darkness and during changing weather conditions. He found that about 80 percent of known mature bucks were never observed during daylight hours. Even though the hunting pressure there was

Big bucks often make small rubs, but a small buck couldn't make a rub like this. His calling card tells the hunter that a trophy lives close by.

was restricted from 1,000 up to 3,000 acres, Larry was aware that some monstrous older bucks had lived their entire lives on the property and were seldom, if ever, seen during the hunting seasons. Where younger deer were given all the feed they could handle—either through food plots or supplemental feeding with mechanical feeders—they quickly

COMPLETE BOOK OF WHITETAIL HUNTING

well regulated and kept at a minimum, Larry found that older bucks became nocturnal, moving only at night. Larry conducted his studies before cameras were available that could snap a photo each time a movement triggered the release. With such devices, researchers have since discovered just how nocturnal whitetails really are—high fences or not. Recent studies reveal that even during the rut, only 20 to 30 percent of mature bucks move during daylight. Cameras and monitors for setting along trails and travel corridors, by the way, are available to hunters who seek information about deer movement at night.

How does a hunter go after nocturnal bucks? Larry Weishuhn recommends hunting hard all day long. Frequently a buck who is primarily nocturnal will move in the middle of the day, when many hunters are back at camp complaining about the fact no whitetails were seen during the morning hunt. By the time most hunters return for an afternoon stint in their tree stands, those deer have already arrived wherever they were headed. Several season ago, I took a good 11-pointer because I happened to be in my stand at high noon. Earlier that morning, I had hunted another stand nearly a half-mile away. It was the second day of the Missouri rifle season, and only a few smaller bucks had worked through the grassy opening. I was watching them from my stand 30 feet up a big black oak. The previous morning, I had hunted a different stand, giving up on the spot about 10:30 in the morning. I returned to the same stand around 3:00 p.m. that afternoon with plans to hunt until dark. I was surprised to see a nice buck had crossed a small creek about 75 yards from where I had sat most of the morning. I knew those tracks had not been there earlier that day.

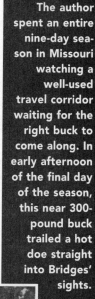

The author spent an entire nine-day season in Missouri watching a well-used travel corridor waiting for the right buck to come along. In early afternoon of the final day of the season, this near 300-pound buck trailed a hot doe straight into Bridges' sights.

Throughout the following morning, I kept thinking about that big buck who had crossed within sight of my stand the previous morning. So when I climbed down out of the big oak shortly after 10:00 a.m., it wasn't to head back to camp. Instead, I made my way back to the same stand where I'd been on opening morning, preparing to stick with it the rest of the day. Less than two hours had passed when I was shocked to see a mature 4.5-year-old buck step out into the grassy clearing less than 50 yards away. As he skirted the opposite side of the opening, I centered the crosshairs of my scope along the rear line of his front shoulder and squeezed off a shot. That big 200-pound white-tail traveled less than 50 yards before it piled up. I immediately climbed down from my stand, rolling up my sleeves prior to field dressing the buck. The time on my watch was 12:30 p.m.!

In recent years, more and more hunters are paying closer attention to the moon's phases and how they affect whitetail movement. Charts are now available which predict the times when deer are most likely to be active. Larry Weishuhn acknowledges the fact that whitetails feed according to the moon's phases and positions in the sky at certain times, and that their movements can be predicted by such charts. Larry has often hunted from daylight to dark, noting the times when deer are most active. It was amazing to him how closely the whitetail's movements coincided with the chart's predictions. On the other hand, he is quick to point out that other factors—such as changes in the weather, food supplies and hunting pressure—can alter a deer's normal movements. Deer are, after all, individuals, and there's always a rebel in every crowd who does things differently.

According to Dick Idol, during the rut—or what he calls the "breeding period"—a mature buck's travel pattern is totally unpredictable. It's the shortest of the fall periods, lasting only two weeks or less. Dick feels that the breeding period begins when the first does come into estrous, and it ends when all receptive does are bred, or when not enough breeding bucks are available to impregnate all remaining receptive does. In most northern and central portions of the whitetail's range, the rut usually begins sometime between November 6 and November 10, winding down just before Thanksgiving.

As Dick Idol explains, during this period bucks are totally preoccupied with does, specifically those receptive for breeding. Unfortunately, the bucks are next to impossible to pattern and can be found almost anywhere within their range. Sign such as rubs and scrapes, which usually enable hunters to pattern a specific buck (or class of buck) during the pre-rut or pre-breeding period, become useless when determining travel patterns. This is especially true with mature, dominant bucks. Dick says that does become the key sign at this stage of the breeding cycle. In other words, where the does are, so go the bucks.

"A buck travels from one family unit to another," Dick points out, "until he

COMPLETE BOOK OF WHITETAIL HUNTING

finds a receptive doe and a situation where his dominance level allows him to retain possession of her. If the competition level is high, the buck may lead his doe to a place where other bucks seldom travel. He will then keep her isolated for a few days until she goes out of heat. In other cases, the doe will remain on a short pattern within her family unit, dictating the pattern of travel which the buck must follow.

The more mature and dominant a buck may be, the more family units he will visit. As Dick says, the buck has been around long enough to know where more does are located. Other factors affecting a buck's travel habits during this period are the buck-to-doe ratios and deer densities. Where the number of bucks and does are in good balance, Idol feels that the mature bucks will keep on the move, visiting a number of family units in search of a doe entering estrous. Where there are many more does than bucks, or where there's a high deer density, causing family groups to stay much closer together, a buck needn't travel far, thereby reducing the amount of travel time. Because of the whitetail buck's unpredictable movements during the breeding period, Dick says this is not the time to try taking a big buck by design, but it's a great time to do so at random. During this period bucks make more mistakes and are more vulnerable than at any

When the rut kicks into high gear, bucks spend all of their time with an estrous doe—or looking for one. Where the does goes, so does the buck.

Whitetail expert Dick Idol says that the peak of the rut is an excellent opportunity to take a trophy buck like this huge Saskatchewan whitetail. He warns, though, that it is a tough time to hunt a particular buck.

wooded fencerow or a tiny clump of brush in an open field. Truly this is the big buck's greatest period of vulnerability.

Mark Drury (M.A.D. Calls) likes to bowhunt in those states—specifically Iowa and Illinois—where the general firearms seasons are scheduled following the peak of the rut. Traditionally, the first of two shotgun seasons in Illinois is scheduled for the weekend prior to Thanksgiving. Most years, this practice puts the season on the downhill side of the rut or breeding period. On the other hand, Iowa's shotgun seasons begin in early December, well after the rut has wound down. One reason why these two states produce high numbers of good bucks for bowhunters each year is because more mature, record book class bucks survive the firearms season. The reason? Because they are not hunted hard at a time when they are most vulnerable. And because Illinois and Iowa do not allow the use of centerfire rifles, bucks who cross open expanses of 200 or 300 yards from a hunter's stand are fairly safe. Even the best slug shooting shotgun with a rifled bore and scope, or a modern in-line percussion muzzleloader with a saboted handgun bullet, have

other time of the season. A buck is frequently caught outside his "core" area as he follows the travel pattern of a doe. Neither the buck nor the doe is nearly as cautious at this time as they would be when traveling alone. Experienced hunters like Dick Idol know that the breeding period is that magical time when a big buck can be spotted in an open field in mid-morning, at noon, or early afternoon. During the breeding period, many good bucks are taken by hunters who jump them from a sparsely

COMPLETE BOOK OF WHITETAIL HUNTING

a maximum effective range less than 200 yards.

The rut doesn't kick into high gear the instant the first doe comes into estrous. The first five or six days of the period represent a transition from the pre-rut, with the activity escalating as more and more does come into heat. The peak of the rut may run only three or four days, but during that period an old whitetail buck can cover a lot of territory in his attempts to tend as many does as possible. In west-central Illinois, where Mark Drury does much of his bowhunting, mid-November generally marks the peak of the rut; but it is often a week early or a week late, depending primarily on the weather. If the fall sea-son has been unusually warm, rut activity is slow to develop and reach its peak. Some whitetail experts place the peak of the rut in the middle of the breeding period. And whereas the start and the end of the rut are usually predictable within a few days, peak activity can begin at almost any time during the breeding period. "The rut can kick into full swing because of any number of occurrences," comments Mark Drury. "One of my favorites is an approaching weather front. It can act almost like a light switch, turning the activity level up to a boil!"

Mark has taken some outstanding bucks during the rut, and he's aware that often some of the best bucks move

During the peak of the rut, staying in the stand all day is often the key to success. Some of the best bucks are shot while many would-be hunters are back at camp eating lunch.

in the middle of the day. He believes in periodic non-repetitive rattling and in utilizing the grunt call during times of high movement, whether that happens at daybreak, noon, early afternoon or evening. Often during the height of the rut, more than one buck will try to tend a hot doe. In the case of high deer densities, it's not uncommon to see three or more good bucks chasing a single doe. According to Mark Drury, that's the perfect scenario for staging a mock battle with the rattling horns. Extremely aggressive clashing of antlers will often get the attention of a buck. Mark begins with an assertive banging of the antlers for 30 seconds or so. Then, after hanging them up, he gets his bow ready for action. If the rattling fails to bring a buck running, Mark turns to his grunt tube.

Will Primos (Primos Hunting Calls) is a firm believer in calling and rattling during the rut, especially during the early stags of the breeding period. Bucks will often increase their scrape activity, trying to catch the attention of does who are beginning to come into estrous. One good example of how effective hunting the early stages of the rut can be is a hunt Will made to Minnesota. He was hunting on an island in the Minnesota River one afternoon during the first week of November, which was then open to bowhunting only, and he found the area covered with bucks and buck sign. The first thing Will did was to freshen a scrape within bow range of his stand, using an estrous doe urine scent. After pouring a few drops into a pawed circle in the leaves, he placed a small amount of deer scent on an overhanging branch. He then climbed into his stand at about 2:30 and immediately began calling, using both grunts and doe bleats. About an hour later he decided to try a short rattling sequence; but just as he started to bring the rattling horns together, he spotted a buck moving directly toward his stand. He quickly chucked the antlers and picked up his bow. The nine-pointer came right to the scrape, nosed the bare earth and began pawing away some leaves that had fallen into the scrape. As the buck licked an overhanging branch, a well-placed arrow ended Will's hunt.

A week later, on another hunt in Pike County (Illinois), Will took one of his best bucks ever. It was during a bow-hunt the week before the opening of the first shotgun season, during the peak of the rut. Several times that morning, Will had rattled and grunted. He knew the rut was going full bore, so instead of rattling aggressively he did short sequences of 10 to 15 seconds, followed by a brief series of grunts. About 8:30 on the morning of November 15, Will had just completed a rattling sequence and was beginning to grunt when he spotted a buck. It came on fast and was headed straight for his stand. He got rid of the rattling antlers in a hurry, grabbed up his bow, and sent a razor-sharp tipped arrow through both lungs. The near 170 class twelve-pointer, which field dressed at more than 265 pounds, went barely 100 yards before going down.

Dick Idol has commented that hunters rely heavily on physical sign, especially rubs and scrapes, to predict the travel patterns of a whitetail buck during the rut preparation and pre-breeding periods. The sign is easier to read, since it clearly marks where the deer has been and allows the hunter to predict the likelihood of a buck's return. Even though rubs are made and scrapes are often worked during the breeding or rut period, however, Idol feels they don't indicate a buck's return with any degree of reliability. During this period, rubs and scrapes are made or worked according to the buck's present location. This, in turn, is greatly influenced by the movements of the receptive doe he is following. For all practical purposes, rubs and scrapes are now of little benefit to the hunter in his efforts to predict the travel patterns of a dominant buck.

Dick Idol notes that understanding the differences in travel patterns from the pre-breeding to the breeding period can be critical. Hunters make the most mistakes at this time of the season, he says, especially in the manner with which they approach hunting a specific area or buck. Scrapes and rubs are visible types of buck sign, and hunters rely heavily on both. Sign of this type becomes more visible during the late pre-breeding and at the outset of the breeding periods. And certain travel patterns become very obvious. Unfortunately, once a hunter has finally figured out a buck's movements, things change quickly as the rut or breeding period advances. When a buck no longer shows himself, many hunters rationalize that the ol' boy has simply become nocturnal, moving little, if at all, during daytime hours. Even though scrapes may be freshened daily, Mr. Big simply never shows. It's not uncommon for a hunter who has tracked a good scrape line diligently never to encounter a mature buck.

"Generally, when a big buck picks up the first doe off his scrape line," Dick Idol comments, "he won't frequent it

Many whitetail experts acknowledge that a hunter should pay more attention to doe areas than to scrapes during the peak of the rut. However, most will admit that it doesn't hurt to spice up fresh scrapes with some doe-in-heat urine to catch the attention of a passing buck.

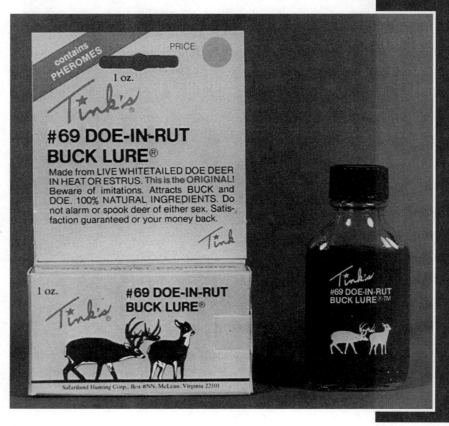

with any regularity during daylight hours for the rest of the breeding period. Instead, the more subordinate bucks—those who do not check these scrapes regularly—may now do so without fear of the dominant but absent bucks. To the casual hunter, such scrapes may appear to be worked regularly by the same buck. Here's a case where sign reading alone won't do the trick. We must know both the beginning and ending dates of this period."

Instead of relying heavily on rubs and scrapes, Dick Idol has learned to look for other sign, especially when he has spent valuable time locating and patterning a huge buck during the pre-breeding period. During the rut or breeding period, he will often spend a lot of time studying tracks. He looks for running tracks primarily, but more specifically he's searching for large and small tracks that run together, indicating what he refers to as a "heavy buck:doe interaction." To be worth anything to the hunter, such sign needs to be fresh, and it must be hunted immediately. The interaction of a dominant buck and receptive doe may be short-lived, or they may move elsewhere in a hurry, especially once the doe is no longer receptive.

Dick also tries to locate the travel routes used by bucks to move from one family unit to another. He first recognized such trails while hunting a buck in Manitoba in the mid-1980s. The area was home to some huge bucks, but overall density was low, meaning that a dominant buck often had to travel a long distance from one family unit to another looking for receptive does. A good track in the snow allowed Dick to follow several sets of tracks, until he had established a recognizable travel pattern. Certain travel routes, he found, were used only by big bucks looking for other family units. Eventually, he was able to put together a plan that enabled him to intercept buck movement. He also discovered that one of the best times to be on stand was during midday.

Larry Weishuhn, an outdoor writer and whitetail biologist, made this observation: "Years of working with whitetails has told me bucks seldom visit their scrapes during the peak of the rut. They are far too busy looking for does to spend time freshening scrapes." Larry also maintains that hunters frequently spend too much time during the peak of the rut hunting over what appear to be well-used scrapes or scrape lines. "It's easy to get suckered into hunting such a spot," he points out, "when there's so much buck sign around. I've even given into the urge."

To show how easy it is to be disappointed, Larry has shared the details of one season when, even though the sign promised a chance at a big mature buck, nothing happened. He was hunt-

ing a ranch he was managing in south Texas. A month before the rut kicked in, Larry found an extremely large, active scrape, one that was used year after year. It was located between a water hole and a feeding area that was covered with big buck tracks. When it appeared that more than one big buck was using the scrape, Larry knew immediately where he'd be hunting when the rut went full swing. "A month later, I was back at the ranch." he recalls,

The author poses with a buck he took during the height of the rut by locating his stand in a heavy deer traffic area. If you're in a good spot, sooner or later a buck will wander in.

"Based on the number of bucks observed chasing does, there was no doubt in my mind the rut was in full swing. I headed immediately for the big scrape, but without taking time to walk anywhere near it for fear of leaving my scent and changing the bucks' routines. Once I found the scrape, I set up a tree stand nearby. I crawled into the stand around lunch time and left after dark. Total number of bucks seen visiting the scrape that first day: zero!"

Larry was convinced a big buck would visit his scrape during the peak of the rut. So the next day he was back in his tree stand watching the scrape and the trails leading to it. During the entire day, he saw several small bucks up close and caught distant glimpses of mature bucks actively chasing does. Two of the younger bucks ran over the top of the scrape as they pursued does, never even acknowledging the scrape's existence. The next morning, Larry moved to a nearby hillside where he could watch over a small brushy creek bottom dotted with other scrapes. He could also keep an eye on the big scrape he had hunted for a day and a half.

At first light, Larry spotted five large bucks chasing does. One was a particularly nice 8-point, with long tines and main beams. Throughout the day, the hunter watched various bucks work the area looking for hot does. Finally, one buck, who looked about 2.5 years old, approached a scrape and sniffed the pawed out earth and the overhanging limb above it. After feeding on the branch and scraping the barren earth with both front hooves, it stepped into the scrape and urinated. Of the 27 bucks Larry Weishuhn observed during his three-day hunt, this was the only one to visit and freshen a scrape. "Hunt scrapes during the rut?" he asks, "Perhaps, but I now hunt primarily in the general area of scrapes, rather than watching the scrape itself. During the peak of the rut, scrapes simply indicate there are bucks in the area, not necessarily the best place to hunt."

Larry feels much the same about horn rattling once the rut peaks. While clashing antlers together is a great way to call in a buck during the pre-rut— or even at the beginning of the rut, when they are competing for receptive does—bucks who are busy tending does generally stay with them rather than possibly loosing a doe to another buck. According to Larry, trying to rattle up bucks during the height of the rut is a common mistake among hunters. He acknowledges, though, that just because a rut is in full swing doesn't mean that bucks no longer fight each other. He feels that bucks are more interested then in looking for does than they are for a fight. He's talking about the "peak" of the rut, not the days leading up to it or winding down, when bucks are still very competitive over receptive does. "In recent years," he remarks, "it seems the rut has spread out longer than it did years ago. Today's rut has more of a 'trickle' effect. In that case, some rattling may work well even during the peak of the rut. It might also

COMPLETE BOOK OF WHITETAIL HUNTING

explain why one day you might rattle in several bucks—and the next day fail to buy a buck with your rattling. Perhaps on those *'no show'* days, the bucks are still pursuing does."

Larry Weishuhn openly admits that one of the biggest mistakes he's made when hunting the rut has been *not* hunting all day long. "I'm a big proponent of hunting from daylight until dark," he says. "Unfortunately, I sometimes don't practice what I preach. But once the peak of the rut begins, bucks begin to move again both day and night. If you're not hunting all day long, you may miss the best opportunity to take a big buck at midday." Over the years, Larry has taken some of his biggest bucks between 10:00 a.m. and 3:00 p.m. One was a huge eight-pointer he shot in southern Texas at midday as Larry was heading to another area. He spotted the buck checking out some does, and from the outline of his rack he knew it was an impressive buck. As the deer turned and began to disappear in the brush, a shot from Weishuhn's .309 JDJ Contender handgun dropped the big buck in its tracks.

Later, on another hunt in northern Missouri, Larry was hunting with a Marlin in-line percussion .50 caliber muzzleloaders during the general firearms season. It was the second week of November and the rut was going full

tilt. His hunting partner convinced Larry to hunt a narrow brush-filled bottom located between two large harvested cornfields. The two men were prepared to hunt all day. Precisely at 11:30 a.m., a doe came running past, followed by two small bucks. Larry readied his muzzleloader just as a mature ten-pointer with eight-inch brow tines followed the same trail moments later, offering an easy shot. "Both hunts came during a full moon," he recalls. "I used to think —before I knew better—that with a full moon there was little reason to hunt

The sight of a half-dozen does wandering near the edge of heavy cover was more than this Nebraska bruiser could withstand. Tony Knight, the renowned rifle inventor, took this rutting buck with a single, well-placed shot.

except at dawn and just before dusk. That was before I began visiting deer camps as a biologist on days following a full moon night. As I drove to the various camps, I often saw lots of bucks chasing does during midday. Later, I began hunting middays during the rut, and especially following full moon nights."

During another season not long ago, Larry Weishuhn and his guide went into town after a morning of hunting in Alberta, Canada. Both men had business to take care of, and after lunch they headed back to their hunting areas. As they drove along the highway at about 12:30 p.m., Larry spotted a

doe carrying her tail at "half mast." They stopped to look, and just as the vehicle came to a stop a monstrous ten-pointer stepped out behind the doe. The buck could have easily gross scored 200 or more Boone & Crockett points. In the blink of an eye, both the buck and doe were gone. Then, a few miles down the road, Larry and his guide spotted another huge buck chasing a doe, followed by another and yet another. By the time they reached their hunting area, the midday flurry of rutting activity had ceased.

"I cannot wait to hunt Alberta again," says Larry. "But this time I will hunt all day long rather than go into town. It's

The author, after locating several scrapes nearly three weeks after the peak of the rut, managed to take this impressive buck during the "secondary rut."

been said that a wise man is one who never repeats a mistake more than once, and who learns from his mistakes. During some 40 years of deer hunting, I've made more than a fair share of mistakes. And I've learned a lot. The truth is, whitetail excite me. I suspect I'll make a few more mistakes in the future. Some I'll have made before, and some will be brand new. That's what whitetail hunting is all about. I wouldn't have it any other way!"

Years ago, I listened to another legendary whitetail hunter share some advice with a fellow hunter. He said something to this effect: "To success-fully hunt the rut, a hunter must know what the whitetails are going to do before *they* know what they're going to do." Well, that was probably 25 years ago, but only in the last decade have I come to truly understand what he was saying. The rut, or actual breed-ing period, is a complex puzzle that may be literally impossible to solve. It's a time when those cautious, secre-tive old bucks have their worlds turned upside down. The same rut-crazed antics that make these deer impossible to pattern are also what make them

so vulnerable. In the end, no one can predict where or when one of these ol' boys will show up—which probably accounts for the fact that many are taken by the most unlikely hunters in the most unlikely places.

Knowing the exact dates(s) when the rut peaks can help a hunter be certain he's where he should be. If you're an ardent bowhunter, or you happen to live where a muzzleloader or general firearms seasons are scheduled during this period, it's possible you'll be in the deer woods as the rut progresses and finally peaks. If you're not sure when the height of the breeding period is in your area, check the nearest state game department for the dates they feel rep-resent the peak in your locale. Game departments maintain accurate records of past ruts. Knowing the moon phases, the length of the days and other factors may pinpoint accurately the exact day the rut will peak. When that time comes, plan a hunt that allows you to be in your stand a day or two before. And follow the advice of the experts featured in this chapter: *hunt the whole day*. That's the formula for success when hunting the whitetail rut. ∎

Chapter Eleven

Hunting Pressured Whitetails

WITH ■ *Richard P. Smith, Whitetail Authority & Outdoor Writer* ■ *Tom Fegley, Outdoor Writer & Photographer*

The floods of 1993 that kept much of the Midwest under water for three to four months played havoc with farm crops along the river and creek bottoms. The wet weather also resulted in a bumper crop of white oak acorns, and every tract of cover I usually haunt during the northern Missouri deer seasons offered plenty of feed for the area's whitetails. With the deer concentrated in the wooded hills, it promised to be an exceptional firearms season. That was good, because I was about to play host to more than a dozen outdoor writers, editors and several hunting industry leaders for the first five days of the gun season. Prior to that, my son Adam, nephew Carl Renfrow and I had spent nearly two weeks in the deer woods, locating enough stands across some 2,000 acres where we planned to hunt. When we had finished, it was clear that with so many hunters coming into camp for the opener, we had forgotten to find stand locations for my two young

helpers. More than once, Adam and I had driven into camp on opening mornings to spot a good buck slipping out of our neighbor's 300-acre tract of timber and ease across a semi-open pasture to take cover in thick brush bordering a small creek. Now my two young hunters each grabbed a portable two-piece climbing stand and headed for the base of the wooded ridge. An hour later, both stands were in place, One was located at the end of a wooded point next to a deep brushy draw and the other was about 300 yards away, where the pasture extended up into a shallow valley that cut into the side of the ridge.

We knew that at least four or five hunters would park along a road running along the top of the ridge. Once they headed for their stands in the pre-dawn darkness of opening morning, they would more than likely push deer from the thick hardwoods. We also knew that the hunters assigned to this

COMPLETE BOOK OF WHITETAIL HUNTING

particular stand of timber tended to be impatient, often leaving their stands early in an attempt to encounter deer in the brushy hardwoods. The two stands were located ideally to intercept any bucks pushed from the area. Thankfully, this was a plan that worked.

In the first light of opening morning, nephew Carl took a shot at a nice buck but missed with his .50 caliber muzzleloader. Just as he finished reloading, he looked up to see a second buck easing down the valley and heading straight for his stand. As the deer eased past at less than 30 yards, Carl dumped the nice ten-pointer with a single, well-placed saboted bullet. It was barely 7 a.m. Less than a half-hour later, my son Adam got his chance. Shortly after he heard Carl's second shot, Adam had spotted the orange jacket of a hunter on the adjacent farm. Now the hunter slowly eased up the side of the ridge about 300 yards above and to the left of his stand. Adam was watching the hunter's progress when a flicker of movement to his right caught his attention. It was a good ten-pointer offering an easy 40-yard shot with his .54 caliber in-line percussion rifle. It was barely 8 a.m. on opening morning and already the two boys had taken respectable ten-pointers, thanks to the other hunters who had unknowingly pushed the deer straight to them.

During the late 1970s, I was fortunate enough to be drawn for a special one-day muzzleloader hunt on the Tennessee National Wildlife Refuge near the Tennessee River. I knew the area was practically overrun with whitetails, and that it would probably be a good hunt. The downside was that no one was allowed to scout the area in advance. I had on numerous occasions fished the river that borders the refuge on the west side, realizing that my best chances for success were to rush to the top of a high ridge along the opposite side of the refuge, then let the other hunters push deer toward me.

The author's son, Adam (right) and nephew Carl Renfrow took this pair of bucks less than 300 yards apart within an hour of each other on opening morning of the Missouri season. They set this up so hunters on an adjacent farm would push the deer toward them.

As soon as the gates to the refuge were opened at 4 a.m., I immediately drove to where a deep valley cut into the side of the towering hardwood ridge. My rifle was loaded, and everything I needed for a full day of hunting was stuffed into my game pouch and the pockets of my fluorescent orange upland game hunting vest. By 4:30, I was making my way up the valley toward the top of the steep ridge. Just as daylight broke, I topped out in a beautiful, open saddle. I couldn't

have found a better place to take a stand if I'd been given a week to scout the area. From high on the side of the ridge, I could observe the headlights of vehicles below as the other hunters— nearly 250 strong—drove along the only road on the refuge and parked along the way to await better light. Throughout the morning, I could hear others snapping a few percussion caps on their muzzleloaders before loading up. I was sure all that vehicle traffic and the sound of hundreds of percussion caps popping below would force deer to the top of the ridge. Fortunately, I was right.

I had barely taken a stand behind the trunk of a downed oak when several does shot past only 40 yards away. Although hunting both sexes was legal, I had promised myself to hold out for a buck until mid-morning before settling for a fat doe. For the next two hours, one doe after another traveled up the same deep valley I had used or along the top of the ridge. Finally, I spotted some antlers. A good eight-pointer was easing along the side of the ridge about 80 yards below my ground stand. As the deer stepped into a small opening, I held to the rear of the front shoulder and

smacked the buck hard with a hefty soft-lead conical bullet. The whitetail piled up only 50 yards away.

Most whitetail hunters dream about having a huge tract all to themselves. That rare kind of solitude has attracted many newcomers to bowhunting, where seasons often last two to four months long. During this period, the number of hunters is still low enough for them to hunt deer that haven't yet experienced any heavy hunting pressure. On the other hand, for those who can only spend four or five days each fall in the deer stand, an abundance of other hunters can actually be a blessing. As outdoor writer Richard Smith points out,

"Opening days of deer season are always special, whether or not a deer is tagged. Those are the days most of us wait all year for. It's a pleasure simply to be in deer country with family and friends. Besides beginning a new season, opening days are a great time to tag a deer. There are normally more whitetails shot on opening day than on any other day of the season, partly because deer and hunter numbers are often highest then."

Indeed, Smith, a 40-year veteran of the deer woods, owed his first "opening day" buck to the fact that other hunters shared the same woods. He had packed in everything he needed

It's difficult for a hunter on foot to still hunt effectively for deer that are always on guard. When approaching pockets of heavy cover that may hold deer, be prepared for a quick shot.

to spend the entire first day of the Michigan firearms season on stand. Except for sighting several does, the morning had been uneventful. Shots were heard coming from every direction, most of them far away. Richard was tempted to leave his ground level stand several times and try his hand at still hunting, but he decided to stick it out. Fortunately, another nearby hunter left his stand at noon for a lunch break. In so doing, he inadvertently pushed a nice six-pointer to Smith, who obligingly collected his first opening-day whitetail.

As Smith explains, more whitetails are harvested on opening day than on any other day of the season. In fact, in many states—including Michigan, Illinois and Missouri—about 60 percent of all the deer taken during the entire firearms season are harvested on the first day. Most hunters tend to stay on stand only until mid-morning before heading back to camp for another cup of coffee and a late breakfast, or perhaps switching to still hunting in hopes of forcing some action. The patient hunter who can remain on a well-placed stand from dawn to dusk has a much better chance of scoring than most of those who ease around on foot looking for a shot—especially those who've returned to camp to eat or catch a nap. The key is to go in prepared to spend the day. Richard learned long ago to pack a lunch before heading out to his stand. Midday can be a most productive time because so many other hunters are headed out of the woods for lunch and won't be back until early

afternoon. The hunter who remains on stand and eats his lunch there is way ahead of the game.

"My lunch usually contains plenty of snack foods, like cookies, granola bars, fruit and candy." Smith explains. "Small items can be eaten quickly without much distraction. Food is wrapped in plastic wrap. I usually cut my sandwiches in half to reduce the size of portions. I always check my surroundings carefully before eating, and I stay as alert as possible while eating. I don't want to reduce my chances of missing a deer. I minimize my movements, too. I seldom carry any liquids other than water, but a cup of hot coffee, soup or chocolate from a thermos bottle can hit the spot on a cold day."

Smith, a dedicated deer hunter, says that after waiting so long for deer season and the rut to roll around each year, he's not about to leave the woods unless it's absolutely necessary. He actually enjoys eating lunch while watching for whitetails. It allows him to maximize his hunting time, with periodic snacks often serving as a reward for sticking with the stand for another hour, and then another. "I realize it's difficult or even impossible for some hunters to remain in one place all day," he admits. "That really isn't necessary in order to take advantage of midday activity. Still-hunting can be alternated with posting (standing), as much to warm up and remain alert as anything else. Midday is also a good time to try rattling and deer calls, as long as you're not attracting the attention of other hunters to your

COMPLETE BOOK OF WHITETAIL HUNTING

location. Calling or rattling could bring a rutting buck who might otherwise have gone unseen."

WHERE DO THEY GO?

After the first few days of hunting season, whitetail that once were abundant seem to disappear—especially good bucks. Sometimes the deer woods can seem as lonely as a small town bus depot at midnight, raising the question all deer hunters ask themselves at one time or another: "Where did they go?" It doesn't take a lot of hunting pressure to make whitetails change their travel patterns or to move into less congested territory. Depending on terrain and habitat, whitetails all react differently to the sudden presence of hunters. Most changes in their patterns, for however long or short a period, are simply maneuvers to avoid being pursued by humans. Wilderness bucks may simply shift to alternate travel routes. Deer inhabiting the fringe of huge wooded areas may move back into heavy pockets of brush, or perhaps a swampy area. Whitetails living in small wood lots surrounded by huge expanses of corn may quickly take refuge in the middle of a standing field, while others who inhabit the wide open prairies of the West may take up residence in tiny secluded pockets of cover far from the creek bottom cover

they normally prefer. Whitetails react quickly to the army of orange-coated hunters who annually invade their home territory. After the first few days of the season, in fact, they may be next to impossible to find, much less get in your rifle sights.

"On Pennsylvania's opening day," writes Tom Fegely of Pennsylvania, "about 60 percent of the total harvest is taken, with another 25 to 30 percent

Steve Mullis shot this buck not far from a landowner's home in cover most hunters would pass up. Pressured whitetail will often take cover in the most unlikely places.

of all bucks tagged the following day or on two subsequent Saturdays. The sheer number of hunters in the woods account for unnatural activity as deer are pushed here and there. The quietest time in the woods occurs in the final week, when hunters must work for their venison. The smart hunter must hit new turf and shift gears as time needed to fill a tag draws to a close." Whether hunting in Pennsylvania, Missouri, North Carolina, Louisiana, or wherever, Tom suggests the following game plan as the season stretches into its final days.

SCOUT NEW COUNTRY

Late season provides little time for scouting, although searching out-of-the way places can pay dividends. Doing so, however, won't come without making sacrifices. With limited hunting time, it's hard to pass up a prime location where you may have bagged bucks on previous openers and instead set foot in unfamiliar territory, even though their locations may be only a half-mail apart. Whitetails who have found a refuge of sorts may still move around within the quiet atmosphere of their new sanctuary, leaving plenty of sign. Fegely says that tracks, droppings, upturned leaves, nipped brush and twigs, even recently scoured scrapes can alert a hunter to a deer's presence. Scouting should be undertaken with sound still-hunting tactics, which includes having your rifle ready at all times. During such late season hunts, Tom Fegely insists, the hunter who carefully and quietly eases through promising cover stands as good a chance of getting a shot as the hunter who spends the entire day perched in a tree stand.

THINK POST-RUT

According to Tom Fegely, the peak rut in Pennsylvania occurs in mid-November. Does who are not bred by then come into estrous 28 days later when the rifle seasons are approaching their end, or when special muzzleloader or archery hunts are about to start. Where the rut is still underway and the does congregate, so do the bucks. Even though the deer may have become somewhat reclusive, certain biological factors still occur, causing whitetails to seek other whitetails. Where a hunter finds abundant fresh buck sign, there's a good chance the deer will return, but perhaps not during daylight hours. The rut, combined with excessive hunting pressure, can wear an old buck down. In one Michigan study, an older, dominant buck who'd been observed chasing does hard for three or four weeks was observed spending more than two days holed up in heavy cover. The old monarch neither drank, fed or bred, even though the rut was still in full swing. Occasionally, the buck would rise, stretch, urinate, then lay back down. "The chosen recuperation site for such animals is almost always dense cover, where they can't be seen and intruders can't enter, at least not without making enough noise to alert the buck," says Tom Fegely.

I recall one hunt in northern Missouri where I could have shot a nice buck

COMPLETE BOOK OF WHITETAIL HUNTING

from the kitchen window of our camp. Shortly after daybreak on the third day of the season, I had dropped an eight-pointer, loaded it onto an ATV four-wheeler and hauled it back to camp. It was still early and I knew it would be several hours before the other men in camp returned from hunting. As I was washing the dishes left from our pre-dawn breakfast, I happened to look out the kitchen window and was shocked to see a really nice buck ease into some heavy cover less than 200 yards from the house. The deer stood there for several minutes, then bedded.

About 20 minutes later, one of the local landowners who had filled his doe tag stopped by to ask if I could help him haul the deer out of the woods. When he told me he hadn't seen a buck yet, I took him into the kitchen and pointed to the ten-pointer bedded within centerfire rifle range of the old farm house. The amazed hunter quickly got out his .270, eased around the house and walked up to a fence post about 150 yards from the buck. After peering through the scope for a long time, he squeezed off a shot. The buck struggled to its feet before a quick second shot downed the 150 class whitetail for good.

Had I not been in camp looking out that window, I doubt anyone would have seen that buck. He was bedded in some very heavy brush. When we went out to recover the deer, we found several other beds nearby which doubtless belonged to the same buck. If it hadn't been spotted from our hunting camp, it would have been virtually impossible to get close to the deer without spooking him. Moreover, an accurate shot at him as he charged through the tangle of saplings and briars would have been equally impossible. Interestingly, the man who shot the buck told me later that it had watched the hunter as he sighted in on it, but with no sign of alarm. Apparently the buck had been bedding close enough to watch the activity around our camp for several days previously.

CONDUCTING A MINI-DRIVE

Once hunting pressure has forced a whitetail to hole up in heavy cover, a lone hunter on foot will find it extremely difficult to get close enough for a well-aimed shot. During late season hunts, the combined efforts of two or more hunters are often a more productive way to bring home some last-minute venison for the freezer, and maybe even a good buck on the wall. I've found that a "two man push" is an effective way to hunt whitetails who are under pressure. This technique works best in relatively small tracts of cover, and it tends to work only when two hunters who know how to work together are involved.

The first step is to keep each other in sight while lining up on opposite sides of cover. One hunter then eases ahead 100 yards or so, then stands still while the other works up to him and passes another 50 to 100 yards closer to the deer. This process is repeated until both hunters are within shooting distance. By alternately walking and

First-time muzzzleloading hunter Deborah Bennett poses with a buck taken with her first shot on her first day of hunting, thanks to a deadly accurate modern in-line ignition muzzleloader.

stopping, a two-man push generally stands a better chance of pushing a whitetail from cover. A lone hunter will too often find himself in the middle of a heavy tangle as his prey goes busting out the other side. A whitetail can be only 50 or 60 yards away, yet remain totally out of sight. But a second hunter who waits patiently 100 yards or so up ahead obviously has the advantage. In a case involving a strip of heavy cover when more than two hunters are needed, a third person working in the center can increase the effectiveness of a push. In that case, the two outside hunters should move ahead first, then wait for the hunter in the center to move through, taking a stand 100 yards ahead. The process is repeated until the cover has been pushed to its completion.

Tom Fegely feels that one hunter who zig-zags his way through a ticket with one or two standers at ready is more likely to produce a clean shot at a buck than when a half-dozen or more drivers push through a pocket of cover.

COMPLETE BOOK OF WHITETAIL HUNTING

He also feels strongly that a late season mini-drive offers equal opportunities for both the driver and the standers. "Don't ignore those seemingly inconsequential plots that are sometimes only an acre or so in size," Fegely warns. "Often deer will be as close as 50 yards from a feeding area and, if not pushed, will stay there throughout the day. Also, when bucks become nocturnal, particularly the older and wiser ones, it takes some effort to move them. Once they've been pushed from one security area, they will slip into another."

SHIFTING GEARS

Throughout most of the U.S., hunting pressure drops off severely after the opening weekend. Other than a spurt of activity during weekends when the general gun season runs several more weeks, the number of hunters headed into the deer woods dwindles quickly as the season progresses. This is true especially during mid-week periods. While still edgy, the whitetails will, following the onslaught of opening weekend, slowly return to their normal travel and feeding routines. Still-hunting late in the season is a great way to take an end-of-the-season whitetail, especially during mid-week toward the end of the season. Tom Fegely is one of those experienced late season still hunters who hunt hard until they get their buck—or run out of time. "Those who respect the visual, auditory and olfactory abilities of whitetails," he says, "can score on late bucks by covering lots of ground—but slowly."

THINK CREATIVELY

Tom Fegely once observed: "The New York hunters who line the state border not far behind our Bradford County (Pennsylvania) hunting camp each opening day always take a buck or two, thanks to our efforts. By the time the Pennsylvania season opens, the New Yorkers have already been afield for more than a week. Deer who live on the edge of both states soon learn that things are quieter on the Pennsylvania side. But all that changes on opening day. Hunters have learned that the deer will return once they've been flushed from the brush on Pennsylvania's opener."

For several years I lived close to the Iowa/Missouri state line and was therefore able to enjoy some great deer hunting on each side. The Missouri firearms season generally opens in mid-November, but the archery season on the Iowa side lasts until the first week of December. Once the Missouri gun season opens, lots of deer scurry across the state line into Iowa, where the only pressure is from bowhunters. It's no surprise that Iowa's archers who hunt along the Missouri border will be in their stands when the lead begins to fly across the line. Once the firearms season winds down in Missouri, many of these same deer are content to stay on the Iowa side, offering some terrific bowhunting. Comes the first weekend in December and the roles are reversed, with Missouri bowhunters waiting in their stands only a mile or two from the Iowa line for a crack at a tremendous buck. ■

Dressing The Part

WITH ■ *Ronnie "Cuz" Strickland, Vice-President, Mossy Oak Camouflage* ■ *Jim Shockey, Canadian Outfitter & Writer* ■ *Kurt von Besser, President, Atsko/SNO-SEAL, Inc.* ■ *Jim Crumley, Founder, Trebark Camouflage*

Chapter Twelve

The stand location seemed ideal. A trail half as wide as an interstate highway ran the full length of a wooded valley. The lower end of the trail crossed over the property line onto another lease—near a steep, narrow point that dropped down from the ridge top. Along the spine of this point was another well-used trail. Where the two intersected seemed the best for getting a bow shot at a buck. A promising rub and scrape line dotted the length of the travel route in the valley.

A smooth-barked hickory with several large limbs 20 feet off the ground was perfectly positioned for a shot at deer on either trail, and the branches promised to offer some cover. I doubted that any deer following the valley trail could spot me, but the upper trail came down from above the height of my stand. When it reached eye level, the deer would be only 30 yards away. I knew I'd have to take extra precautions to avoid moving while deer were using the upper trail. On the other hand, a slight westerly wind was perfect for hunting at this location, so I hung my stand and climbed into it for an afternoon and early evening hunt.

By the time I settled in for the rest of the day, it was about 2 p.m. The early November afternoon was chilly, and the sun danced in and out of a thickening cloud cover. A strong weather front was supposed to push through the area the next day, and I was confident the deer would move. An hour later, a doe and two fawns passed almost directly beneath my stand, feeding on the nettles and other green growth along each side of the travel route. The deer had no idea I was anywhere in the area. Had I wanted to shoot a doe, this big, mature whitetail would have offered a beautiful shot. About a half-hour later, another doe with two fawns came browsing along the same route, but closer to the foot of the ridge. Again, they presented an easy opportunity, but not for me.

About four o'clock, a movement from above caught my attention. I watched as still another doe and pair of fawns came strolling down the upper trail. I could see for some distance, and when it was apparent that no buck was following them, I left my bow hanging from a limb and watched the deer until they were right at eye level. Suddenly, the old doe came to a screeching halt and looked right at me, looking more like an upland bird dog. I had no doubt that I'd been spotted, even though I sat perfectly still and was well-camouflaged. Even the breeze was in my favor. The doe stomped her front feet several times and moved her head back and forth, but without ever taking her eyes off me. She stomped her feet again, then turned slowly and dropped off the back side of the point. Fortunately, she never blew an alarm. A few minutes later, I spotted the doe and her fawns going around the end of the next point about 100 yards away. As they walked out of sight, the old doe stopped and glanced back in my direction.

Not 20 minutes later, a six pointer came walking down the valley, totally unaware that I'd just been discovered by the doe and that I was watching his every movement from above. I let the young

buck pass. Then, as the sun began slipping below a distant ridge, I spotted another movement coming down the upper trail. Through my compact binoculars, I saw that it was another doe and her single fawn—and following 40 or so yards behind them was a fine eight-point buck! The deer were still more than 100 yards away, so I rose up and reached for my bow. An arrow was

For long waits on stands during cold weather, hunters must dress appropriately. Experienced cold weather hunters usually rely on layered clothing.

back to the top of the ridge as well. Once there, the old doe stood and blew at me for another five minutes. Nothing else moved the rest of that memorable day.

That incident took place more than 25 years ago, and ever since I've thought about that day, especially while sitting in a tree stand waiting for whitetails to come along. Then, sometime in the 1980s, I began researching the eyesight of whitetails, reading about ultraviolet light and how special brighteners used in some material dyes and laundry detergents could make even a camouflaged hunter glow like a neon sign. Only then did it dawn on me how easily those two does had spotted me, despite a wind in my favor, my camouflaged face, body, hands—even my portable stand. I've always been conscious about scent and have taken precautions to be as scent-free as possible. My mother got a big kick out of her 15-year-old son washing his hunting clothes with his own unscented detergent. What I didn't know was that detergent makers still use ultraviolet brighteners to make washed clothes look as clean as possible. Kurt von Besser (president of Atsko/SNO-SEAS, Inc.) has built a business

already on the rest, so all I had to do was ease my mechanical release onto the string. I stood ready and the deer kept coming, until the doe and I were at eye level. Just as the previous doe had done, she came to a dead stop and looked straight at me. She stomped her feet and did the same little trick with her head. I guessed she was trying to get me to move. But as she left, she let out a few loud snorts and ran back up the point. The buck scurried around products that neutralize and eliminate these brighteners from hunting clothes. When he first started making claims about how deer see things much differently than humans, von Besser's opinions were met with considerable opposition. Now, most of what he was telling us hunters more than a decade ago has been confirmed by scientific research. Following is an excerpt from Kurt von Besser's book titled, *How Game Animals See & Smell:*

expensive camo outfits, but unless modern camouflage clothing is treated to neutralize the ultraviolet brighteners found in today's clothing dyes, then washed in detergents *without* ultraviolet brighteners, a hunter might as well hunt in a pair of blue jeans and a light colored T-shirt. What appears to our eyes as camouflage can reflect enough ultraviolet light to literally glow in the eyes of a whitetail.

The debate still goes on whether or not deer actually do see hunters as

All aspects of vision depend ultimately on the absorption of light by photopigments. The retinas of white-tailed deer (Odocoileus virginianus), like those of other ungulates, contain a mixture of rod and cone photoreceptors. We have used a noninvasive electrophysiological technique to measure the spectral absorption properties of the photopigments contained in these receptors. In this procedure, electroretinogram (ERG) flicker photometry, light-evoked potentials were sensed by a contact-lens electrode positioned on the eye of an anesthetized deer. The eye was stimulated with a rapidly-pulsed, monochromatic light; variations in pulse rate, stimulus wavelength and adaptation state of the eye allowed preferential access to signals from different classes of photoreceptor. Recordings were obtained from nine white-tailed deer. Three classes of photopigment were detected. One of these is the photopigment contained in the rods; it has a peak sensitivity of about 496nm, a value greatly similar to that found for rod photopigments of other mammals. These measurements also reveal the presence of two classes of cone. One contains a photopigment maximally sensitive in the middle wavelengths (peak value of c. 537 nm); the other cone has a sensitivity peak in the short wavelengths, at about 455 nm. In light of what is known about the relationships between photopigments and vision in other species, these results suggest two likely characteristics of cone-based (i.e. daylight) vision in deer: (1) deer should be relatively less sensitive to long-wavelength lights than many other mammals (e.g. humans) and (2) white-tailed deer would be expected to have dichromatic color vision

What does all this technical jargon mean to the modern whitetail hunter? Primarily, it means that white-tailed deer see things differently than humans. The intricate camouflage patterns found on our hunting clothing now may appeal to our eyes and cause us to purchase

glowing "radioactive" men. I believe that the eyesight of a whitetail is far superior to ours, especially in light gathering, which may include better perception of ultraviolet light. One thing is certain: deer have much better night vision than do humans, in fact,

they appear able to see most everything at times when we hunters can barely make our way through dark woods or down a field road. The next time you see a whitetail's eyes reflect in the headlights of your car, think about why their eyes "shine" and yours don't. The human eye doesn't shine because once light passes through the retina, it is absorbed at the back of the eye. The much larger eye of a deer, however, receives more light than a human eye, including ultraviolet light. This light reception activates the many rods found in a whitetail's eye. Instead of being absorbed at the back of the eye,

the way they are among humans, a special lining called "tapetum" at the rear of a deer's eye recycles the light back through the eye, reactivating photoreceptors many fold. Not only does this result in light reflection, as when a deer looks into the headlights of an oncoming vehicle; it also means that deer have the ability to see far better in low light situations than we do. Their ultraviolet light reception also means that light reflected by the dyes and brighteners of a hunter's clothing can make a hunter visible at all times, whether he's wearing camouflaged clothing or not.

Kurt von Besser's company and several others now market a variety of so-called "U-V eliminators" which are sprayed onto camouflaged clothing, making even fluorescent orange clothing become less visible to deer. Without ultraviolet brighteners to give away a hunter's presence, this brightly-colored cloth (in a human's eye) takes on a yellowish dichromatic tinge in the eye of a whitetail. When wearing blaze orange outerwear that has been treated to eliminate ultraviolet brighteners, a hunter remains visible to other hunters, but in the whitetail's eyes he blends in better with the natural surroundings.

For years, another controversy has stemmed from the use of camouflage made of broken splotches of fluorescent oranges, yellows and greens mixed with blacks and browns. Hunters dressed from head to toe in such camouflage become just as invisible to whitetails as a hunter adorned in the more traditional camouflage of tan, brown, green, gray and black. In other words, these are shades which, to our eye, blend because they are the colors we see when we look at the trunk of a tree, a stand of tall grasses, or a leaf-covered ground.

Hunters have resisted brightly colored camouflage because they feel it makes them stand out. And it does— but only to other hunters, not the deer. On the other hand, game departments have been slow in allowing the use of fluorescent-colored camouflage during the general firearms and muzzleloader seasons. The broken pattern, it was felt,

would make hunters who are fully dressed in such camouflage less visible to other hunters. In reality, a hunter who's dressed in a fluorescent camo outfit is wearing more highly visible colors than a hunter who meets the minimum requirement by wearing a fluorescent vest.

In my part of the country, it's nearly impossible to walk into a small town restaurant at 10:30 a.m. from early October to mid-November without finding at least several bowhunters decked out in one of the latest camouflage patterns. The camouflage industry has indeed become a major part of the hunter's marketplace. A Virginian named Jim Crumley revolutionized the concept of camouflage soon after his graduation from college in the early 1970s. Prior to his introduction of a pattern now widely known as "Trebark," hunters who wanted to break up their outline were forced to hunt with patterns developed for the military. For several seasons I wore the "Tiger Stripe" camouflage worn extensively in Vietnam and quickly became one of Jim Crumley's earliest and best customers.

Jim Crumley

Primarily an archer, Jim Crumley comments, "Camouflage clothing is very important for bowhunting and probably not as important for long range rifle hunting. For a close encounter sport like bowhunting, ridding yourself of a distinct human outline and blending right into your background is extremely important. Camouflage patterns should closely match the surrounding terrain and foliage. Mixing different camo patterns from top to bottom can be a very effective way to do that. However, in the final analysis, the best camo is *Being Still* and learning to move slowly when in a tree stand." His original "Trebark" pattern was a simple pattern which, as the name implies, closely resembled the bark of an oak. The camouflage was made up of varying shades of grays and browns, with a distinct black border around the edges of each piece of bark.

The "Trebark Superflage" now available is an entirely new breed of camouflage. The pattern looks more realistic, and there's better shading of the various hues of grays and browns. The pattern is highlighted with realistic brown and light green leaves closely duplicating the actual size of oak leaves. This new pattern further breaks up the human form with bold images of limbs and branches running both horizontally and vertically. Bill Jordan's "Realtree

COMPLETE BOOK OF WHITETAIL HUNTING

X-tra Gray," "X-tra Brown" and "Advantage" patterns are quite similar in appearance, as is Toxey Haas' "Mossy Oak Treestand" pattern. Some of the later "Mossy Oak" camouflages have gotten away from the distinct lines of tree bark, limbs, branches and leaves. Instead, they are now made up of splotches of browns and grays, with some black to add to the break-up effect.

Actually, camouflage has to fill an almost impossible requirement. An effective pattern must be bold enough to break up the outline of a hunter, yet blend with the natural surroundings so as not to stand out. Some camouflage patterns introduced in recent years seem to have been designed more to attract the hunter's eye than to do the job necessary in the deer woods. In other words, camouflage designers seem more interested in making their patterns "pretty" rather than hiding the hunter effectively.

During one turkey season in the late 1980s, I was hunting in southern Missouri with three other outdoor writers—Jim Zumbo, Tom McIntyre and Wade Bourne. I had dropped Jim and Wade off at different locations and took Tom with me. After several gobblers had totally ignored our calling and

taken us on a merry chase across some rough country, Tom and I returned to where we had left Wade and waited for him to return. Soon Tom motioned across the field and commented, "Here comes Wade now."

I did see someone walking in our direction, but I knew it wasn't Wade because he had been wearing a

Realtree camouflage designer Bill Jordan has devoted years of study and research to making patterns more three-dimensional and more naturally toned.

camouflage outfit. The hunter headed in our direction appeared to be wearing olive drab clothing. At about 100 yards, however, I realized it was Wade after all, but I still couldn't recognize his camouflage pattern until he was only 50 yards away. He might just as well have been wearing olive drab army surplus fatigues.

A lesser known camouflage now on the market is sold under the brand name "A.S.A.T" designed by bow-hunter Jim Barnhart. Instead of trying to duplicate bark, leaves or branches, this pattern features a random overlay of bold, elliptical black and brown slashes printed on a light khaki or tan material. The result is a camouflage pattern that takes on an almost three-dimensional effect. In my opinion it does a better job of breaking up a hunter's outline than any camouflage I've ever worn. One reason why the pattern hasn't been as successful as other, better known products is that it simply isn't as pretty when hanging on a dealer's rack. When it comes to buying camouflage, hunters are often drawn to a more sophisticated, aesthetically appealing pattern rather than one that may not be as nice to look at but is more effective in the deer woods.

Another promising camouflage pattern is "Timberghost," designed by Missourian Kevin Carlile. I was fortunate enough to see early examples of this camouflage in the late 1980s. Kevin had shown me several samples and I was impressed with how realistically the camo resembled the coloring and shading of oak bark. It's only drawback was a lack of boldness. When viewed from a distance, this camouflage looked like a solid, dark gray blotch. I convinced Kevin to make the grain of his pattern larger, which he did. "Timberghost" now ranks among the great camouflages, one that accomplishes what camo is supposed to do: hide the hunter from the sharp eyes of deer and other game.

Since whitetails are hunted throughout the U.S. and across Canada, hunters heading out for the woods during the various seasons must contend with a wide range of weather conditions and temperatures. Even in west-central Illinois where I live, the opener of bow season in early October may involve hunting in 80-degree weather. Fortunately, clothing manufacturers now offer a wide range of camouflaged hunting wear made from extremely light materials designed especially for such warm weather hunting conditions.

During extremely warm weather—especially when there hasn't yet been a cold snap to get rid of the mosquitoes—I've worn the breathable, mesh-type camouflaged tops such as Bug Tamer (Shannon Outdoors, Inc., Louisville, GA) and Bug-Out Outdoor Wear, Inc. (Centerville, IA). These outfits are made mostly from camouflaged "no-see-um"-type meshes that are typically worn over light camo pants and a T-shirt.

Modern thermal insulations provide exceptional warmth without adding cumbersome weight.

clothing. It could be one of the better investments a hunter could ever make.

What about the general firearms seasons, late muzzleloader hunts, or the tail end of the bow season when temperatures reach sub-zero and stay there? Believe it or not, some successful whitetail hunters actually prefer these frigid temperatures over warmer weather, but they've learned how to dress properly for conditions that would force many hunters out of their stands and back to camp to thaw out in front of a stove. Jim Crumley recalls, "Where I grew up, in southwest Virginia, in the '50s, we did not have a deer season. My hunting was limited to small game, upland birds and waterfowl. My first deer hunt didn't happen until I was in college. I thought I was going to freeze to death, and I never saw a deer. I wondered if deer hunting was really all that enjoyable."

The mesh allows the undergarments to breath. In extremely hot weather, the air circulation allows perspiration to evaporate. Some outer clothing of this type consists of two layers of fine mesh, which protects against mosquito bites even better. Those who hunt where mosquitoes or black flies abound should definitely wear this type of mesh

Fortunately, the hunter in Crumley kept him in the game, and he took his first whitetail the year after graduating from college. He remembers that it was a bitterly cold November day. He was carrying his dad's old Winchester .30-30 lever action with open sights. Late in

COMPLETE BOOK OF WHITETAIL HUNTING

the afternoon, a six-pointer came out of a thicket with four does about 75 yards away. Jim took aim, but before he could squeeze off a shot he suffered symptoms of buck fever. He shook all over, his eyes watered and his sight blurred, but finally he got the sight picture he wanted and pulled the trigger. The deer was hit high in the spine and fell. Elated, Jim spent the next two hours dragging that deer back to the truck. By the time he reached the vehicle he was completely encrusted in frost from his own perspiration.

Since those days, Jim has learned how to dress and stay comfortable for those long waits in the stand on cold days. When dressing for extreme cold weather hunting, when temperatures are below zero, he's a firm believer in the layering technique. This is especially true for bowhunting, which doesn't lend itself well to wearing big, bulky insulated coats. Jim often relies on as many as three or four layers of Thermax uppers and bottoms, then pants and shirt. He usually wears a kidney-type belt with pockets for the disposable granular-type

Good camouflages, like Mossy Oak's Fall Foliage, do a great job of duplicating the natural tones and shades of a hunter's surroundings.

Cold weather wear like this insulated jacket and bib from Mossy Oak make it easier to withstand those cold temperatures when whitetails often move the best.

heat packets. Over this he slips on either a heavy pile Polar Fleece or wool top and bottom. When temperatures and wind chills hit the minus side of zero, Jim often wears a GoreTex camouflaged outer garment, which helps hold in heat while at the same time forming a wind breaker. He's a firm believer in using disposable heater packets for

hands, the toes of his boots, and the back of his neck. He has learned that if you want to take a good whitetail, you have to be in the stand. And to stay in the stand for any length of time during frigid temperatures, you have to stay warm.

Ronnie Strickland

Ronnie "Cuz" Strickland of Mossy Oak Camouflage (Haas Outdoors, Inc., West Point, MS) is an ardent hunter with bow, muzzleloader or rifle, but most days he sits in a stand behind a camera producing outdoor TV shows. He does this day in and day out from late September through January in every weather condition and geographical location throughout the U.S. It should come as no surprise that he has learned how to dress for the weather. "I love the cold weather." He exclaims. "Filming for over a decade has taught me how to dress for long sits. I start with thermal underwear, top and bottom. Over this goes a heavy sweatshirt and matching sweatpants, then ten-ounce chamois pants and chamois jacket.

For an outer layer, I slip on an insulated fleece bib and insulated fleece jacket. Lined fleece is one of the best wind stoppers there is for the money. My cold weather boots are heavy, lined icebreaker-type boots rated down to -50 degrees or colder. They're not great for walking but are ideal for long sits in a tree stand. I wear several layers of socks, preferably something loose fitting for better blood circulation in the feet. Last, but not least, I wear a fleece neck gator and a heavy insulated pull-over sock hat. And because I have to run the camera when some deer show up, I wear thin cotton gloves, but I keep my hand tucked into a hand warmer pouch that fits around my waist."

One of the toughest whitetail hunters I know is a good friend and fellow outdoor writer, Jim Shockey, who also happens to be a big game outfitter in Canada. When Jim heads out for a long day's wait at his favorite stand, he resembles a gold prospector headed out of Skagway into the Klondike with a year's supplies on his back. Jim likes to hunt the harshest weather Saskatchewan can dish out, and he knows how to pack in enough cold weather wear to spend the day in the stand in comfort. Often his pack frame is loaded with 60 to 70

Canadian outfitter and outdoor writer Jim Shockey chases trophy whitetail bucks during some of the toughest weather of the season. He keeps warm by dressing in lots of layers.

pounds of additional clothing and other gear. That way, he can sit from daylight 'til dark, even when the temperature has plummeted to -40 degrees. "If you hunt in extreme, bitter cold, where icicles hang from your beard," Jim advises, "you should think about getting some hi-tech outerwear from Northern Outfitters (Orem, Utah). This stuff has been designed and built for guys who live outdoors during extended expeditions. It's not cheap, but it's the best."

The clothing Jim refers to features the latest layering technology, including the finest warmth-retaining insulators and wind-stopping outer shell materials to ensure maximum comfort, even if the wind chill factor is -60 degrees or below. Northern Outfitters uses what they refer to as Vactrex, or "Vapor

COMPLETE BOOK OF WHITETAIL HUNTING

Attenuating & Expelling, Thermal Retaining" insulation. It was developed by leading experts in moisture condensation, nucleation and capillary theory. "It sounds extremely technical—and it is." Jim Shockey says. "But I wouldn't head out on a late November Saskatchewan big buck hunt without it!"

Personally, I prefer a combination of modern materials and the deer hunters old favorite—wool. When the temperatures drop to the minus side of zero, I slip on several layers of Thermax or other polypropylene-type thermal underwear. Over this, I wear a pair of heavy, insulated sweat pants and a wool sweater. Over the sweat pants I put on a pair of heavy wool pants and jacket, like those made by Woolrich or C.C. Filson (I like the heavy wool Filson jackets). When dressed accordingly, with a wool/polyester blend stocking cap and fleece hood, I can sit for hours without discomfort. As for footwear, I prefer the 1000 gram Thinsulate leather boots, such as the Ultimate Hunting Boot produced by Georgia Boot Company (Franklin, TN). With several pair of hi-tech insulated socks, these leather boots keep my feet warm no matter how cold it gets. They're also much easier to walk in than the heavy felt insulated Sorel-type boots.

When there's a long walk to the stand. I often wear a light fleece jacket and pants over undergarments, packing heavier wool garments in a large day pack. Once I've reached my stand, I slip out of the fleece and into the woolies. During those late muzzleloader hunts that stretch into early January, I rely on a unique piece of cold weather gear known as the "Heater Suit." It's like a sleeping bag with legs and feet, no arms and a zipper that works from the inside. First I slip on the insulated booties that came with the suit over my boots, step into the suit, strap an internal harness across my chest, and zip up the front. When a deer comes along, I quietly unzip the front from the inside, whereupon the "Heater Suit" opens like a clamshell. The harness prevents it from dropping down around my feet. Even when wearing moderately insulated clothing, this piece of cold weather wear will keep a hunter warm while other hunters are freezing. The whole thing rolls easily into what looks like a bed roll with shoulder straps.

During one cold day during Iowa's muzzleloading season, I discovered that I could stay out all day when tucked away in a "Heater Suit." While hunting one morning, it began to snow, even though temperatures were right at -20 degrees. Inside my insulated cocoon I was warm and comfortable, in fact, I was so warm and comfortable that I fell asleep. My head was protected from the cold with a wool watch cap and fleece hood, with only my eyes exposed. A week of hard hunting in the bitter cold temperatures had left me exhausted, and the minute I shut my eyes, I began to dream about big bucks. About an hour later, I opened my eyes to find four inches of snow had covered me, while less than 10 yards away stood a big doe eyeing me with a mixture of curiosity and fear. ∎

Chapter Thirteen

Places To Go For Great Deer Hunting

WITH ■ *Dick Idol, Whitetail Expert* ■ *Ronnie "Cuz" Strickland, Vice President, Mossy Oak Camouflage* ■ *Mark Drury, President, M.A.D. Calls* ■ *Larry Weishuhn, Whitetail Biologist & Writer* ■ *Tom McIntyre, Outdoor Writer & Photographer* ■ *Ted Schumacher, Lone Wolf Outfitters* ■ *Jim Shockey, Canadian Outfitter & Writer*

For whitetail hunters, these are indeed the good old days. Some reliable sources claim there are now more deer in North America than when the pilgrims stepped ashore at Plymouth Rock in 1620. We owe this abundance of deer to farming practices that provide such outstanding food sources for deer, with enough cover left over. Hence, the whitetail's amazing ability to adapt to human encroachment, and the millions of sportsmen who see to it that professional deer management throughout the U.S. receives the financial support needed to provide a maximum of recreational hunting opportunities.

The fact is, today's whitetail hunter, no matter where he hunts, now enjoys hunting this great game animal as much, if not more, than was the case 30 years ago. Even so, there still exist numerous areas that are noted for producing excellent opportunities at large numbers of bucks. These include some very special locations where bucks are available in both quantity and quality, the kinds of places where an addicted whitetail hunter's dreams come true.

To begin, there are several states that now boast whitetail populations approaching or exceeding a million deer. Texas alone is home supposedly to more than three million deer, and Alabama claims a deer herd in excess of two million, with Michigan not far behind. Farm states like Iowa and Illinois are home for an unbelievable number of whitetails, producing more and more exceptional bucks each fall. And then there are the "sleepers"— big buck areas that are beginning to produce exceptional whitetail hunting, especially the river drainages of Nebraska and the grassy creek meadows of northeastern Wyoming.

Just because a state—or even an area within a state—boasts a tremendous number of whitetails, it doesn't necessarily mean that a hunter can locate a hot spot and go back home with a monster buck lying in the back of the pickup truck. No matter where one hunts whitetails, they are still wild and running free. Big, older bucks, which are usually the true trophy class animals, are still not pushovers. I know one highly respected outdoor writer who devotes a lot of his time to researching and studying about whitetails. And yet, after spending the better part of a week hunting with a fenced hunting operation in Michigan filled with stocked Boone & Crockett class bucks, he still went home empty-handed. Mature bucks (4.5 years and older) seem to have a survival instinct that makes them next to impossible to find and kill.

Alabama is known for its long, liberal whitetail seasons. The gun season there is nearly three months long, with a legal limit of one buck per day. Even so, the deer herd in that state has reached troublesome proportions. Ronnie "Cuz" Strickland (Moss Oak Camouflage and Haas Outdoors Company and producer of the "Mossy Oak's Hunting The Country" TV show) spends a considerable amount of time in a tree stand each fall. Most of the time Ronnie runs his video camera, taping hunts for his television show. For him, success depends on working where there are enough deer worth hunting in that particular habitat. Ronnie feels that, because of the extremely dense cover where most of Alabama's bulging whitetail population is so thick, spotting deer even during daylight hours is next to impossible. Even though the state is

home to the greatest whitetail density (deer per square mile) of any state, this whitetail hunter (who spends close to three months each fall in a tree stand) claims that Alabama and other southern states with similar habitat are among the toughest places to get off a shot at a good whitetail buck. As Ronnie points out: "I think any whitetails are easier to hunt than the ones in the South. In most deep southern states, the rut is so drawn out that getting big bucks to show themselves is tough. And the cover is much thicker—with more of it. Deer can move, feed, breed, and go about their daily lives in tight places and never expose themselves. Also, there seems to be a greater ratio of does to bucks in the South, which increases your chances of being spotted or scented. Too many sharp eyes and sensitive noses!"

When looking for a successful hunt and taping session, Ronnie likes Illinois, Iowa, Missouri and Kansas in particular. For the serious-minded trophy hunters, these states offer some of the best opportunities. He acknowledges that, at least in those areas, the bucks tend to rut hard for a week or two each November. Then, just before and during the peak of the primary rut, they often become quite visible, including some otherwise reclusive monster bucks. Ronnie Strickland suggests also that hunters who are looking for respectable 140 to 160 class whitetails should consider eastern Idaho, especially the east central region. The herd is beginning to grow there, with

the potential for some "book class" bucks down the road. Apparently the locals are too busy chasing mule deer and elk to hunt the lowly whitetail. Too bad.

My good friend and frequent hunting partner, outfitter Ted Schumacher (Buffalo, Wyoming), claims some excellent whitetail hunting in his area that goes virtually untouched. Almost every creek drainage found on the nearly 80,000 acres he controls is filled with whitetails. Of the 60 or so deer hunters whom Ted books each fall, most prefer

to hunt in the areas just north and east of Buffalo, near Gillette, and the upper northeast corner of Wyoming, where few are interested in hunting whitetails. Even hunters from states like Pennsyl-vania—where tagging a buck with an 18-inch inside spread is tantamount to shooting the whitetail of a life-time—will pass on good upper 150 and 160 class whitetails and settle instead for a so-so 4x4 mulie.

During several fall seasons, I've taken the mandatory guide test and received a Wyoming guide license. That

When hanging a tag on a trophy class whitetail,, don't overlook western states ike Wyoming, Idaho or Montana. Will Primos, of Primos Hunting Calls, took this fine ten-pointer during a muzzleloader hunt in Idaho.

enables me to work with Ted during the month of October, when he conducts the most of his deer hunts. I recall one group of four eastern hunters in particular who came in during the second week of the season. They had driven out in their own motor home and were looking for a remote camp. As I was driving them to one of Ted's leases, I spotted three good 24 or 26-inch mule deer bucks bedded along a deep drainage ditch. Since the season was open, I pointed out the deer, explaining that they were welcome to tag one of the deer. Three of the four hunters immediately grabbed their rifles, made a 100-yard stalk, and dropped the three bucks before they could get out of their beds.

Later that evening, I took the fourth hunter down to a secluded hay field that bordered a large creek. Earlier, I had spotted a couple of mulie bucks in the 28-inch class there and felt we had an honest chance at taking one. As darkness approached, a handsome 160 class ten-point whitetail waltzed out into the field not 70 yards from where we sat. The hunter's tag was good for either mule deer or whitetails, but there was no way I could get him to shoot the buck. Even though he had never seen a whitetail that large in his life, he had

made the trip to Wyoming to shoot a mule deer and wasn't about to go home with a whitetail. Several days later, he happily settled for a 24-inch 4x4 mule deer buck. After the group had left, I returned to the hay field several times to see if I could stick my open deer tag on that same whitetail. Believe it or not, the big buck showed up on the fourth evening and I dropped it with my .50 caliber in-line muzzleloader.

Bucks abound on Anticosti Island, but don't go there looking for a wide-racked, heavy-horned Boone & Crockett class whitetail. This one is typical of the eight-pointer taken on the island (Thomas McIntyre photo)

"The hunters who come here to hunt whitetails almost always take good bucks averaging in the upper 140s or lower 150s," Ted Schumacher told me. "The deer are here, and the hunter who is willing to spend all of his time in whitetail country, instead of glassing the rougher country for mule deer, will very often see some excellent bucks. A lot of them show up in places most eastern whitetail hunters refuse to accept, such as junk yards, abandoned feed lots, outbuildings, even places inside the city limits of some small towns within my hunting area."

Another great place offering high success rates is Anticosti Island, which sits at the mouth of the St. Lawrence River near mainland Quebec. Hunters here are allowed to harvest two deer, and the success rate averages 1.8 deer per hunter each season. But if you're looking for a huge, record book class whitetail, Anticosti Island is not the place. If you simply want to enjoy fantastic hunting with lots of deer, however, you won't find a better place to go. "Anticosti is great, it really is!" exclaims Tom McIntyre, a noted magazine and book author. He has hunted the island several times. During one September hunt, Tom and his guide used "spot and stalk" tactics. Each day they covered a great deal of ground, often walking five or six miles of trails as they glassed the numerous grassy meadows that dotted the heavy spruce and fir growth. He recalls that deer were literally everywhere—and there

should be. This 3,067 square-mile island is home to more than 100,000 whitetails, or more than 30 deer per square mile.

Whitetails are not native to Anticosti. The deer were originally released on the island by a landowner who once lay claim to the entire island. From the original 220 deer he released in 1895, the herd grew quickly. Within 30 years, the whitetail population reached its maximum saturation level, where it has remained ever since. The bucks harvested there are healthy deer who field-dress at 160 to 190 pounds, with the vast majority of bucks harvested being eight-pointers—an Anticosti Island trait.

The island itself has a limestone base, covered with rich soils. The browse found on the island consists mainly of lush, high protein grasses, forbs and a variety of low bush shrubbery. What you won't find on this secluded whitetail hot spot are stands of oaks and other hardwoods, the kind that provide a mast crop, or farmed agricultural lands for the deer to feed on. Thus, the whitetail receive all the nutrients they need from browsing on native grasses and underbrush. At 2.5 years, Anticosti bucks commonly sport nice eight-point racks with 15- to 17-inch spreads. By the time they reach 4.5 or 5.5, they may have added an inch or two to their spread, and grown a rack with noticeably more mass. But the vast majority are still eight-pointers. Tom McIntyre refers to them as "pretty deer"—and they are. Anticosti Island bucks have almost developed a distinct look all their own. Could it be

COMPLETE BOOK OF WHITETAIL HUNTING

Often the memory of a unique hunting experience is what makes a hunt great. On Anticosti Island hunters usually spot and stalk their bucks, something most whitetail hunters rarely experience. (Thomas McIntyre photo)

that in less than a century these white-tails have evolved into their own distinct sub-species?

A number of lodges and guide services are available on Anticosti Island. Rates vary considerably, depending on the lodging, services and meals provided. Hunts are generally five-day affairs, which can run (in 2000) anywhere from slightly over $1,000 to more than $2,000. But on this island deer hunting paradise, everyone goes home with a buck. Deer hunters looking for this unique whitetail hunt should contact Tourism Quebec, 800 Place Victoria, Suite 260, Montreal, QC Canada H4Z 1C3 for the addresses and phone numbers of outfitters on the island. Those who are truly interested in taking a good Anticosti buck should get involved during the earliest hunts in September or during the rut in mid-November. Deer that have not been hunted for more than 10 months show little fear of humans; in fact, they will often stand and watch an approaching hunter. By the end of September, though, good bucks understand they are being hunted and become somewhat more reclusive. But once the rut kicks in, it's an entirely different scene, with bucks chasing does almost constantly, and becoming quite visible.

Tom McIntyre's September hunt on Anticosti rewarded him with a beautiful velvet-covered eight-pointer. Since he knew he would be faced with day-long hikes across the gently rolling terrain, he packed a lightweight .30/06 bolt-action rifle built by Ultra Light Arms.

With a full magazine of 150 grain cartridges, bases, rings and 6x Leupold scope, Tom's rig weighed in at about 8 pounds, which proved ideal for the 100-yard shot he needed to drop his buck. He hunted with Cerf-Sau Lodge, 6145 43rd Avenue, Montreal, Quebec, Canada HIT 2R3, which he highly recommends as a first-class outfitter.

THE GREAT MIDWEST

For Mark Drury, president of M.A.D. Calls and producer of outdoor videos, the Midwest is his favorite whitetail hunting hot spot. Iowa and Illinois, in particular, offer today's trophy-minded hunter the best chance at taking a bragging-sized whitetail buck. He credits that conviction to the following:

1 Both Iowa and Illinois schedule their general firearms seasons after the height of the rut. This allows the whitetails to breed with a minimum amount of hunting pressure. In both states, the archery season is open during the rut and pre-rut, giving bowhunters a great opportunity to go after monster bucks that haven't yet been pressured by gun hunters. That explains why each fall a number of high scoring Boone & Crockett whitetails are taken by bowhunters.

2 Both Iowa and Illinois are "shotgun" states, which means they don't allow hunters to use long range centerfire rifles during the general firearms season. In each case, gun-toting whitetail hunters must pack either a shotgun loaded with slugs or a muzzleloading rifle. To capitalize on shots at big bucks out to 100 yards, more and more Midwestern hunters now turn to scoped modern in-line ignition muzzleloaders in lieu of a shotgun with slugs. Even in the hands of a truly good shot, though, the most advanced in-line muzzleloader or rifled slug-shooting shotgun has a maximum effective range of about 150 yards.

Mark Drury feels that the two factors outlined above allow more mature bucks to reach old age and develop some impressive boney head gear. Illinois and Iowa now produce a number of high-scoring Boone & Crockett bucks every year. In Illinois, the hot spot is a four-county area (Calhoun, Pike, Adams and Brown) located along the western edge of the state, beginning about 40 miles north of St. Louis, Missouri. Often referred to as "The Gold Triangle" by serious whitetail hunters, this region is bordered along the western side by the Mississippi River and on the east by the Illinois River. On the map, the four-county area looks something like an inverted wedge or triangle. Most importantly, it is home to one of the greatest deer densities in the "Prairie State," with some areas of southern Pike and northern Calhoun counties accounting for 40 to 50 whitetails per square mile.

Hunting video producer Mark Drury (left) feels that Midwestern states like Illinois and Iowa harbor the country's best bucks. Here he and brother Terry admire a tremendous Pike County whitetail Mark took with a bow.

In recent years, thanks to expanding trophy management programs, Kentucky has produced some impressive bucks including this Boone & Crockett class ten-pointer taken by David Hale.

COMPLETE BOOK OF WHITETAIL HUNTING

More than one bowhunting expert has told me that there are more Pope & Young bucks here per square mile in these four counties than anywhere else in the U.S.

As for Iowa, hunters should concentrate on those areas along the Missouri state line, especially in the south-central part of the state. Scattered here and there are numerous small tracts of public hunting lands, which can still offer excellent opportunities. Near the small city of Centerville is the state's largest impoundment, Lake Rathbun, which is a U.S. Corps of Engineers reservoir. Surrounding the lake are thousands of acres open to public hunting. Some excellent bucks are taken from this area every year. Another Iowa hot spot (and still something of a sleeper) is a rough geographical area known as the "Loess Hills" in the far western side of the state. The landform there is actually a 100-mile long ridge of sediment left from the ice age, when a mile-deep sheet of ice once covered the earth. The rich soil that was left when the glaciers melted formed the Loess Hills. Scattered along its length are more than 10,000 acres of public hunting and some of the finest big whitetail hunting found in North America.

Iowa is also one of Larry Weishuhn's favorite deer hunting areas. Other than a short "early" muzzleloading season in late October, Iowa's bowhunters have all the action to themselves up to December 1. Then, two back-to-back shotgun seasons allow as many as 200,000 shotgun and muzzleloading hunters to try their hand at taking a whitetail. When these seasons close, the archery season reopens, along with a "late" muzzleloader season that stretches into early January. Larry Weishuhn knows the deer in Iowa are pushed hard during the shotgun seasons, when drives are the favorite method of hunting whitetails, so he waits until the latter part of the late muzzleloading season. Big bucks that eluded shotgun-toting deer drivers and standers settle down a couple of weeks following the early to mid-December onslaught and begin to show themselves again in early January—especially when the temperatures turn cold and snow blankets the ground, forcing the deer to feed. When temperatures dive to -15 degrees to -20 degrees, even wary old bucks can be seen munching in corn fields, trying to maintain body heat.

Larry and I well remember one cold January hunt we shared in Iowa. We were hunting near the end of Iowa's late muzzleloader season as guests of Steve Shoop, owner of J&S Trophy Hunts (Moravia, Iowa). Larry was being taped by a cameraman for a video they were producing together. During the course of the week, Larry and his cameraman had come close to getting a shot at several nice bucks, including one huge eight-pointer they managed to get on camera, but still too far for the scoped .50 caliber in-line rifle Larry was carrying. After a bitterly cold morning on the last day of the hunt, the cameraman was forced to head back without capturing a kill on tape. Larry, too, had to leave the next morning and was preparing to

Whitetail hunting expert Larry Weishuhn claims Texas is a great place for hunting a "good" buck.

COMPLETE BOOK OF WHITETAIL HUNTING

pack up, but I convinced him to stay and hunt the afternoon and evening with me. Several local hunters were conducting some short drives for us, and we nearly had good shots at some 140 to 150 class bucks. As the sun began sinking toward the horizon, I decided that Larry and I should head for a secluded hay field where I had glassed four good 150 class buck feeding a few nights earlier. This was Larry's last shot, but I was prepared to stay four more days.

Here, in Larry's words, are how we ended his Iowa late muzzleloader season:

tree, took aim with my scoped .50 caliber in-line rifle and squeezed off a shot. The buck never got up out of his bed. It turned out to be an older buck about 11 years old. The gnarled rack, while extremely heavy, was not very wide or tall. But still, even though he was worn down from the rut, the buck dressed at 274 pounds.

Canadian outfitter and outdoor writer Jim Shockey, contends that Manitoba, Alberta and especially Saskatchewan provide trophy-minded whitetail hunters with the best chances at putting a deer into the record

"The afternoon was perfect—icy cold and filled with promise. We decided to hunt along the wooded ridge where I had seen a wide-racked buck only a few days earlier, then finish at the hayfield where Toby had glassed several nice bucks. We spotted a few does and were tempted to drop one (to help with the landowner's private management plan), but the promise of a big buck prevented us from squeezing off a shot. Then it happened. A deer that had been bedded in the deep snow 60 yards to our right suddenly stood up. Its head was obscured by branches, but there was little doubt this was one huge buck or doe. I got a solid rest against a small tree, centered the crosshairs on the shoulder and fired.

The deer went down immediately. It was a big buck—the same one we had caught on camera before—with an unbelievably wide rack and short drop tine. As the buck tried to regain its footing, I grabbed Toby's rifle and charged toward the buck to put in a finishing shot. Then I grabbed onto an antler to keep the deer from sliding into the deep draw next to where it had been bedded. I couldn't believe we had taken the same buck I had seen earlier. It had a 28-inch spread with 31-inch main beams. I was smiling so hard from ear to ear that I'm amazed that it wasn't frozen on my face permanently—considering the wind chill that afternoon was pushing -40 degrees!"

A few days later, I was tracking a good buck in fresh snow cover into a cedar thicket. As I topped a small point, I spotted the deer bedded at the base of a big cedar. I crept slowly behind a

books. Statistics easily back up this claim, for when it comes to Boone & Crockett bucks Saskatchewan is the leader (as of 2000). Keep in mind, though, that this province is nearly equal

in size to Minnesota, Wisconsin, Iowa and Illinois combined. If the number of record book heads taken in those four states were combined, square mile for square mile, Saskatchewan can't compete. But when it come to honest opportunities at big bucks, that province wins, hands down.

As Jim Shockey points out, in the past decade Saskatchewan has produced more "Top Ten" contenders than has any other geographical region in North America. That includes the current world record typical buck shot by Milo Hanson in the fall of 1993. His whitetail carried 14 scoring points for a net Boone & Crockett score of 213 5/8 points. Shockey swears he knows of several hunters who have collected sheds in winter and spring that surpass Hanson's buck. Jim and several other respected Saskachewan big buck hunters insist there are at least a half-dozen other bucks roaming the expanses of this province that could score high enough to become new world record holders.

When it comes to whitetail populations, winter in Canada is the "Grim

Reaper." The severity of Canadian weather is a determining factor in how far north whitetails will range. Throughout all of Canada's whitetail habitat, the severity of winter has been a determining factor in the overall whitetail population. Recently, except for the winter of 1994, during which an extended cold spell pushed temperatures down to -60 degrees for more than a month, most of Canada has enjoyed the effect of "El Nino." Winters have been relatively mild and winter losses almost nonexistent. The survival rate of whitetails has been outstanding, hence the carryover of big, mature bucks explains why so many high-scoring bucks have been harvested in Saskatchewan and its neighbors, Alberta and Manitoba. For updated information on hunting in Saskatchewan, contact: Saskatchewan Environment and Resource Management, 3211 Albert Street, Regina, Saskatchewan, Canada S4S 5W6.

Dick Idol, the whitetail hunting expert, says "Some hunters spend too much time searching for an animal to hunt, while others spend good hunting time in areas where no deer that meets their standards exist. It's been said many time before—you can't kill 'em if they ain't there! If you're looking for a buck that scores at least 150 Boone and Crockett points, and there isn't one anywhere near the area you're hunting, I can guarantee you won't kill one. It's such a basic premise that telling it hardly seems appropriate, yet I see it happening all the time across North America."

Dick often finds himself using the term "big buck" without really defining it. To him, "big" is relative. When hunting the hill country of Texas, "big" takes on an entirely different value than when he's hunting in Alberta. If it didn't, Dick reminds us, there would be no reason for him ever to hunt an area that couldn't produce a predetermined minimum score. He knows only too well that his chances of taking a 170 class whitetail buck depend on where such bucks are taken on a regular basis—not where there's been only one big buck taken in the past ten years or more. So if your goal is to harvest a buck that has an honest chance of making it into the Boone and Crockett record book, first do some homework. States like Texas and Alabama may hold a tremendous number of whitetails, and they may offer dozens of opportunities for harvesting a 120 to 130 class buck; but if only one or two bucks per every 100,000 harvested during the season score high enough to get into the book, those places would be poor choices for someone who wants to take a magnificent book class whitetail.

Dick Idol knows that the meaning of "big" varies from one hunter to another, based on each hunter's experience, personal hunting goals, time available for the hunt, and so on. The typical progression, he explains, begins with the novice hunter who is happy to take a few bucks of any size, but who, as he gains experience, holds out for bigger deer. The minimum standard for a hunter with a bow, Dick says, is often lower than for the same person during a firearms season. Dick is as serious a big buck hunter as you'll find anywhere in North America. Before heading off on a hunt in the U.S., Canada or Mexico, he does his homework to improve his odds of hunting in the best possible areas where he might find the kind of buck he's looking for, whether it's a 150 class buck in a particular area, or a monster Boone and Crockett class whitetail big enough to make an ardent whitetail hunter's mouth water. Dick maintains close contact with other experienced big buck hunters all across the continent, and he listens closely when they talk about huge bucks inhabiting tracts of land whose size afford opportunities to pattern and hunt a specific kind of buck. Often he will follow up on reports of monster sheds being found, or he will check out the hunting opportunities in a region where an unusually high number of big bucks are being harvested. In other words, he doesn't wait until he reads about these hot spots in a hunting magazine. By that time, the best opportunities have already passed by and the hunter can expect plenty of competition from other big buck hunters. Instead, Dick and other experienced hunters spend a lot of time talking to hunters from the various areas.

Several years ago, Dick shared with me a hunting experience he had once in Wyoming. He had been contacted by a rancher there who claimed he had the biggest whitetail buck in the state running the creek bottoms on his ranch. It would score high in the record book,

the rancher promised, and he'd be honored if Dick would join him in the hunt. The rancher's story seemed too good to be true, but Idol decided to give it a shot. Since he had five full days to get his crosshairs on the buck, Dick reluctantly passed on a nice 150 class buck early that first morning. During the first three days, he saw numerous 130 to 140 class deer but kept holding out for the "big one." Finally, on the fourth morning of the hunt, he spotted the nice buck he had seen earlier. Again, he decided to pass on the deer, hoping he'd have an opportunity on the final day of the hunt should that big buck fail to show up. But Mr. Big still didn't appear. Shortly after daybreak on the last morning of the hunt, the 150 class ten-pointer waltzed out into a hay field in front of Dick's stand and was immediately dropped with one well-placed shot. Shortly after hearing the report of the shot, the rancher roared up in his 4x4 to where Dick stood with the fallen buck. As he jumped out of the truck, the rancher shouted out, "Halleluyah. . . you got that ol' devil!" Dick never told him it was the same buck he had passed on twice.

When hunting a big buck, one that has a chance of qualifying for the Boone & Crockett record book, Dick Idol likes the prairie provinces of Canada, where he has taken some impressive bucks in both Alberta and Saskatchewan. Montana boasts some whitetail hot spots as well. The prairies and river bottom country of eastern Montana are now turning out some big

Trophy hunter Jim Shockey finds the prairie provinces of Canada to be his favorite place for taking a trophy buck. Here he poses with a few of the many trophies taken there.

racks, with quite a few bucks qualifying for the record books. Another often overlooked whitetail hunting area in Montana is the southwestern corner of the state, west of Bozeman. This area produces plenty of excellent 140 to 160 class whitetails which score high enough to make their way into both the archery and muzzleloader record books.

"I spend a lot of time in the woods and shoot very few bucks," remarks Dick Idol. "For me, it's the love of the outdoors and the hunt that's most important. I like to win the game once in a while, and fortunately I do. When that happens, success is so sweet. When I don't succeed, there's always next year."

After more than 35 years of pursuing whitetails across the country, I've also developed a number of favorite whitetail hunting areas. The following information includes my personal picks of hunting areas where a hunter has a better than average chance of taking a nice 130 to 160 class whitetail buck with bow, muzzleloader, shotgun with slug, or centerfire rifle.

BOW

I believe in a home court advantage because it allows me to spend enough time scouting and patterning bucks that score above 130. It helps when my backyard happens to be "The Golden Triangle" of western Illinois. Of the four counties that make up this region, I like northern Calhoun and southern Pike counties, which is where I live. This area has the highest deer density in the state, with some areas holding more than 50 deer per square mile, including a good number of bucks. I like hunting early whitetails with a bow, starting as soon as the season opens on October 1. When the whitetails are feeding heavy on white oak acorns, I'll place my favorite stands in a well-used feeding area or along a travel route that leads into these areas.

Some of the best bowhunting of the year kicks in during the third or fourth week of October and on into early November. This is basically the pre-rut period in my area, and the bucks become quite active. Rubs and scrapes become more numerous. More important, the bucks tend to cover more ground in their search for hot does. While most does won't come into estrous until the primary rut of mid-November, the bucks are ready—and looking. Hunters who can use the various deer calls with proficiency and who know how to rattle can make things happen, The first good cold spell of the year—when a hard frost sets in and temperatures drop to freezing—seems to spur this activity ever more.

Illinois maintains several small public hunting areas within the "Golden Triangle", and portions of the Mark Twain National Wildlife Refuge are also open to bowhunting. The best hunting, though, is found on private lands. A unique program, known as Access Illinois Outdoors, is operated by the Illinois Department of Natural Resources to help hunters gain access to prime private lands for modest trespass fees.

COMPLETE BOOK OF WHITETAIL HUNTING

Most out-of-state hunters, however, book their hunts with one of more than a dozen outfitters who operate within the "Golden Triangle."

MUZZLELOADER

One of my favorite hunts has always been Nebraska's special muzzleloader season held in early December. When trying to decide where to hunt, I'm torn between two different areas: the extreme south-central or extreme north-central regions of Nebraska. While both offer tremendous whitetail hunting, what makes the muzzleloader season particularly attractive is the fact that nonresident hunters, who find it difficult to obtain one of a limited number of tags available for either area during the general firearms season, can walk into any Nebraska Game and Parks Commission regional office and purchase a muzzleloader tag across the counter.

The whitetails have already been pressured some during the centerfire rifle season in mid-November, but as a rule they've settled back down and become less difficult to hunt. Only about 5,000 muzzleloader tags are issued each year, so the pressure is spread out. In most areas, there won't be another muzzleloading hunting in sight. I've hunted the area around Arapaho, Nebraska, several times during the muzzleloader season, and on most days I've spotted at least several good bucks. Often they're well out of muzzleloader range, so hunters may have to look at a lot of deer in the distance before one finally steps out within a muzzleloader's 150-yard effective range. The Republican River runs through this south-central area, and the numerous river bottom stands of timber and thick brush provide excellent cover for deer. There's no public hunting in this area and visiting whitetail hunters may have to knock on a few doors before finding a place to hunt. For a very reasonable trespass fee, though, most will find doors open. Several outfitters operate within this area as well, leasing some of their prime habitat. For the names of outfitting services in the Republican River area, or of large landowners who allow hunting in exchange for trespass fees, contact the Chamber of Commerce, Arapaho, Nebraska.

When hunting deer in the north-central part of the state, I concentrate my efforts along the Niobrara River, from west of Valentine to east of Bassett. This is one of the rare "sleeper" areas in the country. I've hunted there a few times and have seen some tremendous bucks, not to mention some of the prettiest deer country I've ever set foot on.

Brad Arrowsmith owns and operates a working cattle ranch of 18,000 acres north of Bassett. During the fall hunting seasons he books a limited number of whitetail hunters—either modern centerfire rifle or muzzleloading—and for a very reasonable fee will put on one of the country's finest big buck hunts. The terrain there changes from numerous river bottom hay fields to thick oak brush, from gentle slopes to towering

Ponderosa pines along the high ridges. Each year, Brad's hunters take solid 150 to 180 class bucks. In fact, there's a monster buck (191 typical) hanging on Brad's living room wall that he shot himself.

SHOTGUN WITH SLUG

As a premier shotgun state, Iowa offers some good big buck opportunities during the general firearms seasons held in early to mid-December. Being an old muzzleloader buff, I'd probably opt for shooting a modern scope-sighted in-line ignition muzzleloader stuffed with modern saboted projectiles. A rig like that would easily stretch my effective range out to about 150 yards. State regulations allow hunters to use a frontloading rifle like this one during the shotgun seasons.

During the general firearms seasons,

the area around Centerville, Iowa, where outdoor writer Larry Weishuhn and I once shared a bitterly cold January muzzleloader hunt, also ranks among the top whitetail-producing areas of the state. Several extremely good bucks are taken here regularly by local hunters who tend to spend the vast majority of their time making large-scale drives. A visiting hunter who asks around may find a local group or two that would welcome another driver or stander (some drives held here may consist of 40 or more hunters). Drives of such magnitude move a lot of deer, and they're not always headed in the direction of the posted standers. Hunters who stay on the fringes of such drives may often find themselves covered with deer. On the other hand, hunters who look for whitetails after 20 or 30 drivers have thoroughly pushed out an area will find whitetails scarce. As a rule, outfitters in the Centerville area won't allow drives, but a few outfitting services there will lease some prime hunting lands. Hunting pressure on surrounding properties can push a lot of deer into these "quiet" zones, offering a shotgun-toting hunter some easy shots at close ranges.

CENTERFIRE RIFLE

If I wanted to take my best shot at an upper 140 to 150 class whitetail buck with a centerfire rifle, I'd head for the northeastern corner of Wyoming. This area consists mostly of large expanses of pines and spruces, interlaced everywhere with clear running rivers and small creeks with numerous hayfields along their banks. Whitetails are numerous there and at times quite visible, especially during the rut. Traditionally, the season in the area around Devil's Tower is open throughout November and encompasses the pre-rut and rut periods. The month-long centerfire rifle season provides ample opportunities for hunters to find a good buck in the crosshairs of his scope. Most local and out-of-state hunters converge on this region during the first ten days of the season. By the middle of November, most will find they've got the entire place to themselves. The area does have several large expanses of National Forest and other lands administered by The Bureau of Land Management, all offering fine public hunting. The best opportunities for a good whitetail buck, however, are found mostly on private ranches. Several outfitters offer complete package hunts that ensure an extremely high rate of success. One outfitter in the area, who usually books around 24 hunters each month, has maintained better than a 90 percent success rate on bucks scoring from 140 to the upper 160s. This outfitter charges only half of what a good hunt for the same class buck would cost on one of the better Texas ranches.

For more information on permit application and season dates in Wyoming, plus a list of outfitters to contact, write to Wyoming Game and Fish Department, 5400 Bishop Boulevard, Che-yenne, Wyoming 82006. ■

Chapter Fourteen

How To Manage & Control Deer Hunting On Your Property Or Lease Successfully

WITH ■ *Larry Weishuhn, Biologist & Writer* ■ *Dr. Grant Woods, Wildlife Biologist* ■ *Toxey Haas, CEO Mossy Oak, Haas Outdoors* ■ *Stan Potts, Wildlife Manager & Bowhunter* ■ *Mark Drury, M.A.D. Calls & Producer of Drury Outdoors Videos*

Never before have sportsmen been so interested in the management of privately owned or leased properties for the benefit of wildlife. Perhaps it's because we have come to realize that, with better management, the properties concerned can provide for significantly larger game populations while producing bigger and healthier game animals. Either way, both wildlife and landowners emerge winners. And because of "private wildlife management," more and more whitetail hunters can enjoy some of the finest deer hunting in history.

"Micro management" is a term most professional game managers use to describe how whitetail herds are so closely managed by the state, or regions within a state, into small, specified zones. That allows state game departments to control and monitor the hunting pressure and harvest on the deer within each specific zone. During

the late 1950s and early 1960s, many states practiced "micro management" in an attempt to distribute whitetail populations more evenly within a state's boundaries. Illinois, where I grew up and still reside, is an excellent example of "micro management" of whitetails.

I first began hunting deer in 1963 as a 14-year-old. The first year I hunted the big deer woods of southern Illinois, only a third of the state was open to deer hunting. Most open counties were located in either the southern portion of the state—where the Shawnee National Forest stretches across the state from the Ohio River to the Mississippi River— or in the northwestern part where open counties bordered the Mississippi River. Few, if any, of the intensely farmed counties in the middle of the state were open to deer hunting, primarily because so few deer were available for hunters. In 1963, the deer herd in Illinois probably

Older bucks with inferior racks, such as this wide-racked Nebraska six-pointer taken by Wade Bourne, should be culled from the herd to prevent future bucks of this kind.

numbered only 100,000 animals. By closely regulating the number of permits issued for each open county, while keeping others closed to deer hunting altogether, the Department of Natural Resources (referred to then as the Illinois Department of Conservation) has transformed this once sparsely populated state into one of the country's top meccas for big bucks with a statewide whitetail population approaching one million deer. Still, those deer hunters in Illinois who use firearms must apply for a specific county, and the permit is good for that county only. Even though every county in the state now boasts a healthy population of deer, the Department of Natural Resources continues to practice "micro management," mostly to prevent hunters from overhunting a particularly good deer-producing county or region. Most other Midwestern states also enjoy tremendous growths in whitetail populations, thanks largely to similar "micro management" practices. Indeed, some are beginning to experience a similar problem: too much of a good thing. Where once there were no deer, now there are too many—at least in the minds of some.

Bowhunter Stan Potts manages thousands of acres in western Illinois, one of the state's top deer-producing areas. Whitetail populations have grown to densities of 40 to 60 deer per square mile, which is more than

Too many does can create competition for prime food sources, resulting in bucks who never reach full potential.

COMPLETE BOOK OF WHITETAIL HUNTING

most landowners can support. During summer, late in the evening, hordes of whitetails converge on young soybean fields doing serious damage to the harvest. Because of the exceptional deer hunting found here in this area, lease lands now bring a premium. And while the farmers enjoy this new source of revenue from outfitters and hunting clubs, their real source of income—farming—is now at risk. Wildlife managers like Stan Potts are now encouraging a heavier harvest of does in an attempt to reach a zero population growth among the deer herds. "Shoot a doe so the herd won't grow!" has become something of a battle cry for Potts.

Whitetail authorities like Larry Weishuhn, who hails from Uvalde, Texas, is a firm believer in harvesting does to maintain the quality of buck-hunting in overpopulated areas. Some whitetail authorities claim that, among whitetail fawns who are born each year, more than half are bucks. Larry Weishuhn feels the mix is closer to fifty-fifty, but he also recognizes that buck fawns have a slightly higher mortality rate than doe fawns. Still, for the sake of proper herd management, Larry supports an equal harvest of does and bucks as a way to maintain good herd balance—and to produce higher quality bucks.

Back when deer herds were first being re-established in many parts of the country, game departments often mandated a "Buck Only" harvest. Everyone knew that when you shot a doe, you also took away future deer.

Even when deer numbers reached unheard of levels, changing that mind-set became an almost impossible task. Older hunters who'd spent long days in the deer woods during those "lean years" without ever seeing a whitetail, much less shooting one, still resisted the idea of harvesting does, and so the deer herds continued to grow. With so many hunters with their sights set on taking bucks only, the buck-to-doe ratio went out of balance in a hurry.

Larry Weishuhn recognizes that when the buck:doe sex ratio gets too lopsided, problems arise that are more evident than merely poor buck hunting. When the ratio is allowed to go out of whack—with fewer bucks and a sky-rocketing population of does—food supplies can become endangered. In extreme cases, high numbers of does can consume all available forage, especially when bitter cold temperatures and snow set in for several months without letup. In other cases, a drought can result in a total loss of the mast crop and poor agricultural grain crops, and an over-population of whitetails can deplete existing food supplies. In any event, the result can be a severe die-off. Even when the deer manage to survive such harsh conditions, they may come out of it in such poor condition that they become susceptible to acute diseases and parasitic problems. The result is the same: severe death rates, with the very young and old among the first to succumb.

Through the years, Larry has worked as a professional wildlife biologist in Texas

Whitetail manager Larry Weishuhn preaches and practices doe harvest as a means of producing better quality bucks, as well as superior hunting experiences.

and, more recently, as a consulting wildlife biologist for large landowners who seek improvement in the quality of deer hunting on their lands. One ranch he managed in particular is a prime example of how buck-hunting can be greatly improved through the controlled harvest of antlerless (doe) deer. After touring a 3,000 acre high-fenced tract, Larry's initial population census indicated a whitetail population of around 300 deer, or one deer per 10 acres. After an ongoing study of the confined herd, he determined it was made up of approximately 50 bucks, 200 does and 50 fawns. Accordingly, he established a 1:4 buck to doe ratio and an estimated fawn survival rate of 40 percent.

The landowner's stated purpose for the property was to develop a quality deer herd so as to provide top quality trophy buck hunts. Larry's first suggestion, therefore, was to reduce the amount of cattle grazing on the property. He had worked with ranches made up of similar forage and knew that with more tightly controlled grazing and supplemental feeding for the whitetails, this ranch could easily support one deer per 10 acres. While the deer density was well within the capacity of the forage, Larry knew the buck:doe ratio needed work, and that the age class of the bucks being harvested was not old enough to produce the kind of deer the rancher and his hunters preferred.

Larry also suggested that no bucks were to be harvested that year, and that the rancher and his hunters must crop 100 adult does from the herd.

The landowner followed these harvest guidelines, reduced grazing pressure, planted several fertilized food plots, and established supplemental mineral licks around the property. The next fall census revealed the herd now consisted of approximately 70 bucks, 100 does, and 150 fawns, or a total of 320 whitetails and an increase of 20 deer. In only one season, the buck:doe ratio had been narrowed to about 1:1.4. Larry then recommended harvesting 20 bucks and 60 does during the second season.

The third fall census revealed the landowner's whitetail population within the high-fenced 3,000 acre tract to be 110 bucks, 110 does and 80 fawns, for a total of 300 deer. The ranch had now reached the magical 1:1 ratio in only three years. That fall there was a harvest of 40 bucks and 40 does, a ratio that continues to this day. Hunters can now harvest bucks who are three years or older, while all does taken are carefully studied to make certain they are full-grown adults. Thanks to the expert "micro management" of this 3,000 acres of whitetail cover, the quality of hunting there has been greatly improved through the regular—and mandatory—harvest of does.

A few years back, I accepted Larry Weishuhn's invitation to help thin down the wild hog population on several ranches he managed near his hometown of Uvalde, Texas. The hunters who owned these ranches were concentrating on harvesting big bucks, leaving the doe and hog harvest to Larry and the ranch hands. On one of the ranches

Landowners now spend millions of dollars annually to provide high protein, nutrient-enriched food sources for whitetail living on their properties.

the hogs had practically overtaken the property. Whenever one of the supplemental feeders kicked on, the hogs would beat the deer to the corn and feed pellets as they were kicked out onto the ground. As soon as the motorized feeders kicked on, as many as 30 hogs would appear almost instantly, beating the hungry deer to the corn and feed pellets. In only a few days, Larry and I filled the back of his pickup truck with those feral hogs more than once.

What caught my attention on this particular ranch was its ongoing deer management program. The deer quality had been improved dramatically by maintaining a one to one ratio of bucks and does. The landowners were also

trying to improve the quality of their bucks through the introduction of superior genes. A spacious enclosure of 40 or 50 acres contained a huge 170 class northern whitetail buck and a half dozen local does. The idea was for the buck to impregnate these deer, then return the does to the wild. Their offspring would thus carry the genetic makeup of the larger northern sub-species of whitetails. This same process was repeated again and again through the rut and the following year.

Larry admits that such crossing among breeds can have an affect on the quality of the bucks, but more is gained, he feels, by maintaining a proper herd balance and supplementing natural forage with food sources and minerals that are highly nutritious. Admittedly, the introduction of a larger sub-species, genetically speaking, may not always result in the desired result, especially when the buck's genes are introduced in a setting where the forage is insufficient to produce deer of the donor's original potential. Larry can recall several experimental efforts where some four-month-old fawns were larger than their mothers.

In Illinois, where Stan Potts struggles to maintain high quality buck hunting for paying clients, thinning the doe population back to a 1:1 ratio is out of the question. Most of the land parcels are 40 to 300 acres in size, and they seldom border each other. Even if the state allowed a drastic doe reduction on a few parcels of land, deer from adjoining properties would soon replace them. The high fences that surround most of the ranches Larry Weishuhn manages in Texas aren't there to keep the deer in—they are there to keep other deer out!

Potts and other private wildlife managers in the Midwest have adopted some strict hunting regulations to improve the quality of the deer they oversee. First, where bowhunters are allowed to harvest more than one deer, many managers limit the hunt

to one buck while encouraging their archers to harvest an additional doe. I once took part in a hunt in western Kentucky where my buck tag didn't become valid until I took a doe. The buck:doe ratio was unbelievably lopsided, with one mature buck for every 20 or 30 does. Also, most outfitters and private land managers now stress the importance of harvesting only mature bucks that are at least three years old. So if you want larger bucks, you'll have to let the young ones walk. Some hunting clubs and outfitters frequently impose

Private game manager Stan Potts, left, knows the importance of harvesting excess does and supplemental feeding programs that enable young bucks to reach maturity. His goal is to produce fine trophies like the one taken by Terry Drury.

The number of points isn't the only way to judge a trophy. Here the author admires a tremendous eight-pointer with a 26-inch inside spread and 31-inch main beams—a trophy in anyone's book.

requirements for a "shooter buck," one that is at least an eight-pointer. The thinking is that if hunters are restricted to shooting only bucks with eight or more points, then all the spikes, forkhorns and six-pointers will have a chance to grow. There may be some merit to this, but in most of the places where I've hunted, the majority of bucks were eight or ten pointers, and most of them were 1 1/2 or 2 1/2 years old. An "eight points or better" rule wouldn't do much to increase the age class of the bucks harvested.

A more reasonable approach would require hunters to harvest only those bucks displaying a certain outside spread—at least as wide as their ears—

or those which the knowledgeable hunter feels will score 130 to 150 or so points. It might also be an elderly buck with a pot-bellied stature, huge body size, or perhaps a heavy horn mass that displays neither length or width. Aging bucks on the hoof can take a trained eye, and the definition of a "quality" buck easily changes from one part of the country to another, and in the eyes of the hunter. To improve the quality of the bucks on any sizable piece of property, whoever is in charge of managing the herd should impose some standards to shoot for, but he should also never lose sight of the fact that not all hunters are "trophy" hunters. For a 14-year-old deer hunter, a 2 1/2-year-old eight pointer with a 15- or 16-inch spread could be the deer of a lifetime.

For Stan Potts, the spread is an accurate method of determining a mature buck. "The overall spread works best for me," he explains. "A buck wider than his ears, with an inside spread of 16 inches or so, is a shooter. That eliminates 100 percent of the 1 1/2-year-old bucks harvested, and probably 70 to 80 percent of the 2 1/2-year-olds. Once we've eliminated harvesting these deer, we don't have to worry about the 3 1/2-year-old bucks. They and their elders will take care of themselves. They are survivors. You can never overhunt true mature bucks. They are too smart, and you cannot do it!"

Mark Drury (M.A.D. Calls) knows the importance of letting younger bucks go in order to build the age-class structure and put older bucks in the woods. He offers the following tips for judging the age of a buck more accurately.

1 1/2 YEARS: *These young bucks have small, slender bodies and long, lanky legs. Their waists taper from the chest cavity to the haunches, creating the illusion of a thin waist. Its face is also long and slender, and its color is still not well defined. These young ones have a wide-eyed appearance and long noses. But probably the quickest indicator is the antler spread. Seldom will the maximum outside spread extend past the tips of the ears.*

2 1/2 YEARS: *At this age, bucks are hard to recognize. They look like either a big 1 1/2-year-old or a small 3 1/2-year-old. They still have slender bodies and a lanky appearance, even though most are now noticeably larger than the 1 1/2-year-olds. Their noses are still long and their antler spread most often remains within the spread of the ears. They are slightly heavier and often taller now than their younger siblings.*

3 1/2 YEARS: *By now, the whitetail buck has begun to show more definition. He has a larger chest cavity and his waist has begun to fill out. Facial coloration is more evident and he is slowly taking on characteristics that can vary considerably from buck to buck. One of the best clues to a buck who has reached this age is the size of the antlers. Assuming it has inherited good genes and been fed proper nutrition, a buck who reaches this age will commonly sport his first true "trophy" rack, which surpasses the tips of the ears and often displays some mass.*

4 1/2 YEARS AND BEYOND: *These older bucks begin to move with less fluidity, as if they were becoming arthritic. The chest cavity is now more barrel-like, its neck seemingly like an extension of the chest. The head is big and blocky, and its legs look short and stubby. Accordingly, racks are heavier, with most of the bucks sporting their very best antlers between 5 1/2 to 7 1/2 years—assuming they've survived by then. Once a whitetail buck becomes 9 1/2 or more, he becomes more pot-bellied and his back begins to sway. Some studies reveal that during their golden years a buck's antler growth declines, or the rack regresses. The rack of a really old whitetail buck may not display much width or tine length, but its antlers are massive.*

Let Him Go . . . So He Can Grow

QUALITY DEER MANAGEMENT ASSOCIATION

During most state firearms seasons, most of the bucks harvested are the young 1 1/2-year-olds. Where permits are good for either sex, nearly 40 percent of the "antlerless" deer harvested are actually yearling "button" bucks. In some states, such as in Missouri, close to 60 percent of the entire buck population is harvested by hunters each fall. It's evident that without proper private management very few bucks would ever get the chance to reach their full potential. Managing for quality via the selective harvesting of bucks also means culling inferior or odd-horned bucks from the herd. Biologists agree that genetic flaws responsible for an inferior rack can be passed on to future generations; therefore, such deer should be eliminated. But in recent years a debate has arisen over harvesting spikes. For years the "experts" argued that a buck sporting spikes at 1 1/2 years of age would never amount to much. Larry Weishuhn contends that bucks develop spikes as their first set of antlers for a number of reasons, including accidents,

illness, lack of proper nutrition, or some other biological or environmental causes. As far as Larry is concerned, the jury is still out on whether "spike" 1 1/2-year-old bucks are genetically inferior and should be removed from the herd. On a closely managed range, he submits, any spike buck who appears to be 1 1/2 or older should be harvested and removed from the gene pool. The same applies to odd-horned bucks, especially those cases where one side is normal and the other is a simple spike or fork-horn. Whether such abnormalities are the product of poor genetics or simple accidents, the risk of letting such deer pass on similar horn characteristics isn't worth the payback.

On private properties where he hunts around the country, Mark Drury always practices quality deer management. While the practices discussed in this chapter are extremely important in producing the kind of bucks every serious whitetail hunter dreams about, he also believes that quality deer hunting begins with each state game department.

COMPLETE BOOK OF WHITETAIL HUNTING

The states of Iowa, Illinois, Kansas, Nebraska and Missouri all share basically the same trophy potential. Each state is heavily farmed, providing an excellent food source for whitetails on a year-round basis. They all encourage healthy doe harvests in an attempt to maintain a relatively stable buck:doe balance. Drury feels that Illinois, Iowa and Kansas offer big buck hunters their best chance of hanging a tag on a real wall-hanger. For this Mark credits the game departments who schedule the general firearms deer season at the tail end or following the peak of the rut—not during the high activity period of the breeding season, when mature bucks are the most vulnerable. Many readers may think just the opposite—that a state where the season falls in the middle of the rut offers the best chance of harvesting a mature buck—and they are probably right. In fact, the vulnerability of bucks during this period is exactly why Missouri and Nebraska each offer a lower trophy potential. Bucks who fall within the older age class in these two states are considerably smaller in number. There are simply more mature deer available to hunt in Illinois, Iowa and Kansas. Both Illinois and Iowa are also "shotgun/muzzleloader only" states where long range centerfire rifles are not allowed. The short range capability

While many hunters don't consider it "hunting," high-fenced areas now produce exceptional bucks, like this Boone & Crockett class buck taken by Larry Weishuhn at a large Michigan enclosure.

Small food plots of less than an acre can be easily prepared and sown at minimal cost, but they pay big dividends in deer numbers and quality.

of a shotgun with slugs or a muzzle-loader allow more big bucks to reach those golden years.

Not everyone is in a position to hunt prime private deer country, join an established hunting club or lease huntable acres, much less own the land on which they hunt. Millions of deer hunters must hunt deer on state or federally-owned public hunting areas, such as state and national forests, state wildlife management areas, or property owned by the U.S. Corps of Engineers. But just because a tight budget may prevent a hunter from enjoying his sport on private lands doesn't mean he has to settle for a less than ideal experience. Many state and federal agencies now

do a much better job of managing wildlife, especially on lands that have been officially designated as "Wildlife Management Areas." Improvements in deer habitats usually include planting food plots and establishing year-round water sources, all with the intent to increase the population of whitetails.

One great example of cooperative wildlife management is found in western Iowa. Running parallel with the Missouri River is a geographical area known as the Loess Hills (see also chapter 13), a long ridge of sediment left from the glacial period of 100,000 years ago. The rolling, often rough ground is covered with a patchwork of oak forests and farmed agricultural fields. Along

Harold Knight, of Knight & Hale Game Calls, took this exceptionally wide buck from an area he personally manages for quality deer.

the 100-mile length of the Loess Hills hunters will also find a scattered patchwork of public hunting areas totaling more than 10,000 acres. Smaller 300 and 400 acre tracts, completely surrounded by privately owned lands, are also available. In some of the larger areas, the Iowa Department of Natural Resources allows farmers to farm much of the land on a cooperative basis, leaving portions of their crops as a food source for deer, turkey and upland game. Smaller, more remote food plots are located throughout each area. This is state wildlife management at its best, for these areas now provide outstanding, top-quality deer hunting for residents and nonresident hunters who have no access to private lands.

Other states are undertaking similar work on large wildlife management areas. In Arkansas, for example, one finds numerous large tracts of public hunting, some covering more than 100,000 acres. The Wildlife Resources Agency in Tennessee administers dozens of such areas, and similar work is underway on certain tracts of National Forest, such as the 250,000 acre Shawnee National Forest of southern Illinois and the 500,000 acre Mark Twain National Forest in southern Missouri. Throughout the country are sprinkled numerous U.S. reservoirs admin-

QUALITY DEER MANAGEMENT AREA

NO HUNTING OR TRESPASSING WITHOUT PERMISSION

istered by the Army Corps of Engineers. Practically all are surrounded by thousands of acres of exceptional whitetail hunting, especially where some sort of wildlife management plan has been implemented.

When faced with hunting on public lands, there are many things a hunter can do to help improve the quality of deer hunting. Are there any conservation organizations nearby that handle habitat improvements on a volunteer basis, including food plot work or other management tasks associated with the public hunting areas? Also check with the agencies in charge of the hunting areas. Are hunters allowed to establish mineral licks there that can add to the nutrients and thus promote a healthier whitetail population? It's easy to complain about "poor hunting," but it takes someone who's serious about whitetail hunting to actually do something about improving the quality of deer hunting. When hunting public areas, even those that have already been intensely managed, don't forget that government agencies are faced with providing maximum hunting opportunities for many thousands of hunters. Instead of managing a 3,000-acre tract of land to produce 20 to 40 trophy class 3 1/2-year-old bucks for an elite group of hunters, they try to provide quality hunting for a hundred or more hunters eager to utilize the area season after season. As Mark Drury notes, "Managing for quantity is worlds apart from managing for quality."

Toxey Haas, founder of Mossy Oak

Toxey Haas

Camouflage, has built his business around the whitetail hunting industry. Like thousands of serious hunters throughout the U.S. and Canada, he owns and manages a sizable tract of prime habitat for the deer he loves to hunt. Instead of building a high fence to prevent deer from leaving his property, Toxey has learned how to keep them on his land by making his property the best habitat and food source within the area. When given everything they need, the deer should have no reason to leave. Part of Toxey's management plan is to provide the most palatable food source he can grow on his numerous food plots. During a few hunting trips earlier to New Zealand, Toxey toured several large deer farming operations where a special forage for various species of deer had been developed. The plants were extremely high in nutrients and quite digestible, allowing the deer's digestive system to better absorb these nutrients. The result was noticeably larger horn growth and heavier body development.

Since these deer farming operations marketed both venison and antlers, quick growth and maximum development are key to being profitable. Toxey had some of his own food plots joined with these forage plants and was amazed at how eagerly the whitetails took to the food source, and how quickly they seemed to benefit from its higher nutritional value. He immediately joined forces with wildlife biologist Dr. Grant Woods to form a new company,

More and more, trophy-minded white-tail hunters are leaving less to chance. There is now more emphasis than ever on producing quality whitetails, such as this buck munching on some Mossy Oak BioLogic forage.

COMPLETE BOOK OF WHITETAIL HUNTING

called Mossy Oak's BioLogic. Its goal was to bring to private wildlife managers across the country the same scientifically developed forage products that had increased so dramatically the venison and horn growth among New Zealand's deer farmers. "Many of today's wildlife biologists spend too much time planting the same crops farmers have used for cattle, like wheat, oats, corn and soybeans," notes Dr. Woods. "When deer are hungry, they will come out and eat it. However, when these crops are analyzed nutritionally, there's just not a lot there the deer can digest."

Dr. Woods points out that deer, unlike cattle, don't have the same bacteria in their stomachs and guts. While the digestive system of cattle can break down rough grasses and heavy grains to provide some nutritional value, the digestive system of a whitetail simply cannot break these forage feeds down properly so as to be of any real benefit. Deer may feed heavily on grain crops like corn and soybeans, especially during extremely cold weather, but most of what they take in passes straight through without much nutritional transfer. "Kind of like garbage in—garbage out!" Woods comments.

Grant Woods acknowledges that when most grasses and grain crops first sprout, the shoots are tender and are easily digested by whitetails. But once these plants begin to grow and the stalks become more fibrous and woody, the cell walls become much too tough for the deer to digest. The nice green

fields that have dotted southern deer country for decades may attract deer, especially when the mast crops are scarce or consumed by wildlife, but the deer get little nutritional value from most of what is being planted as a supplemental food source for whitetails. As Toxey Haas states, "The traditional grain fields that everybody plants, such as rye and other winter grasses, are basically useless as a nutritional source for deer."

Both Woods and Haas point out that whitetails are very selective feeders. They will always move wherever the most palatable and most nutritious food sources are available. Mossy Oak's BioLogic forage blends were developed to provide private wildlife managers with a superior source of nutrition, one the deer find palatable and feed on readily. Best of all, these specially developed forage plants provide 30 to 38 percent crude protein and are 80 percent digestible by whitetails. Compare that to most native grasses with only six to nine percent protein, or with most clovers yielding 18 to 23 percent crude protein. Only 30 to 40 percent of these foods is digestible by deer.

Mossy Oak's BioLogic lineup consists of a "Summer Management Blend," a "Fall Attractant" forage blend, and a "Fall Premium Perennial" blend. The *Summer Management Blend* is planted once daytime temperatures hit 60 degrees consistently during the day while overnight temperatures remain above 40 degrees. This blend consists

Dr. Grant Woods

of various forages which mature at different times throughout the warm summer months. The forages contain nutrients aimed at antler development and weight gain. The latter is especially important in helping young fawns later to produce bigger fawns with better survival rates. The *Fall Attractant* is a lush, highly palatable blend of forages designed primarily to attract and hold whitetails in a specific area. Like the summer blend, it includes plants that mature at different times, maintaining a highly nutritional forage for the deer through the fall and hunting seasons. Both are annuals and should be replanted each year for best results. The *Fall Premium Perennial* blend, on the other hand, should be planted only once every three to five years. This forage will do much of what the other two blends accomplish, but hardy enough to provide highly nutritional feed into the winter months, when whitetails often need it the most.

One of the misconceptions of providing supplemental forage sources for whitetails is that all efforts are aimed at producing bucks with larger antlers. That observation is far from the truth. The payback for costly, time-consuming private deer management should rightly

be the harvesting of bigger and healthier bucks within three to five years, but landowners should never lose sight of the fact that their efforts benefit the does equally. Big, healthy does produce big, healthy fawns, which in turn mature into big, healthy bucks; that is, provided they have the proper genetic structure, are given the proper nutrition, and are allowed to reach a ripe old age. Forage that's high in nutrition will also help pull whitetails through winter's stress period. "The rut is a huge energy drain on deer," observes Grant Woods. "When I was studying at the University of Georgia, our deer were in a half-acre pen. The three bucks and three does were given all they could eat, and yet the bucks still lost 25 percent of their body weight. Think about the cost of the rut on bucks out in the wild. It takes a lot of energy, a lot of nutrition for a deer to survive, and to be in good shape to grow antlers next year."

Where it's legal, the use of feeders to provide pellet-sized feed or loose rations, such as corn, has grown in popularity. A feeder set up within sight of a hunting cabin or a farmhouse is a great way to observe deer on a regular basis. Unless the landowner is prepared to continue supplemental feeding of this nature, most efforts will amount to little

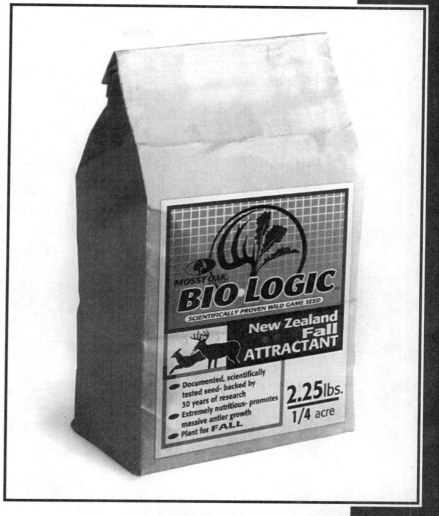

more than "baiting." Whitetails are opportunists and will readily come to automatic feeders dispensing such feeds on a regular basis. While short-term feeding prior to and during the hunting season does little to benefit whitetails, it does bait the deer to an area. Larry Weishuhn feels that supplemental feeding efforts should be part of an overall management plan, not some easy method of attracting and holding whitetails. Such feeding programs, he feels, can have a beneficial impact on the deer, provided their feedings are

The Mossy Oak BioLogic forages have been developed specifically to put more weight and heavy antlers on whitetails.

Realtree camouflage designer Bill Jordan shows off an extremely wide-racked south Texas buck, the product of an extensive whitetail management program (including supplemental feeding). Note the feeder in background.

COMPLETE BOOK OF WHITETAIL HUNTING

conducted on a timed, around-the-clock basis and over a long period of time.

If you cannot afford to feed deer on a year-round basis, but you want to feed them at times when it will have the most impact on the quality of deer being managed, the harsh winter months and late spring through early summer periods are probably the best times to "pour on the feed." As Grant Woods points out, the rut can take its toll on whitetails, sending them into winter overly stressed. At this time of the year, the deer can use a handout to help them better survive extreme cold. A doe who emerges from winter in top condition is more likely to have healthy fawns. And while most deer will turn to natural forages during the spring and summer months, the supplemental feeding of high protein pellets can have a dramatic impact on antler development. At any rate, once a feeding program has been started, you have to see it through. But before you start, check with your state game agency to make sure everything is legal!

While the overall goal of private deer management should be to produce a healthier whitetail population, there is no denying it: the short-term goal of most hunting clubs, outfitters and individual hunters is to produce bigger, heavier antlered bucks. For decades, hunters everywhere have established "salt licks" in their attempts to lure and hold deer close to favored hunting spots. Even when the attraction of salt—which deer truly love during warmer weather—is combined with the strong mix of minerals, some biologist still question their nutritional value. Larry Weishuhn advises that mineral licks should be a part of any management plan. The deer may not actually benefit as much as some claim, but supplemental mineral licks certainly don't hurt. They will attract and help hold whitetails to the point where other management practices come into play.

Larry says that when looking for a suitable loose mineral supplement, choose one that includes at least 12 percent calcium and 12 percent phosphorous, along with trace minerals and elements like zinc, selenium, copper, magnesium, iodine, manganese and other minerals. Deer are naturally drawn to natural mineral licks, but often a mixed supplement can have a bitter taste. Whitetails may shun a lick made up entirely of loose-grained or block minerals. Mixing the supplement with salt can make the mixture more palatable.

Over the years, I've created several well-used mineral licks. I begin by digging a hole two feet deep, 18 to 20 inches wide and about 30 inches long. Into the bottom of the hole I set down two 50-pound mineral blocks. Next, I mix 50 or 100 pounds of loose salt with the dirt taken from the hole to carefully cover the mineral blocks with the mixture. If the lick is located in a well-used feed area or along a regular travel route, late spring and summer whitetails will usually start using the lick within a few days. By the end of the first month, they'll have pawed their way down to the mineral blocks.

One day several years ago, near the end of May, I left two mineral blocks sitting on top of the ground, near where I had made a lick as described above. By the end of August, the deer had nearly uncovered the two mineral blocks that had been buried. They were nearly half licked away, while the two blocks sitting on the ground were virtually untouched. The following spring, upon returning to freshen up the much-used lick, I noticed the two unburied blocks had dissolved some but were still 75 percent there. It wasn't until the end of summer that the deer began using the spot where I had placed the two blocks on top of the ground. But even then they seemed to be licking the dirt away from where the now thoroughly dissolved blocks had been placed. The longer a mineral salt lick remains in the same spot— assuming it's freshened up each year —the more deer will use it. Remember, the first deer to use a lick must first discover this new source of salt and minerals. After that, the lick quickly becomes a daily part of a doe's life, as well as her fawns, and ad infinitum. A well-established ten-year-old mineral lick can serve that many generations of deer as well. Over a ten-year period,

Thanks to supplemental feeding of high protein pellets, this 1 1/2-year-old buck is off to a great start toward becoming a super buck in another three to five years.

COMPLETE BOOK OF WHITETAIL HUNTING

I've put nearly 1,000 pounds of salt and minerals into a single northern Missouri lick. Today there is a hole in the ground large enough almost to bury a small pickup. Whitetails will use a lick heavily during the warm days of spring and through the hot weather of summer and early fall. But by the time hunting season rolls around, only a few deer, especially good bucks, will be using

such licks. And yet, many game departments still make licks illegal, thinking erroneously that they give the hunter some sort of advantage. Game departments who think this way, along with hunters who feel a good lick gives them an ace up their sleeves, are both wrong.

Anyone interested in establishing a successful private deer management program should contact the Quality

HOW TO MANAGE & CONTROL DEER HUNTING

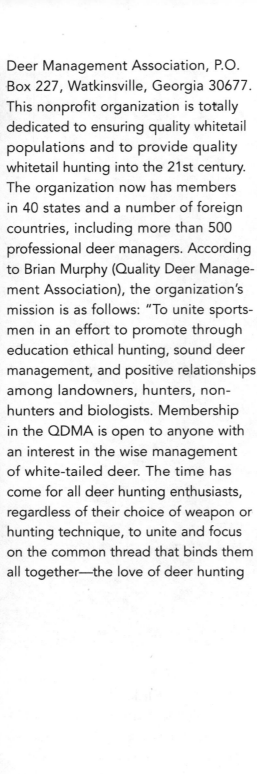

Deer Management Association, P.O. Box 227, Watkinsville, Georgia 30677. This nonprofit organization is totally dedicated to ensuring quality whitetail populations and to provide quality whitetail hunting into the 21st century. The organization now has members in 40 states and a number of foreign countries, including more than 500 professional deer managers. According to Brian Murphy (Quality Deer Management Association), the organization's mission is as follows: "To unite sportsmen in an effort to promote through education ethical hunting, sound deer management, and positive relationships among landowners, hunters, non-hunters and biologists. Membership in the QDMA is open to anyone with an interest in the wise management of white-tailed deer. The time has come for all deer hunting enthusiasts, regardless of their choice of weapon or hunting technique, to unite and focus on the common thread that binds them all together—the love of deer hunting and the desire that future generations will be able to experience the great tradition of deer hunting."

The organization is currently the source for some of the finest videos and books on white-tailed deer management. Their 322-page edition of "Quality Whitetails - The Why and How of Quality Deer Management" is sure to become the standard reference book on the topic. The book was written by 24 of the most knowledgeable white-tailed deer biologists and managers in North America. It includes valuable management procedures, biological information, nutritional guidelines, tips and how-to projects for landowners or managers who seek to improve the quality of the deer on their properties, whether they own or control 40 acres, or 10,000 acres. As Toxey Haas reminds us: "Private deer management is a 365-days-a-year commitment, not just a little work in the spring or summer, or throwing out a salt block here and there." ■

After The Harvest

WITH ■ *John Sloan, Bowhunter & Outdoor Writer* ■ *Ted Schumacher, Outfitter, Lone Wolf Outfitters*
■ *Brian Murphy, Quality Deer Management Association*

It's unfortunate, but tons of excellent venison are wasted each season because of poor handling in the field and improper care after the deer is hung on the meat pole. Many a fine trophy headed for the taxidermist has met a similar fate as well. While a nice rack can usually be salvaged from a spoiled head and cape, a good set of horns hanging on the wall doesn't have the same impact as a full shoulder mount, nor does it offer recollections of a great hunt. Once the trigger is pulled or the arrow released and a whitetail has been harvested, it doesn't take much more effort or money to properly care for it after it's on the meat pole. The enjoyment of fine eating and a beautiful trophy are all part of the whitetail hunting experience. Letting meat spoil unnecessarily, or failing to provide the respect and recognition which an outstanding set of antlers deserves, detracts from the experience and reduces deer hunting to little more than a thrill killing. Some states have even passed laws that make "wanton waste" of game illegal. Many conscientious hunters feel that all states should impose fines and even possible jail time on those who are convicted of killing deer and then deliberately allowing the meat to spoil.

Outdoor writer John Sloan, who once co-hosted a weekly outdoor television show, known as the Tennessee Outdoorsman," is often asked by viewers how exactly does he get the wild taste out of deer meat. "I'll tell you straight away," he answers. "there is no wild taste in deer meat. It simply tastes like deer meat. If you want it to taste like choice beef, throw away the venison and buy choice beef."

Whether he goes into the field with a bow, rifle or muzzleloader, this ardent hunter harvests about ten deer a year, all of which are consumed by the Sloan family. John contends that once an

When a buck drops on the spot, it usually indicates a solid hit into the vitals—and also some fine eating.

arrow is released or a bullet leaves the muzzle and a deer goes down, the quality of meat to be set on the dinner table is greatly influenced by what the hunter does in the next two hours. Sloan claims that probably 75 percent or more of deer hunters really don't know how to care for a deer once they've killed it. Following are some recommendations offered by John Sloan for making better-tasting venison:

urinary tract, etc.). Washing partially digested food from inside the body cavity as soon as possible can help prevent the meat from souring or acquiring that "gamey" taste so many hunters complain about. And second, a thorough wash-down promotes proper cooling of the carcass. Getting the carcass clean and cool as quickly as possible is extremely important in serving a great-tasting venison steak

Once the deer has been shot, the quicker you can field dress it the better. Try not to cut an internal organ. Do a clean job. The mandate that says you must remove the tarsal glands when field-dressing a whitetail is an old wives' tale. The big discolored glands that are found on the insides of both back legs can spoil the flavor of the meat only if the tarsal glands come into contact with it. The hunter who cuts these glands from the legs first before proceeding with the field-dressing stands to ruin the meat by getting the tarsal gland secretions on his knife or hands. The edict here is simply to leave the glands alone. Don't touch them. To be safe, wash your hands before proceeding.

When I first began hunting whitetails, many of the older hunters swore up and down that it was strictly taboo to wash down a deer carcass. Instead, they insisted, it should be wiped down with dry cloths. Well, that's another old wives' tale. According to John Sloan, "Once a deer has been field dressed, wash it out. Throw it into a creek or lake, use a hose, snow, ice—something —and wash it out!"

Hosing out a deer carcass—or rinsing it out with clean creek water—serves two important purposes. First, it cleans the body cavity. This is extremely important when the bullet or arrow has clipped the digestive tract (stomach, intestines,

or roast. As John Sloan says, "Get that deer to a cool location as quickly as possible. Don't ride around town showing it to your friends. They don't want to see it anyway. That deer needs to be hung up as soon as possible in a cool, dry place that's free of insects."

John prefers to hang his deer by the head, which allows the remaining blood and body fluids to drain out of the body cavity. When a deer is hung by the hind legs, these same fluids tend to collect in the chest cavity, which in turn can sour the taste of the meat. Once the deer has been hung in a dry, cool place, John likes his venison to age with the skin on. "My personal preference," he says, "is to hang a deer, hide on, with the temperature at 36 degrees for up to 14 days. In the south, you need a walk-in cooler. In cold weather, use your garage."

Up to this point, John and I pretty much agree on how to handle a harvested deer. However, I'm not a fan of aging venison. Other than the time it takes to hang a deer on a meat pole in camp or in a garage prior to skinning it out, I leave the hide on for the shortest time possible. Once the hide comes off,

the carcass can be butchered and put in the freezer within only a few hours.

One problem with skinning a deer and aging it with the hide off is that the meat develops a tough, leathery film, which makes butchering more time-consuming. True, this leathery film can be trimmed from the meat as it's butchered. But doing this results in loss of edible meat since it's impossible to trim away the film without leaving some meat with every cut. When there's room in my chest freezer, I like to lay the

COMPLETE BOOK OF WHITETAIL HUNTING

quarters or leg and shoulder sections on layers of freezer paper and allow them to chill down almost to the freezing point. This firms up the meat and makes it much easier to cut. As for aging, I prefer to marinate my cuts, allowing the meat to age in the solution for 24 hours before cooking. The result is meat as tender as any that's been hanging for two weeks—skin on or skin off.

Many will argue that a really old buck must hang and be aged or the meat will be too tough to chew. I disagree. Choice steaks and the backstrap can be cut from the carcass and marinated in a simple solution of Worcestershire sauce, garlic powder and pepper. I guarantee it will cook up as tender as aged venison. Other cuts from a 4 1/2-year-old (or older) whitetail should be set aside for summer sausage, bratworst or perhaps jerky. The venison from a younger buck or doe can make good eating when properly butchered into steaks, roasts and stew meats.

Ted Schumacher (Lone Wolf Outfitters, Buffalo, Wyoming) often guides whitetail hunters more than 100 miles from his home base. Instead of heading back to camp after a morning hunt, Ted often finds a shady spot where he can catch a nap during the midday heat of an early October rifle hunt. Should one of his hunters prove successful that morning, it could mean the harvested whitetail will be subjected to 12 to 18 hours of 80 to 90 degree heat before the meat is carried back to camp and into Ted's walk-in cooler. Fortunately,

Wyoming's north-central and northeastern regions, where Ted conducts his hunts, are laced with cool, clear streams. Once photographs have been taken and the deer is field dressed, Ted will often tie a rope around one antler and toss the entire deer into one of those streams. The water temperature is usually around 60 degrees, so the entire carcass can cool down completely in several hours. Before heading out for an evening hunt, the deer is often hung in the shade of a tree or an old abandoned ranch building where it can drain and dry.

If there's a chance that you may have to drag a deer through muddy water, along a dusty roadway, across a dry creek, or anywhere that could result in debris getting inside the deer, it's advisable to wait until the deer has been carried past these areas before field dressing it. This will help protect the meat from contamination.

"When hunting this far from camp," Ted Schumacher advises, "I always fill a large cooler with bags of ice, which stays pretty well frozen all day. Once we have the deer we took that day loaded into the back of my truck, we fill the chest cavities with several bags. Then, back at camp, we hang the deer by the antlers and allow them to drain out. Then the cavity is wiped dry with paper towels before the deer are hung in the cooler for the night. The season opens the first of October in some of our areas, and temperatures can soar into the 90s. But by making sure the meat is fully cooled down before transporting the deer 100 miles or more, we don't lose any."

The longer it takes to track and find a wounded deer, the quicker a hunter needs to get the deer field dressed. During a warm weather hunt, venison can spoil quickly unless it's allowed to cool thoroughly.

COMPLETE BOOK OF WHITETAIL HUNTING

Ted has also arranged for a local meat cutter to come into camp every couple of days to process deer that are headed home with non-resident hunters, many of whom are headed back east where early October temperatures can still push close to 100 degrees. Before the meat is packed away in insulated coolers for the long ride home, it's frozen in chest-type freezers. This procedure should do the job for about 24 hours; but if a hunter is flying home with the meat, or taking a two-day drive home, Ted suggests that they place several pounds of dry ice in their cooler along with the meat, then seal the cooler tightly with duct tape.

When traveling, I almost always carry several large coolers. In one, I place the boned meat, separating the major muscle groups in different plastic bags (to keep the meat from getting soaked in water from melting ice). In the other cooler, I carry a half-dozen bags of ice in case we have to replenish our supply of ice in the cooler. Every two hours or so, I drain the water from that cooler as well. Remember, good-tasting venison is no accident; it's the result of good care, preparation and forethought.

Having the right knives is vital to the proper field dressing and butchering of a deer. Most knowledgeable deer hunters recommend a fixed or lock blade knife, one that has a three to five-inch blade for all field dressing chores. Don't pack one of those foot-long "Rambo" specials when headed into the deer woods—they are practically useless. When field dressing a buck, start by rolling the deer over onto its back. Make an incision all the way around the anal opening. Then carefully cut off the penis and testicles (unless state law requires that they remain attached) and cut along each side of the pelvic bone where the two rear hams come together. This allows the legs to lay down flat and out of the way. Now open the body cavity by first making a small incision about where the rear haunches come together. Take extra precautions not to cut or puncture the intestines.

To make the long cut, slip your forefinger and the middle finger of one hand into the incision, with the palm upward. Insert the knife blade with the cutting edge facing upward as well. Then with your two fingers, pull upward on the internal membrane, skin and hair, slowly making an incision toward the sternum. By sliding the two fingers, along with the blade that rests between them, you're less likely to hook the stomach or intestines with the point of the knife. While many hunters hack their way through the sternum, or breast bone, there's really no reason to. Once the cavity is open, reach inside and roll out the stomach, liver, intestines and lower organs.

The diaphragm separates the heart and lungs from other internal organs. To remove these, cut around the outside edge of the diaphragm, then reach up inside the chest cavity with one hand and grasp the wind pipe and esophagus. Then, with the knife in the other hand, reach up inside and cut these parts. Then, with one solid pull, everything should spill out of the body cavity. You may have to cut around the anal tract some more to pull it all free. Everything that was on the inside at the start should now be on the outside. Most makers of hunting knives now offer models featuring a "gut hook," which has a sharpened, hook-type contour along the top of the blade. This is used to "hook" the hair-covered skin and internal membrane of the belly and then pull forward to open the cavity. However, I find it more difficult to do a good clean job with a gut hook than when I use my two fingers to guide the blade of a good sharp knife up the belly.

Everyone, it seems, has a different opinion on how a deer should be butchered. I always jerk out the backstraps first and save them for the grill. Then I'll cut a few steaks from some of the major muscle groups, trim up a few roasts, and cut most of the remaining meat into soup and stew chunks. I love chili made with venison burger, so with at least one deer I take each fall I'll have some of the meat ground. I prefer a very coarse grind, though, not the fine grind most often associated with hamburger meat. I like to mix just a little beef suet with my burgers so they brown well in the skillet. According to John Sloan, "There are only three cuts of meat: steaks, roasts and stew meat. The backstrap filet mignon on a whitetail is number one. It lies along the spine on each side. The two front

shoulders make excellent pot roasts, while the hindquarters provide great steaks and roasts. I don't care how good your mother's neck roast is, the rest of the deer is stew meat, which can also be made into hamburger, salami or sausage."

Another thing John and I tend to agree on is the need to bone venison completely. The bone marrow tends to give the meat some of the "wild taste" many associate with venison. And since most commercial processors use a band saw liberally, most cuts are well doused with bone marrow and bone dust—but not on any meat that's headed for *my* table! When cutting meat into final cuts, use a good, sharp six to eight-inch bladed knife. And take all the time necessary to remove all fat and muscle membrane, which also gives meat an off taste and is what often makes cuts seem tough. When packaging meat for the freezer, always use airtight plastic wrap and waxed freezer paper to keep air out. It's also a good idea to mark each package as to its contents and the date it was packaged. And finally, for best taste all venison should be consumed within six months, unless it's been made into processed salami. Even then, meat that's been in the freezer for up to a year begins to taste stale.

TROPHY PREPARATION

Just as great-tasting venison reflects the hunter's attention to field dressing, cleaning and cooling of the carcass, a great-looking mount on the wall is generally the result of similar attention

COMPLETE BOOK OF WHITETAIL HUNTING

to detail and forethought. Always remember, even the best taxidermist cannot make a mount into something that's not there. By way of explanation, I once operated a taxidermy shop that specialized in big game mounts. I've never been excited by a great fish mount and I hated the thought of working on ducks. Novelty mounts, like having a bunch of squirrel mounts arranged to form a band, bordered on the ludicrous. On the other hand, I greatly admired good taxidermy of an impressive whitetail buck, but I now receive even greater satisfaction when

taking a recently harvested deer head and giving it a true, lifelike look.

Actually, for me taxidermy was a hobby that simply got out of hand. After doing a few mounts for myself and for several friends each year, I wound up doing 150 or more deer heads each fall and winter. During the half-dozen years I operated the shop, one of my biggest gripes was how poorly hunters cared for the head they wanted to be mounted. Fully one-third of the heads I received came in with the cape (head and neck skin) cut too short to allow a deer to be mounted on a full

A medium-sized knife, similar to this model from Thompson/Center Arms, is the ideal size for handling almost all field dressing and skinning needs.

shoulder form. Worse yet, on a few occasions I encountered heads with their throats cut, while others had been lying around on the garage floor for two to three weeks after the deer had been skinned. And yet, every one of those proud hunters demanded that their trophy be mounted "exactly" like that beautiful full-shouldered ten-pointer that hung on my shop wall.

My friend John Sloan once told me, "The two greatest enemies of the taxidermist, when asked to create a beautiful shoulder mount from a deer head, are time and the hunter. The hunter can fail to do some simple things—or time can ruin the hide." Following is a list of pointers John has offered for creating a better-looking wall mount:

• *Never cut the deer's throat. It will ruin the cape. Even the best seamstress cannot sew one back so it won't show.*

• *Don't cut any farther than the sternum when field dressing a deer. A cut made into the brisket is almost impossible to hide.*

• *Cool down the deer in a hurry. The neck is one of the last areas to cool down.*

• *During an exceptionally warm hunt, skin the deer and cape the neck* and head. If there's access to a freezer, roll up the entire hide with the head, place in a plastic trash bag and freeze it. Before dropping the head and skin into the freezer, though, take time to wipe away any blood and dirt from the head and antlers. This will make the job much easier for the taxidermist.

• If you are faced with caping the complete head (total removal of the skin from the neck and skull), first be sure you know what you're doing.

• A few wrong cuts and the mount will be ruined. Before making any cuts, take a few measurements, as follows: Measure a) from the front corner of the eye to the end of the nose; b) measure from the base of the antler to the end of the nose; c) measure the diameter of the neck where it meets the head, and again at its largest circumference. These measurements will aid the taxidermist in obtaining the proper-sized form and getting the rack set properly on the form.

• When cutting off excess hide from the cape, check to make doubly sure you're cutting far enough back to allow for a full shoulder mount. A good guide is to cut the hide off from behind the rear line of the front shoulder. When cutting, make sure the cut is "square."

• When caping, cut back at an angle from the rear base of each antler to a point six to eight inches at the rear of the rack, making a kind of Y-shaped cut. Instead of cutting all the way to the rear of the cape, make only about a foot-long incision down the rear center of the neck. This will provide enough room to skin out the neck.

• Take extra precaution when removing the skin from around the bases of the antlers, and even more care when skinning out the eye, mouth and nose areas. A cut through the skin here could result in an unsightly blemish in the mount.

• Unless you're in a remote wilderness camp, leave the fleshing to the taxidermist. If you must flesh the cape, do so with great care, avoiding cuts in the hide and especially around the eyes, nose and lips. Salt the hide well (using non-iodized salt) and roll it up, flesh side in. If there's access to a freezer, roll the hide up, flesh side in, place in a plastic bag and freeze.

Several don'ts arise when hanging a deer or skinning it for mounting. Never drag or hang a deer with a rope around it's neck. This can break fragile hairs or even wear hair off the hide, leaving an unsightly ring. When making any cuts, always insert the point or blade of the knife and cut the skin from the inside out. This prevents cutting off long hairs, which may be needed to hide sewn seams. When skinning a deer for the butcher, you'll end up with less hair on the meat if the knife is used in the same manner; i.e., make cuts through the hide from the inside out.

Brian Murphy (Quality Deer Management Association) says that skull mounts —or European mounts as they are often called—are probably the oldest form of taxidermy. Since this work requires a minimum of time and equipment, such mounts are usually very affordable or they can be done completely by the hunter. Following are the basic steps:

1 Remove the hide and fleshy parts with a sharp knife. Boil the head in a large pot, taking care to keep the base of each antler out of the water. To help reduce the oils produced by the boiling, add about 1/2-cup of powdered laundry detergent. Brian Murphy recommends that once the water begins to boil, reduce the heat so that the water simmers the flesh from the head. When more water needs to be added, always use hot water to prevent cracking the teeth. The boiling process will remove much of the flesh, but a knife and scrub brush are usually needed to remove stubborn tissue. A stiff wire will break up and remove brain matter from the opening located on the rear underside of the skull. Changing the water and detergent several times usually results in a better job.

2 Bleaching the skull also results in a much better-looking trophy. It produces a beautiful white skull by mixing pow-dered bleach with hydrogen peroxide until it takes on a foam-like consistency. Wearing rubber gloves, coat the entire skull with the mixture (all but the antlers) and place the skull portion in a clear plastic bag. Set the bag on a white surface in direct sunlight. Be sure to keep the mixture on the skull moist for two to three days, until the bones are bright white. When this bleaching process is completed, wash the skull thoroughly with mild soap and water, rinse and let dry.

3 The skull can now be mounted or left whole. If it is destined for a wall, the bottom portion of the skull can be cut off, using a meat/bone saw, fine toothed band saw, or even a hacksaw. For the best-looking skull mount, keep the cut below the eye sockets and nasal bones. Cutting the bottom of the skull will offer a flat surface that fits flush on a wooden plaque. The skull can be attached to the plaque with wood screws and epoxy or wire loops. An uncut skull makes a nice addition to a fireplace mantle, a large table top, or it can be hung on the wall or over a doorway without a plaque.

Whether the deer you've harvested is destined for a trophy room or a simple horn mount over the door of a hunting camp, always treat the game you've harvested with respect. If it's thrown around like so much dead meat, the sport of deer hunting will lose some of its special meaning. ■

The Future Of Whitetail Hunting In North America

WITH ■ *Brian Murphy, Exec. Dir., Quality Deer Management Association* ■ *Larry Wieshuhn, Whitetail Biologist & Outdoor Writer* ■ *Tom Fegely, Outdoor Writer & Photographer* ■ *Richard P. Smith, Outdoor Writer* ■ *Tom and Rhonda Baker, Owners, Buck Hollow Ranch*

The young six-pointer nibbled away at the late September soybeans, unaware that he was being glassed from just 100 yards away. Hard to believe, but this racked buck appeared to be that year's fawn. Its neck was small and slender, and I could still make out spots along its sides. Once or twice in my life, I had seen buck fawns sporting three or four-inch spikes, but this one actually carried a well-developed 3 x 3 set of antlers with only about a 10-inch spread. If it was indeed a fawn, the young whitetail was a real credit to the outstanding genetics of the deer herd living in south central Iowa.

Crouched next to me in shoulder-high weeds was a 12-year-old boy, known as "A.J.," with a youth deer permit in his back pocket. We had hunted in the morning and evening of the previous day without spotting a buck. It has been opening day of the special "Youth Deer Hunt" conducted by the Iowa Department of Natural Resources,

an annual affair during which several thousand young deer hunters participate late each September and early October. While practicing earlier that summer with a scoped .50 caliber in-line percussion muzzleloading rifle, A.J. informed me that he'd be more than happy to shoot a doe on this, his first, hunt. He also let me know that if, at all possible, he would rather pull the trigger on a large buck.

So here we were, shortly after day-break of the second morning, watching a young six-pointer feeding well within the effective range of A.J.'s rifle and load. The boy, knowing he was about to get the shot he'd been dreaming about, was naturally excited. I, in turn, was faced with a decision. Should I allow A.J. to take the shot and harvest his first whitetail, or should I explain to him that it would be against basic deer management principals to harvest such a young buck with so much potential? After thinking about it for a few minutes,

I decided there was no way I could rob the boy of an opportunity to take his first whitetail buck.

The young hunter and I made our way slowly to a pile of rotting logs that had been bulldozed there several years earlier. A.J. eased up to the crest, lay the forearm of his rifle across a log, and took careful aim, slipped off the safety and eased back on the trigger. It was as if he'd been doing it all his life. At the roar of the .50 caliber muzzleloader, the buck dove for the heavy cover of some nearby timber, then hit the dirt after a few yards and lay there as we approached a few minutes later. I could recall having the same feelings of excitement and joy on the morning I took my first whitetail some 35 years

earlier. As we loaded the deer into the back of my pickup, I knew I had made the right decision. The local deer herd may have lost a buck with tremendous potential, but the world of deer hunting was now one hunter richer.

The numbers of deer hunters in the U.S. are on the decline. Although hunting permits for firearms, muzzleloaders and archers combined are up in many parts of the country, the total number of hunters buying these permits has dropped. In some states the decline has been significant. On the other hand, the resource has never been stronger. Thanks largely to modern conservation practices and game management, whitetail herds across the country are at an all-time high. Equally important has been the interest in hunting whitetails. Without the monetary support from the hunting public, many of the programs that have resulted in greater deer numbers would never have gained the necessary funding to get off the ground, let alone rescue America's favorite big game animal from extinction.

More deer and fewer hunters should mean better hunting—and in most regions it still does. Each year, one state or another will enjoy a previous record harvest, and in many states where 300,000 deer hunters once harvested 100,000 deer, approximately the same number of hunters now check in around 200,000 deer. Liberal bag limits and additional hunting opportunities have encouraged a growing number of whitetail hunting fans to participate in more than one season. It's no wonder that the number of archery and muzzle-loading hunters has been on the increase, most of them having crossed over from the ranks of modern gun hunters. Some never go back, preferring the less crowded hunting of the lengthy bow seasons, or the "first shot" opportunities of an early muzzleloader hunt. Other hunters participate in all three, which accounts for the overall increase in the number of permits issued in some states. Without question, today's whitetail hunter displays an increased interest in "quality" hunting and is doing more than ever to improve the quality and quantity of deer inhabiting the land they own, lease or simply hunt. Millions of private dollars are spent annually by individuals, hunting

clubs and deer hunting organizations to improve the whitetail habitat and the overall quality of the deer herd. Tom Baker, now of Warm Springs, Arkansas, is among the dedicated individuals who have been responsible for the upsurge in these improvements.

Tom and his wife Rhonda own a 2,700-acre piece of whitetail hunting heaven, called Buck Hollow Ranch, which is located in the northeastern corner of Arkansas, only a few miles south of the Missouri state line. This area of the eastern escarpment of the so-call Ozark Plateau has always been rich in game and was the favored hunting ground of the Cherokee and Osage tribes. The abundance of whitetails and wild turkey were also a lure to settlers during the early 1800s. But as in so many other states, subsistence and market hunting decimated the deer populations to a point where, in the 1930s, fewer than 500 whitetail were said to remain in the entire state.

Through its widespread refuge system and trapping/restocking efforts, the Arkansas Game and Fish Commission has rebuilt the deer herd to record numbers. Currently (as of mid-2000) more than 700,000 whitetails roam the state's timbered ridges, river and creek bottoms and farmland woodlots. When Tom and Rhonda bought what is now Buck Hollow Ranch in 1994, the property boasted a good deer density, but the quality of the bucks harvested by local hunters during recent seasons was poor.

Tom Baker

Since whitetail hunting was the primary reason for buying the property, Tom and Rhonda immediately initiated Quality Deer Management principals (see below). As a result, they have witnessed a remarkable improvement in the quality of bucks taken on their ranch.

Several years after the Bakers began their own management plan, the Arkansas Game and Fish Commission initiated a statewide Quality Deer Management plan, which also helped improve the quality of deer that came and went on Buck Hollow Ranch (Arkansas regulations now allow hunters to harvest two does each in an effort to establish a more desirable buck:doe ratio; all bucks taken must now have

at least three points on one antler). In addition to extensive food plots planted with high protein food sources throughout their 2,700 acre parcel, the Bakers also provide the deer with supplemental minerals through high phosphorus and calcium licks. The Bakers allow only the harvesting of mature bucks, which means that any buck shot must have at least four points on one antler. They also recognize the need to harvest more does than bucks, a program whose efforts are paying off. The average buck taken on Buck Hollow Ranch now scores 20 to 30 points higher (Boone and Crockett scoring) than those tagged during the Baker's first season in 1994. In addition, their supplemental food

plots are producing bucks in excess of 200 pounds, a good 50 pounds heavier than they were only four years earlier. "Quality Deer Management is more than just a management approach." states Brian Murphy of the Quality Deer Management Association. "It is a philosophy—an attitude. As deer hunter numbers continue to decline across much of the country, it is my contention that the quality of hunters is becoming more important than sheer numbers. Since Quality Deer Management hunters are generally more active and more knowledgeable, they give more back to the resource than most deer hunters. They are raising the standard by which others will be measured in the future."

With plenty of deer to hunt, there is at present a nationwide interest in improving the quality of the deer we hunt. Efforts like those made on Buck Hollow Ranch are being repeated everywhere the whitetail is found—and not always on such large tracts of land. In fact, the Quality Deer Management Association recognizes that most habitat improvement projects are now taking place on privately owned parcels of 40 acres or less in size, and many of their programs target smaller landowners. Nevertheless, old

QUALITY DEER MANAGEMENT
IS PRACTICED ON THIS PROPERTY

QUALITY DEER MANAGEMENT ASSOCIATION

THE QDMA PROMOTES:

- Safe and ethical hunting
- Adequate harvests of adult does
- Restraint in harvesting young bucks
- Hunter involvement in education and management
- Cooperation with biologists and law enforcement
- Adherence to wildlife and trespass laws
- Stewardship and appreciation of all wildlife

habits are hard to break, and one of the most difficult obstacles game departments face is getting veteran hunters to shoot does. I remember well those early years of deer hunting in my home state of Illinois, when it was a rarity merely to catch a glimpse of a deer during an entire season. We all knew it was the does who birthed the next generation of whitetails, and while

Organizations like the Quality Deer Management Association have brought a new awareness to what it will take to ensure quality whitetail hunting in the future.

I grew up hunting either sex, not many hunters in our camp would shoot a doe—not until the last day anyway. We've unknowingly created a problem by not harvesting enough does. As a result, we simply have too many deer. Just because we have nearly ten times as many whitetails as where I once hunted as a kid, it doesn't necessarily mean that we have ten times as many bucks. In fact, where once there was one buck for every four or five does, the ratio is now one buck for every 10 to 20 does. Faced with these numbers, we can understand the need for increased doe harvests. Indeed, most states currently offer bonus "antlerless" tags to ensure that enough female deer are being harvested.

"Not only is the harvest of antlerless deer good whitetail management," advises whitetail hunting authority Richard Smith, "but it's the best way to produce quality bucks with the biggest racks. A primary goal of deer management is to keep population levels low enough so there's enough natural food to go around during critical times of the year, especially in winter. This increases the potential for healthy herds with little or no stress or starvation losses. Healthy herds consistently produce bucks with the biggest antlers."

Where years of "buck only" regulations have been allowed to continue, there is often a large number of deer but few mature bucks. Throughout much of the country, young 1.5-year-old bucks make up the highest percentage of bucks harvested each season. In Missouri, for example, as many as 60 percent of all antlered bucks are taken by hunters each fall. Even though a high number of bonus "antlerless" tags ensures some harvesting of does in Missouri, along with other states having similar bag restrictions, many experts now question the validity of all general firearms tags marked "buck only." There's a feeling that more does would be taken by hunters if all tags issued were "either sex." A hunter who spends four or five days without seeing a buck will likely settle for a big, tasty doe rather than go home empty-handed. And when it comes down to harvesting a deer just for the meat, wouldn't it be better for a hunter to take one of the overly abundant does than a young buck?

High deer densities are creating new problems for wildlife managers, especially where high deer numbers coincide with high human numbers. Whitetail have nearly taken over many suburban areas and even ventured into the city limits of major metropolitan areas. In some parts of the country, it's easier to spot a huge trophy class buck easing its way through someone's back yard than it is way out in the country somewhere. The deer instinctively know that these areas, lacking any hunting pressure, offer something of a refuge. Many bucks that are now city dwellers live to be old timers decked out with very impressive head gear. In fact, the current reigning World Record non-typical whitetail buck (as of mid-2000) was a deer found dead along an intrastate highway inside the city limits of St. Louis, Missouri.

COMPLETE BOOK OF WHITETAIL HUNTING

Outstanding trophy bucks, like the one Mark Drury harvested in Texas, will always capture the imagination of serious deer hunters. The opportunities to harvest one have never been greater.

Adam Bridges, the author's son, with a buck he took all on his own at age 12. He's since taken much bigger deer, but none as memorable as this one.

Where large numbers of deer are living amongst a large human population, there has to be conflict. When deer first began showing up inside U.S. cities 20 to 30 years ago, the novelty of seeing one of these graceful critters turned many suburban residents against deer hunting. "How could anyone shoot Bambi?" These same people now wish Bambi didn't live in their backyard, munching away on their prized flowers, shrubbery and gardens. Moreover, deer darting across the road have created a real driving hazard, one which most insurance companies are pressuring state game department to eliminate.

Where deer densities approach 30 to 50 or more deer per square mile, diseases can spread quickly. In recent years, periodic outbreaks of EHD (epizootic hemorraghic disease) have decimated whitetail populations within specific geographical areas. A severe case in Montana's Milk River area several years ago practically wiped out an entire population of whitetails. If the deer population can't be curbed, future epidemics may become widespread. In one short period of time, 50 years of whitetail management could be wiped out. Where deer live in close proximity to livestock and humans, there's also the possibility that whitetails may even have an impact on human health. Tuberculosis is often detected in whitetails, especially those living in captivity, and many biologists feel that deer could serve as reservoirs for this disease that once had a major impact on humans.

As anyone can clearly see—more is not always better. Deer numbers are higher now than when the Pilgrims stepped ashore on this continent. In southern Pike County, Illinois, where I live, there's an expanse of land sandwiched between the Mississippi and Illinois Rivers. Archeologists consider this one of the richest areas in the country, historically speaking, and excavations within a mile of my home have produced chipped flint points that are 10,000 to 12,000 years old. We know that deer hunting in this region was—and remains—a tradition as old as man's existence, at least in this hemisphere.

Most whitetail biologists and wildlife managers would feel more comfortable if deer populations were 20 to 25 percent smaller than they are currently. Fortunately for those who enjoy pursuing this great game animal, hunting for sport has become the only effective means of controlling deer numbers. In a few metropolitan area where gun hunting has become a thing of the past, bowhunting simply doesn't result in enough harvesting to be effective. Sometimes a city government may be forced to hire professional sharpshooters as a way to reduce deer herds, but such edicts usually run into opposition from nearby residents. As ridiculous as it may sound, attempts have even been made to feed deer with pellets containing birth control substances.

The plain fact is, we are not harvesting enough whitetails, especially the females. And as the multiplier factor

continues to kick in, the deer herds keep growing. A prime example of how the balance between deer, humans and habitat can quickly get out of control is northeastern Virginia, not far from our nation's capitol. There, the expanding suburbs keep taking up more and more of the whitetail's traditional habitat. And as the human population of the area skyrockets, the hunting of deer has either been curtailed in many neighborhoods, or government regulations have become more restrictive. During the 1970s and 1980s, much of the U.S. was open to deadly accurate centerfire rifles. As new homes replaced our wide-open spaces, hunting regulations increasingly required the use of short-

ranged, less effective shotguns and slugs for deer hunting. In an interview only a few years back, a top official with the Virginia Department of Game and Inland Fisheries confessed that serious thought was being given to making some of the heavily populated (by humans) regions "muzzleloading only." The one-shot aspect of muzzleloading offers a still safer means of harvesting a whitetail population that has gone totally out of control. As we head into the 21st century, game managers certainly have their work cut out for them.

Our ever-changing social values means that more single-parent homes have been created, which translates into less parental guidance for our children.

COMPLETE BOOK OF WHITETAIL HUNTING

Unfortunately, it also means that fewer fathers have the time it takes to introduce their sons and daughters to hunting, much less pass down the traditions of deer hunting. That's unfortunate. "Like heirlooms handed down generation to generation," Tom Fegely points out, "kids exposed to deer camps seldom throw away the memories. Most young hunters gain entry to a camp courtesy of a father, uncle or some special person who thought enough of them to share the experience and mystique. It's called passing on the tradition."

The average age of the modern deer hunter is considerably more than it was 20 or 30 years ago. During the 1960s and 1970s, it wasn't uncommon for schools in many parts of the country to shut down for the opener of the annual deer season, thus allowing young hunters to spend the day afield with family and friends in pursuit of whitetails. Since then, we've put too much emphasis on life styles that have become increasingly more complicated, stress-filled and time-consuming. Kids aren't allowed to be kids anymore. It's as though we can't wait to pressure them into becoming young adults. They don't have time to share the

Young hunters are too often chastised for harvesting small bucks. Never discourage a young hunter from taking a good shot during the early stages of deer hunting.

deer woods with Dad. They're too busy with organized sport, surfing the Internet, or trying to get into the college of their choice. Whereas hunters in the 15-25 age bracket once made up a healthy percentage of those who went after deer each fall, that same age range now represents the largest void among the ranks of deer hunters nationwide.

Fortunately, hunting the whitetail continues to play an important economic role in many local areas throughout the country. Hundreds of thousands of workers owe their jobs to the fascinating aspects of hunting deer. In some states, the annual deer seasons pump millions of dollars into local economies, from the small cafes where out-of-town hunters enjoy pre-dawn breakfasts and late evening dinners, to motel lodgings and the fees we pay to landowners and outfitters for the right to hunt in prime locations. Like it or not, hunting the white-tailed deer is big business. As Larry Wieshuhn puts it, "Increased costs are all too often given as reasons for not hunting whitetails these days. Sometimes those statements are valid. . . and sometimes they are not. It simply comes down to a matter of priorities."

Larry also points out that despite the boost in local economies that are credited to healthy whitetail herds almost everywhere, escalating costs involved in hunting deer now make it increasingly difficult for average wage earners to enjoy a quality hunt. This is especially true for hunters seeking a "top-of-the-line" buck. That doesn't mean, according to Larry Wieshuhn, that just because a hunter cannot afford the "big bucks" needed to hunt big bucks, he or she will never get the chance to enjoy a quality hunt. Many landowners and outfitters are still faced with the problem of harvesting a large number of does and some lesser bucks, which can make such hunts available at reasonable prices a reality.

Ironically, the future of deer hunting in North America is both bright and bleak. On the bright side is a tremendous whitetail population that continues to prosper. Along with the current interest in quality deer, we're seeing a much greater harvest of exceptional bucks each fall. On the down side, there's the decline in the number of deer hunters. If ever fewer young hunters take to the woods, while the number of older hunters dwindles as we grow older, the loss in numbers of hunters may become severe in another 20 to 30 years. Should the numbers become so small as to negate the maintenance and preservation of good whitetail habitats, we stand the chance of losing one of the oldest traditions this continent has to offer.

So, if you have not yet introduced your own children to whitetail hunting, don't wait until it's too late. Other conflicting interests and commitments can take over quickly and easily. And if you don't have a child to share the deer hunting tradition with, do as I did at the beginning of this chapter with A.J.—go out and borrow one! ■

Index